# Encyclopedia of Robust Control: Design Methods

# Volume III

# Encyclopedia of Robust Control: Design Methods Volume III

Edited by **Zac Fredericks**

New Jersey

Published by Clanrye International,
55 Van Reypen Street,
Jersey City, NJ 07306, USA
www.clanryeinternational.com

**Encyclopedia of Robust Control: Design Methods**
**Volume III**
Edited by Zac Fredericks

International Standard Book Number: 978-1-63240-202-8 (Hardback)

Printed in the United States of America.

# Contents

**Permissions**

**List of Contributors**

# Preface

This book gives a broad overview of theoretical and design advances with the help of selected applications. Robust control has been a topic of extensive research in the last three decades resulting in H_2/H_\infty and \mu design methods followed by studies on parametric robustness, earlier motivated by Kharitonov's theorem, the extension to non-linear time delay systems, and other recent methods. This book includes contributions by experts in this field from all over the world. It covers special topics in robust and adaptive control. It also includes topics on robust control and problem specific solutions. This book serves as a complete guide for researchers, students and other interested individuals in the field of robotics and mechatronics.

This book has been the outcome of endless efforts put in by authors and researchers on various issues and topics within the field. The book is a comprehensive collection of significant researches that are addressed in a variety of chapters. It will surely enhance the knowledge of the field among readers across the globe.

It is indeed an immense pleasure to thank our researchers and authors for their efforts to submit their piece of writing before the deadlines. Finally in the end, I would like to thank my family and colleagues who have been a great source of inspiration and support.

Editor

# Special Topics in Robust and Adaptive Control

# Robust Attenuation of Frequency Varying Disturbances

Kai Zenger and Juha Orivuori
*Aalto University School of Electrical Engineering*
*Finland*

## 1. Introduction

Systems described by differential equations with time-periodic coefficients have a long history in mathematical physics. Applications cover a wide area of systems ranging from helicopter blades, rotor-bearing systems, mechanics of structures, stability of structures influenced by periodic loads, applications in robotics and micro-electromechanical systems etc. (Rao, 2000; Sinha, 2005). Processes characterized by linear time-invariant or time-varying dynamics corrupted by sinusoidal output disturbance belong to this class of systems. Robust and adaptive analysis and synthesis techniques can be used to design suitable controllers, which fulfill the desired disturbance attenuation and other performance characteristics of the closed-loop system.

Despite of the fact that LTP (Linear Time Periodic) system theory has been under research for years (Deskmuhk & Sinha, 2004; Montagnier et al., 2004) the analysis on LTPs with experimental data has been seriously considered only recently (Allen, 2007). The importance of new innovative ideas and products is of utmost importance in modern industrial society. In order to design more accurate and more economical products the importance of model-based control, involving increasingly accurate identification schemes and more effective control methods, have become fully recognized in industrial applications.

An example of the processes related to the topic is vibration control in electrical machines, in which several research groups are currently working. Active vibration control has many applications in various industrial areas, and the need to generate effective but relatively cheap solutions is enormous. The example of electrical machines considered concerns the dampening of rotor vibrations in the so-called critical speed declared by the first flexural rotor bending resonance. In addition, the electromagnetic fields in the air-gap between rotor and stator may couple with the mechanic vibration modes, leading to rotordynamic instability. The vibration caused by this resonance is so considerable that large motors often have to be driven below the critical speed. Smaller motors can be driven also in super-critical speeds, but they have to be accelerated fast over the critical speed. Active vibration control would make it possible to use the motor in its whole operation range freely, according to specified needs given by the load process. Introducing characteristics of this kind for the electric drives of the future would be a major technological break-through, a good example of an innovative technological development.

In practice, the basic electromechanical models of electrical machines can be approximated by linear time-invariant models with a sinusoidal disturbance signal entering at the so-called critical frequency. That frequency can also vary which makes the system model time-variable. The outline of the article is as follows. Two test processes are introduced in Section 2. A systematic and generic model structure valid for these types of systems is presented in Section 3. Three types of controllers for active vibration control are presented in Section 4 and their performance is verified by simulations and practical tests. Specifically the extension to the nonlinear control algorithm presented in Section 4.4 is important, because it extends the optimal controller to a nonlinear one with good robustness properties with respect to variations in rotation frequency. Conclusions are given in Section 5.

## 2. Problem statement

The control algorithms described in the paper were tested by two test processes to be discussed next.

### 2.1 An electric machine

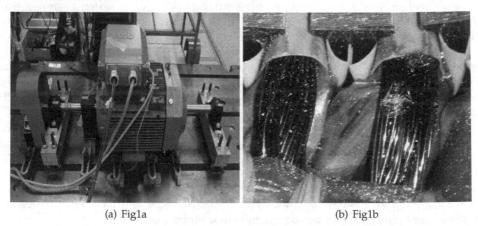

|                 (a) Fig1a                 |                 (b) Fig1b                 |

Fig. 1. Test machine: A 30 kW three-phase squirrel cage induction motor with an extended rotor shaft (a) and stator windings (b)

In electrical motors both radial and axial vibration modes are of major concern, because they limit the speed at which the motor can be run and also shorten the lifetime of certain parts of the motor. The fundamental vibration forces are typically excited at discrete frequencies (critical frequencies), which depend on the electrodynamics of the rotor and stator (Inman, 2006). In some machines the critical frequency can be passed by accelerating the rotor speed fast beyond it, but specifically in larger machines that is not possible. Hence these machines must be run at subcritical frequencies. It would be a good idea to construct an actuator, which would create a separate magnetic field in the airgap between the stator and rotor. That would cause a counterforce, which would attenuate the vibration mode of the rotor. Running the rotor at critical speeds and beyond will need a stable and robust vibration control system, because at different speeds different vibration modes also wake.

In Fig.1 a 30 kW induction machine is presented, provided with such a new actuator, which is a coil mounted in the stator slots of the machine (b). The electromechanical actuator is an extra winding, which, due to the controlled current, produces the required counter force to damp the rotor vibrations. The actuator is designed such that the interaction with the normal operation of the machine is minimal. More on the design and modelling of the actuator can be found in (Laiho et al., 2008).

Some of the machine parameters are listed in Table 1. The vibration of the rotor is continuously measured in two dimensions and the control algorithm is used to calculate the control current fed into the coil. The schema of the control arrangement is shown in Fig.2. The idea is to

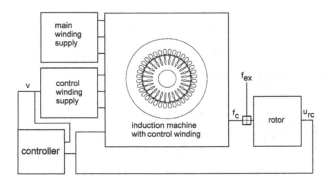

Fig. 2. Rotor vibration control by a built-in new actuator

generate a control force to the rotor through a new actuator consisting of extra windings mounted in the stator slots. An adaptive model-based algorithm controls the currents to the actuator thus generating a magnetic field that induces a force negating the disturbance force exited by the mass imbalance of the rotor. The configuration in the figure includes an excitation force (disturbance) consisting of rotation harmonics and harmonics stemming from the induction machine dynamics. The control force and the disturbance exert a force to the rotor, which results in a rotor center displacement. If the dynamic compensation signal is chosen cleverly, the rotor vibrations can be effectively reduced.

In practical testing the setup shown in Fig.3 has been used. The displacement of the rotor in two dimensions (xy) is measured at one point with displacement transducers, which give a voltage signal proportional to the distance from sensor to the shaft. A digital tachometer at the end of the rotor measures the rotational frequency. The control algorithms were programmed in Matlab/Simulink model and the dSpace interface system and the Real-Time Workshop were used to control the current fed to the actuator winding.

### 2.2 An industrial rolling process

The second tests were made by a rolling process consisting of a reel, hydraulic actuator and force sensor. The natural frequency of the process was 39 Hz, and the hydraulic actuator acts both as the source of control forces and as a support for the reel. The actuator is connected to the support structures through a force sensor, thus providing information on the forces acting on the reel. The test setup is shown in Fig.4 and the control schema is presented in Fig.5.

| Parameter | Value | Unit |
|---|---|---|
| supply frequency | 50 | Hz |
| rated voltage | 400 | V |
| connection | delta | - |
| rated current | 50 | A |
| rated power | 30 | kW |
| number of phases | 3 | - |
| number of poles | 2 | - |
| rated slip | 1 | % |
| rotor mass | 55.8 | kg |
| rotor shaft length | 1560 | mm |
| critical speed | 37.5 | Hz |
| width of the air-gap | 1 | mm |

Table 1. Main parameters of the test motor

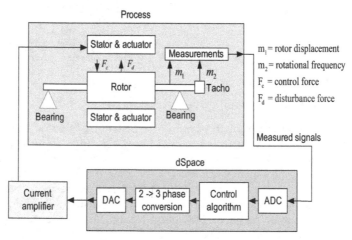

Fig. 3. Schema of the test setup (motor)

## 3. Modeling and identification

Starting from the first principles of electromagnetics (Chiasson, 2005; Fuller et al., 1995) and structure mechanics, the vibration model can for a two-pole cage induction machine be written in the form (Laiho et al., 2008)

$$\dot{q} = Aq + Bv + Gf_{ex}$$
$$u_{rc} = Cq \tag{1}$$

where $q$ denotes the states (real and complex) of the system, $v$ is the control signal of the actuator, $f_{ex}$ is the sinusoidal disturbance causing the vibration at the critical frequency, and $u_{rc}$ is the radial rotor movement in two dimensions. The matrices $A$, $B$, $G$ and $C$ are constant. The constant parameter values can be identified by the well-known methods (Holopainen et al., 2004; Laiho et al., 2008; Repo & Arkkio, 2006). The results obtained

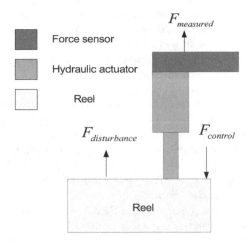

Fig. 4. The test setup (industrial rolling process)

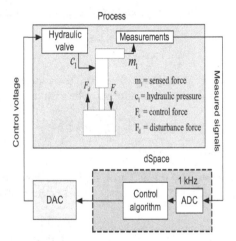

Fig. 5. The controller schema

by using finite-element (FE) model as the "real" process have been good and accurate (Laiho et al., 2007), when both prediction error method (PEM) and subspace identification (SUB) have been used. Since the running speed of the motor was considered to be below 60 Hz, the sampling rate was chosen to be 1 kHz. A 12th order state-space model was used as the model structure (four inputs and two outputs corresponding to the control voltages, rotor displacements and produced control forces in two dimensions). The model order was chosen based on the frequency response calculated from the measurement data, from which the approximate number of poles and zeros were estimated.

In identification a pseudo random (PSR) control signal was used in control inputs. That excites rotor dynamics on a wide frequency range, which in limited only by the sampling rate. However, because the second control input corresponds to the rotor position and has a big influence on the produced force a pure white noise signal cannot be used here. Therefore the model output of the rotor position added with a small PSR signal to prevent correlation was used as the second control input. After identification the model was validated by using independent validation data. The fit was larger than 80 per cent, which was considered to be adequate for control purposes. The results have later been confirmed by tests carried out by using the real test machine data, and the results were found to be equally good.

The model structure is then as shown in Fig.6, where the actuator model and electromechanic model of the rotor have been separated, and the sinusoidal disturbance term is used to model the force that causes the radial vibration of the rotor. In Fig.6a the models of the actuator and rotor have been separated and the disturbance is modelled to enter at the input of the rotor model. The internal feedback shown is caused by the unbalanced magnetic pull (UMP), which means that the rotor when moved from the center position in the airgap causes an extra distortion in the magnetic field. That causes an extra force, which can be taken into consideration in the actuator model. However, in practical tests it is impossible to separate the models of the actuator and rotor dynamics, and therefore the model in Fig.6b has been used in identification. Because the models are approximated by linear dynamics, the sinusoidal disturbance signal can be moved to the process output, and the actuator and rotor models can be combined.

In Fig. 6a the 4-state dynamical (Jeffcott) model for the radial rotor dynamics is

$$\dot{x}_r(t) = A_r x(t) + B_r u_r(t)$$
$$y_r(t) = C_r x(t)$$

(2)

where $y_r$ is the 2-dimensional rotor displacement from the center axis in xy-coordinates, and $u_r$ is the sum of the actuator and disturbance forces. The actuator model is

$$\dot{x}_a(t) = A_a x_a(t) + \begin{bmatrix} B_{a1} & B_{a2} \end{bmatrix} \begin{bmatrix} y_r(t) \\ u(t) \end{bmatrix}$$
$$y_a(t) = C_a x_a(t)$$

(3)

where $y_a$ are the forces generated by the actuator, and $u$ are the control voltages fed into the windings. The self-excited sinusoidal disturbance signal is generated by (given here in two dimensions)

$$\dot{x}_d(t) = A_d x_d(t) = \begin{bmatrix} 0 & 1 & 0 & 0 \\ -\omega_d^2 & 0 & 0 & 0 \\ 0 & 0 & 0 & 1 \\ 0 & 0 & -\omega_d^2 & 0 \end{bmatrix} x_d(t)$$

$$d(t) = C_d x_d(t) = \begin{bmatrix} 1 & 0 & 0 & 0 \\ 0 & 0 & 1 & 0 \end{bmatrix} x_d(t)$$

(4)

where $\omega_d$ is the angular frequency of the disturbance and $d(t)$ denotes the disturbance forces in xy-directions. The initial values of the state are chosen such that the disturbance consists of two sinusoidal signals with 90 degree phase shift (sine and cosine waves). The initial values are then

$$x_d(0) = \begin{bmatrix} x_{\sin}(0) \\ x_{\cos}(0) \end{bmatrix} = \begin{bmatrix} 0 \\ A\omega_d \\ A \\ 0 \end{bmatrix}$$

where $A$ is the amplitude of the disturbance. The models of the actuator, rotor and disturbance can be combined into one state-space representation

$$\dot{x}_p(t) = A_p x_p(t) + B_p u(t) = \begin{bmatrix} A_r & B_r C_a & B_r C_d \\ B_{a1} C_r & A_a & 0 \\ 0 & 0 & A_d \end{bmatrix} x_p(t) + \begin{bmatrix} 0 \\ B_{a2} \\ 0 \end{bmatrix} u(t)$$

$$y_r(t) = C_p x_p(t) = \begin{bmatrix} C_r & 0 & 0 \end{bmatrix} x_p(t) \tag{5}$$

with

$$x_p = \begin{bmatrix} x_r \\ x_a \\ x_d \end{bmatrix}$$

As mentioned, the actuator and rotor model can be combined and the disturbance can be moved to enter at the output of the process (according to Fig. 6b). The state-space representation of the actuator-rotor model is then

$$\dot{x}_{ar}(t) = A_{ar} x_{ar}(t) + B_{ar} u(t)$$
$$y_{ar}(t) = C_{ar} x_{ar}(t) \tag{6}$$

where $u$ is a vector of applied control voltages and $y_{ar}$ is vector of rotor displacements. The whole system can be modeled as

$$\dot{x}_p(t) = A_p x_p(t) + B_p u_p(t) = \begin{bmatrix} A_{ar} & 0 \\ 0 & A_d \end{bmatrix} x_p(t) + \begin{bmatrix} B_{ar} \\ 0 \end{bmatrix} u(t)$$

$$y_r(t) = C_p x_p(t) = \begin{bmatrix} C_{ar} & C_d \end{bmatrix} x_p(t) \tag{7}$$

with

$$x_p(t) = \begin{bmatrix} x_{ar}(t) \\ x_d(t) \end{bmatrix}$$

The process was identified with a sampling frequency of 1 kHz, which was considered adequate since the running speed of the motor was about 60 Hz and therefore well below 100 Hz. Pseudorandom signals were used as control forces in both channels separately, and the prediction error method (PEM) was used (Ljung, 1999) to identify a 12th order state-space representation of the system.

The identified process model is compared to real process data, and the results are shown in Figs.7 and 8, respectively. The fit in x and y directions were calculated as 72.5 % and 80.08 %, which is considered to be appropriate. From the frequency domain result it is seen that for lower frequency the model agrees well with response obtained form measured data, but in higher frequencies there is a clear difference. That is because the physical model used behind the identification is only valid up to a certain frequency, and above that there exist unmodelled dynamics.

## 4. Control design

In the following sections different control methods are presented for vibration control of single or multiple disturbances with a constant or varying disturbance frequencies. Two of the methods are based on the *linear quadratic gaussian* (LQ) control, and one belongs to the class of *higher harmonic control* algorithms (HHC), which is also known as *convergent control*. If the

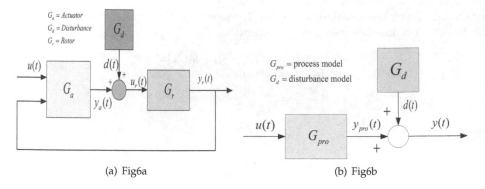

(a) Fig6a                                                              (b) Fig6b

Fig. 6. Process models for the actuator, rotor and sinusoidal disturbance

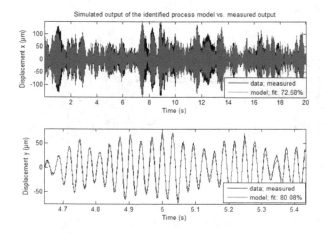

Fig. 7. Validation of the actuator-rotor model in time domain

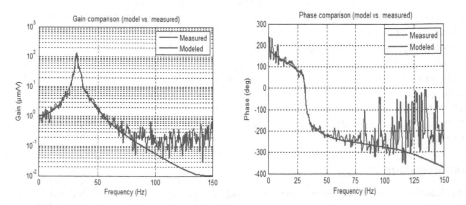

Fig. 8. Validation of the actuator-rotor model in frequency domain

sinusoidal disturbance frequency signal varies in frequency, the algorithms must be modified by combining them and using direct frequency measurement or frequency tracking.

## 4.1 Direct optimal feedback design

In this method the suppressing of tonal disturbance is posed as a dynamic optimization problem, which can be solved by the well-known LQ theory. The idea is again that the model generating the disturbance is embedded in the process model, and that information is then automatically used when minimizing the design criterion. That leads to a control algorithm which inputs a signal of the same amplitude but opposite phase to the system thus canceling the disturbance. The problem can be defined in several scenarios, e.g. the disturbance can be modelled to enter at the process input or output, the signal to be minimized can vary etc. Starting from the generic model

$$\dot{x}(t) = Ax(t) + Bu(t) = \begin{bmatrix} A_p & 0 \\ 0 & A_d \end{bmatrix} x(t) + \begin{bmatrix} B_p \\ 0 \end{bmatrix} u(t)$$

$$y(t) = \begin{bmatrix} C_p & C_d \end{bmatrix} x(t)$$

(8)

the control criterion is set

$$J = \int_0^\infty \left( z^T(\tau)Qz(\tau) + u^T(\tau)Ru(\tau) \right) d\tau$$

(9)

where $z$ is a freely chosen performance variable and $Q \geq 0, R > 0$ are the weighing matrices for the performance variable and control effort. By inserting $z(t) = C_z x(t)$ the criterion changes into the standard LQ form

$$J = \int_0^\infty \left( x^T(\tau)C_z^T QC_z x(\tau) + u^T(\tau)Ru(\tau) \right) d\tau$$

(10)

The disturbance dynamics can be modelled as

$$\dot{x}_d(t) = A_d x_d(t) = \begin{bmatrix} A_{d1} & \cdots & 0 & 0 \\ \vdots & \ddots & \vdots & \vdots \\ 0 & \cdots & A_{dn} & 0 \\ 0 & \cdots & 0 & -\epsilon \end{bmatrix} x_{dn}(t)$$

$$d(t) = C_d x_d(t) = \begin{bmatrix} C_{d1} & \cdots & C_{dn} & 0 \end{bmatrix} x_{dn}(t)$$

(11)

where

$$A_{dn} = \begin{bmatrix} 0 & 1 \\ -\omega_{dn}^2 & -\epsilon \end{bmatrix}, \quad i = 1, 2, ..., n$$

and the initial values

$$x(0) = \begin{bmatrix} x_{d1}^T(0) & \cdots & x_{dn}^T(0) & b \end{bmatrix}^T$$

According to the formalism a sum of $n$ sinusoidal disturbance components (angular frequencies $\omega_{dn}$) enter the system. The very small number $\epsilon$ is added in order the augmented system to be stabilizable, which is needed for the solution to exist. The damping of the resulting sinusoidal is so low that it does not affect the practical use of the optimal controller.

The constant $b$ can be used for a constant bias term in the disturbance. Compare the disturbance modelling also to that presented in equations (4) and (5).

To minimize of sinusoidal disturbances the following performance variable can be chosen

$$z(t) = \left[ C_p \vdots [C_{d1} \cdots C_{dn} \; 0] \right] x(t) = \left[ C_p \vdots C_d \right] x(t) = C_z x(t) \tag{12}$$

which leads to the cost function (10)

The solution of the LQ problem can now be obtained by standard techniques (Anderson & Moore, 1989) as

$$u(t) = -Lx(t) = -R^{-1}B^T S x(t) \tag{13}$$

where $S$ is the solution of the algebraic Riccati equation

$$A^T S + SA - SBR^{-1}B^T S + Q = 0 \tag{14}$$

It is also possible to choose simply $z(t) = x(t)$ in (9). To force the states approach zero it is in this case necessary to introduce augmented states

$$x_{aug}(t) = \int_0^t (y_{ar}(\tau) + d(\tau)) \, d\tau = [C_{ar} \; C_d] \int_0^t \left( [x_{ar}(\tau)^T \; x_d(\tau)^T]^T \right) d\tau \tag{15}$$

The system to which the LQ design is used is then

$$\dot{x}(t) = \begin{bmatrix} \dot{x}_p(t) \\ \dot{x}_{aug}(t) \end{bmatrix} = \underbrace{\begin{bmatrix} A_p & \vdots & 0 \\ \cdots & \vdots & \cdots \\ [C_{ar} \; C_d] & \vdots & 0 \end{bmatrix}}_{A_{aug}} x(t) + \underbrace{\begin{bmatrix} B_p \\ \cdots \\ 0 \end{bmatrix}}_{B_{aug}} u(t)$$

$$y_r(t) = \underbrace{[C_p \; 0]}_{C_{aug}} x(t)$$

$$\tag{16}$$

In this design the weights in $Q$ corresponding to the augmented states should be set to considerably high values, e.g. values like $10^5$ have been used.

Usually a state observer must be used to implement the control law. For example, in the configuration shown in Fig.6a (see also equation (5)) that has the form

$$\dot{\hat{x}}(t) = A_p \hat{x}(t) + B_p u(t) + K (y_r(t) - \hat{y}_r(t))$$
$$y_{obs} = \hat{x}(t) \tag{17}$$

The gain in the estimator can be chosen based on the duality between the LQ optimal controller and the estimator. The state error dynamics $\tilde{x}(t) = x(t) - \hat{x}(t)$ follows the dynamics

$$\dot{\tilde{x}}(t) = (A_p - KC_p) \, \tilde{x}(t) \tag{18}$$

which is similar to

$$\dot{x}_N(t) = A_N x_N(t) + B_N u_N(t) \tag{19}$$

with $A_N = A_p^T, B_N = C_p^T, K_N = K^T$ and $u_N(t) = -K_N x_N(t)$. The weighting matrix $K_N$ can be determined by minimizing

$$J_{obs} = \int_0^\infty \left( x_N(t)^T Q_{obs} x_N(t) + u_N(t)^T R_{obs} u_N(t) \right) dt \tag{20}$$

where the matrices $Q_{obs}$ and $R_{obs}$ contain the weights for the relative state estimation error and its convergence rate.

The optimal control law (13) can now be combined with the observer model (17). Including the augmented states (15) the control law can be stated as

$$\dot{x}_{LQ}(t) = \begin{bmatrix} \dot{\hat{x}}(t) \\ \dot{x}_{\text{aug}}(t) \end{bmatrix} = \underbrace{\left( \begin{bmatrix} A_p - KC_p & 0 \\ C_p & 0 \end{bmatrix} - \begin{bmatrix} B_p \\ 0 \end{bmatrix} L \right)}_{A_{LQ}} x_{LQ}(t) + \underbrace{\begin{bmatrix} K \\ 0 \end{bmatrix}}_{B_{LQ}} y_r(t)$$

$$u_{LQ}(t) = \underbrace{-L}_{C_{LQ}} x_{LQ}(t) \tag{21}$$

where $y_r$ is the rotor displacement, $u_{LQ}$ is the optimal control signal, and $A_{LQ}, B_{LQ}$ and $C_{LQ}$ are the parameters of the controller.

## 4.2 Convergent controller

The convergent control (CC) algorithm (also known as instantaneous harmonic control (IHC) is a feedforward control method to compensate a disturbance at a certain frequency (Daley et al., 2008). It is somewhat similar to the well-known least means squares compensator (LMS), (Fuller et al., 1995; Knospe et al., 1994) which has traditionally been used in many frequency compensating methods in signal processing. A basic schema is presented in Fig.9. The term $r$ is a periodic signal of the same frequency as $d$, but possibly with a different

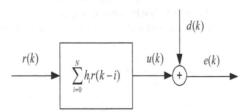

Fig. 9. Feedforward compensation of a disturbance signal

amplitude and phase. The idea is to change the filter parameters $h_i$ such that the signal $u$ compensates the disturbance $d$. The standard LMS algorithm that minimizes the squared error can be derived to be as

$$h_i(k+1) = h_i(k) - \alpha r(k-i) e(k) \tag{22}$$

where $\alpha$ is a tuning parameter (Fuller et al., 1995; Tammi, 2007). In the CC algorithm the process dynamics is presented by means of the Fourier coefficients as

$$E_F(k) = G_F U_F(k) + D_F(k) \tag{23}$$

where $G_F$ is the complex frequency response of the system and the symbols $E_F$, $U_F$ and $D_F$ are the Fourier coefficients of the error, control and disturbance signals. For example

$$E_F^{\omega_n} = \frac{1}{N} \sum_{k=0}^{N-1} e(k) e^{-2i\pi kn/N} \approx e(k) e^{-i\omega_n t}$$

where $N$ is the number of samples in one signal period, and $n$ is the number of the spectral line of the corresponding frequency. If the sampling time is $T_s$, then $t = kT_s$.
The criterion to be minimized is $J = E_F^* E_F$ which gives

$$U_F = -(G_F^* G_F)^{-1} G_F^* D_F = -A_F D_F \tag{24}$$

where $*$ denotes the complex transpose. The pseudoinverse is used if necessary when calculating the inverse matrix. In terms of Fourier coefficients the Convergent Control Algorithm can be written as

$$U_F(k+1) = \beta U_F(k) - \alpha A_F E_F(k) \tag{25}$$

where $\alpha$ and $\beta$ are tuning parameters. It can be shown (Daley et al., 2008; Tammi, 2007) that the control algorithm can be presented in the form of a linear time-invariant pulse transfer function

$$G_{cc}(z) = \frac{U(z)}{Y(z)} = \beta \frac{\mathrm{Re}\left(G_F\left(e^{i\omega_k}\right)^{-1}\right) z^2 - \alpha \mathrm{Re}\left(G_F\left(e^{i\omega_k}\right)^{-1} e^{-i\omega_k T_s}\right) z}{z^2 - 2\alpha \cos\left(\omega_k T_s\right) z + \alpha^2} \tag{26}$$

where $Y(z)$ is the sampled plant output and $U(z)$ is the sampled control signal.
The convergent controller can operate like an LMS controller in series with the plant, by using a reference signal $r$ proportional to the disturbance signal to be compensated. The 'plant' can here mean also the process controlled by a wide-frequency band controller like the LQ controller for instance.

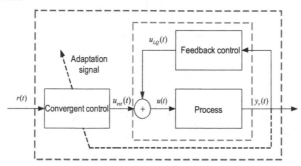

Fig. 10. Convergent controller in series with a controlled plant

Alternatively, the CC controller can be connected in parallel with the LQ-controller, then having the plant output as the input signal. Several CC controllers (tuned for different frequencies) can also be connected in parallel in this configuration, see Fig.11.

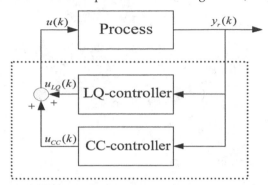

Fig. 11. Convergent controller connected in parallel with the LQ controller

### 4.3 Simulations and test runs

The controller performance was tested in two phases. Firstly, extensive simulations by using a finite element (FE) model of the electrical machine and actuator were carried out. Secondly, the control algorithms were implemented in the test machine discussed in Section 2.1 by using a dSpace system as the program-machine interface. The disturbance frequency was 49.5 Hz, and the controller was discretized with the sampling frequency 1 kHz. Time domain simulations are shown in Figs. 12 and 13. The damping is observed to be about 97 per cent, which is a good result.

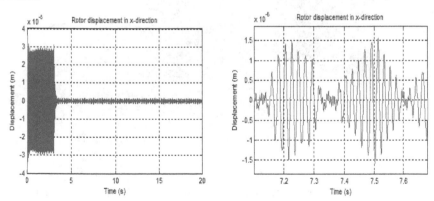

Fig. 12. Simulation result in time domain (rotor vibration in x-direction)

The critical frequency of the 30 kW test motor was 37.7 Hz. However, due to vibrations the rotor could not be driven at this speed in open loop, and both the identification and initial control tests were performed at 32 Hz rotation frequency. In the control tests the LQ controller was used alone first, after which the CC controller was connected, in order to verify the performance of these two control configurations. Both controllers were discretized at 5 kHz sampling rate.

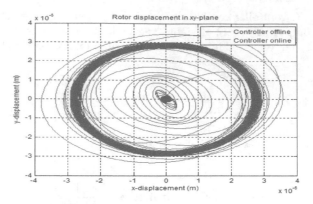

Fig. 13. Simulated rotor vibration in xy-plot

The test results are shown in Figs. 14-17. In Fig.14 the control signal and rotor vibration amplitude are shown, when the machine was driven at 32.5 Hz. The LQ controller was used first alone, and then the CC controller was connected. It is seen that the CC controller improves the performance somewhat, and generally the vibration damping is good and well comparable to the results obtained by simulations. The same can be noticed from the xy-plot shown in Fig.15.

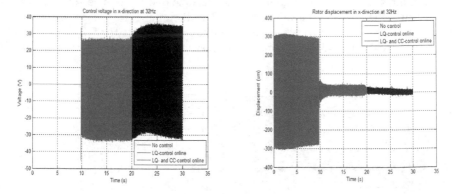

Fig. 14. Test machine runs at 32 Hz speed: Control voltage and rotor displacement in x-direction

Next, the operation speed was increased to the critical frequency 37.5 Hz. Controller(s) tuned for this frequency could be driven without any problems at this speed. Similar results as above are shown in Figs.16 and 17. It is remarkable that now connecting the CC controller on improved the results more than before. So far there is no clear explanation to this behaviour.

### 4.4 Nonlinear controller
If the frequency of the disturbance signal is varying, the performance of a controller with constant coefficients deteriorates considerably. An immediate solution to the problem involves the use of continuous gain scheduling, in which the controller coefficients are modified according to the current disturbance frequency. To this end the disturbance

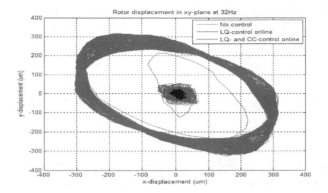

Fig. 15. Test machine runs at 32 Hz speed: xy-plot

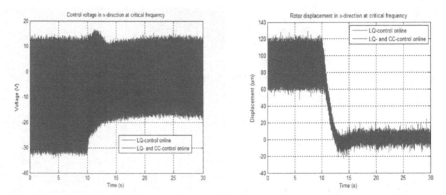

Fig. 16. Test machine runs at 37.5 Hz critical speed: Control voltage and rotor displacement in x-direction

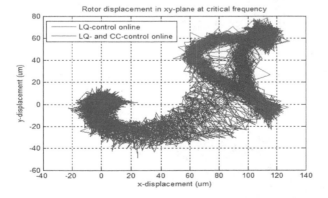

Fig. 17. Test machine runs at 37.5 Hz critical speed: xy-plot

frequency (usually the rotating frequency) has to be measured of tracked (Orivuori & Zenger, 2010; Orivuori et al., 2010). The state estimator can be written in the form

$$\dot{\hat{x}}(t, \omega_{hz}) = (A(\omega_{hz}) - K(\omega_{hz})C)\hat{x}(t, \omega_{hz}) + Bu(t) + K(\omega_{hz})y(t) \tag{27}$$

where it has been assumed that the model topology is as in Fig.6b and the disturbance model is included in the system matrix $A$. The matrix $K$ changes as a function of frequency as

$$K(\omega_{hz}) = \left[ f_1(\omega_{hz}) \; f_2(\omega_{hz}) \; \cdots \; f_n(\omega_{hz}) \right]^T \tag{28}$$

where $f_i$ are suitable functions of frequency. Solving the linear optimal control problem in a frequency grid gives the values of $K$, which can be presented like in Fig.18 The functions $f_i$

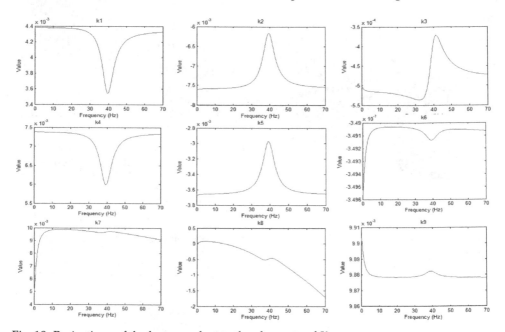

Fig. 18. Projections of the hypersurface to the elements of $K$

can be chosen to be polynomials, so that the feedback gain has the form

$$K(\omega_{hz}) = \begin{bmatrix} a_{11} & a_{12} & \cdots & a_{1m} \\ a_{21} & a_{22} & \cdots & a_{2m} \\ \vdots & \vdots & \ddots & \vdots \\ a_{n1} & a_{n2} & \cdots & a_{nm} \end{bmatrix} u_\omega(\omega_{hz}) \tag{29}$$

where $a_{ij}$ are the polynomial coefficients and

$$u_\omega(\omega_{hz}) = \left[ \omega_{hz}^{m-1} \cdots \omega_{hz}^2 \; \omega_{hz} \; 1 \right]^T \tag{30}$$

The optimal control gain $L(\omega_{hz})$ can be computed similarly.
The controller was tested with the industrial rolling process presented in Section 2.2. A sinusoidal sweep disturbance signal was used, which corresponds to a varying rotational speed of the reel with constant width. The rotation frequency ranged over the frequency range 5 Hz..50 Hz. Before the practical tests the theoretical performance of the controller was analyzed. The result is shown in Fig.19, which shows a neat damping of the vibration near the critical frequency 39 Hz. Simulation and practical test results are shown in Figs.20 and

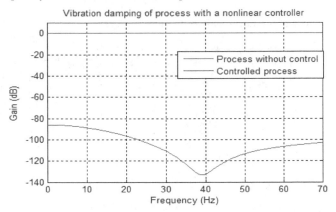

Fig. 19. Theoretical damping achieved with the nonlinear controller

21, respectively. The controller turns out to be effective over the whole frequency range the damping ratio being 99 per cent in simulation and about 90 per cent in practical tests. The result of the good performance of the nonlinear controller is further verified by the output spectrum of the process obtained with and without control. The result is shown in Fig.22.

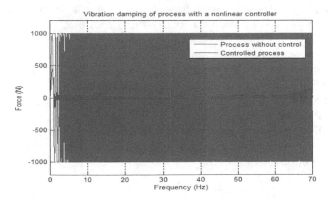

Fig. 20. Simulated performance of the nonlinear controller

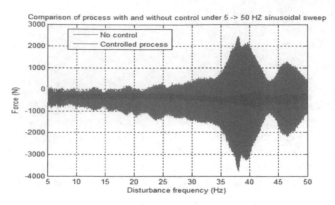

Fig. 21. Real performance of the nonlinear controller

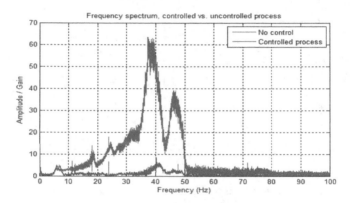

Fig. 22. Frequency spectra of the process output with and without control

## 5. Conclusion

Vibration control in rotating machinery is an important topic of research both from theoretical and practical viewpoints. Generic methods which are suitable for a large class of such processes are needed in order to make the analysis and controller design transparent and straightforward. LQ control theory offers a good and easy to learn model-based control technique, which is effective and easily implemented for industrial processes. The control algorithm can be extended to the nonlinear case covering systems with varying disturbance frequencies. The performance of such an algorithm has been studied in the paper, and the performance has been verified by analysis, simulation and practical tests of two different processes. The vibration control results have been excellent. In future research it is investigated, how the developed methods can be modified to be used is semi-active vibration control. That is important, because active control has its risks, and all industrial users are not willing to use active control methods.

## 6. Acknowledgement

The research has been supported by TEKES (The Finnish Funding Agency for Technology and Innovation) and the Academy of Finland.

## 7. References

Allen, M. S. (2007). Floquet Experimental Modal Analysis for System Identification of Linear Time-Periodic Systems, In: *Proceedings of the ASME 2007, IDETC/CIE*, 11 pages, September 2007, Las Vegas, Nevada, USA.

Anderson, B. D. O. & Moore, J. B. (1989). *Optimal Control: Linear Quadratic Methods*, Prentice-Hall, Englewood Cliffs, NJ.

Chiasson, J. N. (2005). *Modeling and High Performance Control of Electric Machines*, John Wiley, IEEE, Hoboken, NJ.

Daley, S.; Zazas, I.; Hätönen, J. (2008). Harmonic Control of a 'Smart Spring' Machinery Vibration Isolation System, In: *Proceedings of the Institution of Mechanical Engineers, Part M: Journal of Engineering for the Maritime Environment*, Vol. 22, No. 2, pp. 109–119.

Deskmuhk, V. S & Sinha, S. C. (2004). Control of Dynamical Systems with Time-Periodic Coefficients via the Lyapunov-Floquet Transformation and Backstepping Technique, *Journal of Vibration and Control*, Vol. 10, 2004, pp. 1517–1533.

Fuller, C. R.; Elliott, S. J.; Nelson, P. A. (1995). *Active Control of Vibration*, Academic Press, London.

Gupta, N. K. (1980). Frequency-shaped cost functionals: Extension of linear-quadratic-Gaussian design methods, *Journal of Guidance and Control*, Vol. 3, No. 6, 1980, pp. 529–535.

Holopainen, T. P.; Tenhunen, A.; Lantto, E.; Arkkio, A. (2004). Numerical Identification of Electromechanic Force Parameters for Linearized Rotordynamic Model of Cage Induction Motors, *Journal of Vibration and Acoustics*, Vol. 126, No. 3, 2004, pp. 384–390.

Inman, D. J. (2006). *Vibration With Control*, Wiley, Hoboken, NJ.

Knospe, C. R.; Hope, R. W.; Fedigan, S. J.; Williams, R. D. (1994). New Results in the Control of Rotor Synchronous Vibration. In: *Proceedings of the Fourth International Symposium on Magnetic Bearings*, Hochschulverlag AG, Zurich, Switzerland.

Laiho, A.; Holopainen, T. P.; Klinge, P.; Arkkio, A. (2007). Distributed Model For Electromechanical Interaction in Rotordynamics of Cage Rotor Electrical Machines, *Journal of Sound and Vibration*, Vol. 302, Issues 4-5, 2007, pp. 683–698.

Laiho, A.; Tammi, K.; Zenger, K.; Arkkio, A. (2008). A Model-Based Flexural Rotor Vibration Control in Cage Induction Electrical Machines by a Built-In Force Actuator, *Electrical Engineering (Archiv für Elektrotechnik)*, Vol. 90, No. 6, 2008, pp. 407–423.

Ljung, L. (1999). *System Identification: Theory for the User*, 2nd Ed., Prentice Hall, Upper Saddle River, NJ.

Montagnier, P.; Spiteri, R. J.; Angeles, J. (2004). The Control of Linear Time-Periodic Systems Using Floquet-Lyapunov Theory, *International Journal of Control*, Vol. 77, No. 20, March 2004, pp. 472–490.

Orivuori, J. & Zenger, K. (2010). Active Control of Vibrations in a Rolling Process by Nonlinear Optimal Controller, In: *Proceedings of the 10th International Conference on Motion and Vibration Control (Movic 2010)*, August 2010, Tokyo, Japan.

Orivuori, J.; Zazas, I.; Daley, S. (2010). Active Control of a Frequency Varying Tonal Disturbance by Nonlinear Optimal Controller with Frequency Tracking, In: *Proceedings of the IFAC Workshop of Periodic Control Systems (Psyco 2010)*, August 2010, Antalya, Turkey.

Rao, J. D. (2000). *Vibratory Condition Monitoring of Machines*, Narosa Publishing House, New Delhi, India.

Repo, A-K. & Arkkio, A. (2006). Numerical Impulse Response Test to Estimate Circuit-Model Parameters for Induction Machines, *IEE Proceedings, Electric Power Applications*, Vol. 153, No. 6, 2006, pp. 883–890.

Sinha, S. C. (2005). Analysis and Control of Nonlinear Dynamical Systems with Periodic Coefficients, In: *Proceedings of the Workshop on Nonlinear Phenomena, Modeling and their applications*, SP-Brazil, Eds. JM Balthazar, RMLRF Brasil, EEN Macau, B. R. Pontes and L C S Goes, 2-4 May, 2005.

Tammi, K. (2007). *Active Control of Rotor Vibrations - Identification, Feedback, Feedforward and Repetitive Control Methods*, Doctoral thesis, VTT Publications 634, Espoo: Otamedia.

Sievers, L. A.; Blackwood, G. H.; Mercadal, M.; von Flotow, A. H. (1991). MIMO Narrowband Disturbance Rejection Using Frequency Shaping of Cost Functionals, In: *Proceedings of American Control Conference*, Boston, MA, USA.

# 2

# Robust Feedback Linearization Control for Reference Tracking and Disturbance Rejection in Nonlinear Systems

Cristina Ioana Pop and Eva Henrietta Dulf

*Technical University of Cluj, Department of Automation, Cluj-Napoca*
*Romania*

## 1. Introduction

Most industrial processes are nonlinear systems, the control method applied consisting of a linear controller designed for the linear approximation of the nonlinear system around an operating point. However, even though the design of a linear controller is rather straightforward, the result may prove to be unsatisfactorily when applied to the nonlinear system. The natural consequence is to use a nonlinear controller.

Several authors proposed the method of feedback linearization (Chou & Wu, 1995), to design a nonlinear controller. The main idea with feedback linearization is based on the fact that the system is no entirely nonlinear, which allows to transform a nonlinear system into an equivalent linear system by effectively canceling out the nonlinear terms in the closed-loop (Seo *et al.*, 2007). It provides a way of addressing the nonlinearities in the system while allowing one to use the power of linear control design techniques to address nonlinear closed loop performance specifications.

Nevertheless, the classical feedback linearization technique has certain disadvantages regarding robustness. A robust linear controller designed for the linearized system may not guarantee robustness when applied to the initial nonlinear system, mainly because the linearized system obtained by feedback linearization is in the Brunovsky form, a non robust form whose dynamics is completely different from that of the original system and which is highly vulnerable to uncertainties (Franco, *et al.*, 2006). To eliminate the drawbacks of classical feedback linearization, a robust feedback linearization method has been developed for uncertain nonlinear systems (Franco, et al., 2006; Guillard & Bourles, 2000; Franco *et al.*, 2005) and its efficiency proved theoretically by W-stability (Guillard & Bourles, 2000). The method proposed ensures that a robust linear controller, designed for the linearized system obtained using robust feedback linearization, will maintain the robustness properties when applied to the initial nonlinear system.

In this paper, a comparison between the classical approach and the robust feedback linearization method is addressed. The mathematical steps required to feedback linearize a nonlinear system are given in both approaches. It is shown how the classical approach can be altered in order to obtain a linearized system that coincides with the tangent linearized system around the chosen operating point, rather than the classical chain of integrators. Further, a robust linear controller is designed for the feedback linearized system using loop-shaping techniques and then applied to the original nonlinear system. To test the robustness of the method, a chemical plant example is given, concerning the control of a continuous stirred tank reactor.

The paper is organized as follows. In Section 2, the mathematical concepts of feedback linearization are presented – both in the classical and robust approach. The authors propose a technique for disturbance rejection in the case of robust feedback linearization, based on a feed-forward controller. Section 3 presents the $H_\infty$ robust stabilization problem. To exemplify the robustness of the method described, the nonlinear robust control of a continuous stirred tank reactor (CSTR) is given in Section 4. Simulations results for reference tracking, as well as disturbance rejection are given, considering uncertainties in the process parameters. Some concluding remarks are formulated in the final section of the paper.

## 2. Feedback linearization: Classical versus robust approach

Feedback linearization implies the exact cancelling of nonlinearities in a nonlinear system, being a widely used technique in various domains such as robot control (Robenack, 2005), power system control (Dabo et al., 2009), and also in chemical process control (Barkhordari Yazdi & Jahed-Motlagh, 2009; Pop & Dulf, 2010; Pop et al, 2010), etc. The majority of nonlinear control techniques using feedback linearization also use a strategy to enhance robustness. This section describes the mathematical steps required to obtain the final closed loop control structure, to be later used with robust linear control.

### 2.1 Classical feedback linearization
### 2.1.1 Feedback linearization for SISO systems
In the classical approach of feedback linearization as introduced by Isidori (Isidori, 1995), the Lie derivative and relative degree of the nonlinear system plays an important role. For a single input single output system, given by:

$$\dot{x} = f(x) + g(x)u \qquad \qquad (1)$$
$$y = h(x)$$

with $x \in \Re^n$ is the state, $u$ is the control input, $y$ is the output, $f$ and $g$ are smooth vector fields on $\Re^n$ and $h$ is a smooth nonlinear function. Differentiating $y$ with respect to time, we obtain:

$$\dot{y} = \frac{\partial h}{\partial x} f(x) + \frac{\partial h}{\partial x} g(x)u \qquad \qquad (2)$$
$$\dot{y} = L_f h(x) + L_g h(x)u$$

with $L_f h(x): \Re^n \to \Re$ and $L_g h(x): \Re^n \to \Re$, defined as the Lie derivatives of h with respect to f and g, respectively. Let $U$ be an open set containing the equilibrium point $x_0$, that is a point where $f(x)$ becomes null – $f(x_0) = 0$. Thus, if in equation (2), the Lie derivative of $h$ with respect to $g$ - $L_g h(x)$- is bounded away from zero for all $x \in U$ (Sastry, 1999), then the state feedback law:

$$u = \frac{1}{L_g h(x)} \left( -L_f h(x) + v \right) \qquad \qquad (3)$$

yields a linear first order system from the supplementary input $v$ to the initial output of the system, $y$. Thus, there exists a state feedback law, similar to (3), that makes the nonlinear system in (2) linear. The relative degree of system (2) is defined as the number of times the output has to be differentiated before the input appears in its expression. This is equivalent to the denominator in (3) being bounded away from zero, for all $x \in U$. In general, the relative degree of a nonlinear system at $x_0 \in U$ is defined as an integer $\gamma$ satisfying:

$$L_g L_f^i h(x) \equiv 0, \forall x \in U, i = 0,...,\gamma - 2$$
$$L_g L_f^{\gamma-1} h(x_0) \neq 0 \tag{4}$$

Thus, if the nonlinear system in (1) has relative degree equal to $\gamma$, then the differentiation of $y$ in (2) is continued until:

$$y^{(\gamma)} = L_f^\gamma h(x) + L_g L_f^{\gamma-1} h(x) u \tag{5}$$

with the control input equal to:

$$u = \frac{1}{L_g L_f^{\gamma-1} h(x)} \left( -L_f^\gamma h(x) + v \right) \tag{6}$$

The final (new) input – output relation becomes:

$$y^{(\gamma)} = v \tag{7}$$

which is linear and can be written as a chain of integrators (Brunovsky form). The control law in (6) yields $(n-\gamma)$ states of the nonlinear system in (1) unobservable through state feedback.

The problem of measurable disturbances has been tackled also in the framework of feedback linearization. In general, for a nonlinear system affected by a measurable disturbance $d$:

$$\dot{x} = f(x) + g(x)u + p(x)d$$
$$y = h(x) \tag{8}$$

with $p(x)$ a smooth vector field.

Similar to the relative degree of the nonlinear system, a disturbance relative degree is defined as a value $k$ for which the following relation holds:

$$L_p L_f^i h(x) = 0, i < k - 1$$
$$L_p L_f^{k-1} h(x) \neq 0 \tag{9}$$

Thus, a comparison between the input relative degree and the disturbance relative degree gives a measure of the effect that each external signal has on the output (Daoutidis and Kravaris, 1989). If $k < \gamma$, the disturbance will have a more direct effect upon the output, as compared to the input signal, and therefore a simple control law as given in (6) cannot ensure the disturbance rejection (Henson and Seborg, 1997). In this case complex feedforward structures are required and effective control must involve anticipatory action for the disturbance. The control law in (6) is modified to include a dynamic feed-forward/state feedback component which differentiates a state- and disturbance-dependent signal up to $\gamma$–$k$ times, in addition to the pure static state feedback component. In the particular case that $k = \gamma$, both the disturbance and the manipulated input affect the output in the same way. Therefore, a feed-forward/state feedback element which is static in the disturbance is necessary in the control law in addition to the pure state feedback element (Daoutidis and Kravaris, 1989):

$$u = \frac{1}{L_g L_f^{\gamma-1} h(x)} \left( -L_f^{\gamma} h(x) + v - L_p L_f^{\gamma-1} p(x) d \right) \qquad (10)$$

### 2.1.2 Feedback linearization for MIMO systems

The feedback linearization method can be extended to multiple input multiple output nonlinear square systems (Sastry, 1999). For a MIMO nonlinear system having $n$ states and $m$ inputs/outputs the following representation is used:

$$\begin{aligned} \dot{x} &= f(x) + g(x) u \\ y &= h(x) \end{aligned} \qquad (11)$$

where $x \in \Re^n$ is the state, $u \in \Re^m$ is the control input vector and $y \in \Re^m$ is the output vector. Similar to the SISO case, a vector relative degree is defined for the MIMO system in (11). The problem of finding the vector relative degree implies differentiation of each output signal until one of the input signals appear explicitly in the differentiation. For each output signal, we define $\gamma_j$ as the smallest integer such that at least one of the inputs appears in $y_j^{\gamma_j}$ :

$$y_j^{\gamma_j} = L_f^{\gamma_j} h_j + \sum_{i=1}^{m} L_{g_i} \left( L_f^{\gamma_j-1} h_j \right) u_i \qquad (12)$$

and at least one term $L_{(g_i)}(L_f^{\gamma_j-1}) h_j) u_i \neq 0$ for some $x$ (Sastry, 1999). In what follows we assume that the sum of the relative degrees of each output is equal to the number of states of the nonlinear system. Such an assumption implies that the feedback linearization method is exact. Thus, neither of the state variables of the original nonlinear system is rendered unobservable through feedback linearization.

The matrix $M(x)$, defined as the decoupling matrix of the system, is given as:

$$M = \begin{bmatrix} L_{g_1}\left(L_f^{r_1-1} h_1\right) & \cdots & L_{g_m}\left(L_f^{r_1-1} h_m\right) \\ \cdots & \cdots & \cdots \\ L_{g_1}\left(L_f^{r_p-1} h_m\right) & \cdots & L_{g_m}\left(L_f^{r_p-1} h_m\right) \end{bmatrix} \qquad (13)$$

The nonlinear system in (11) has a defined vector relative degree $r_1, r_2, \ldots r_m$ at the point $x_0$ if $L_{g_i} L_f^k h_i(x) \equiv 0$, $0 \le k \le r_i - 2$ for i=1,...,m and the matrix $M(x_0)$ is nonsingular. If the vector relative degree $r_1, r_2, \ldots r_m$ is well defined, then (12) can be written as:

$$\begin{bmatrix} y_1^{r_1} \\ y_2^{r_2} \\ \vdots \\ y_m^{r_m} \end{bmatrix} = \begin{bmatrix} L_f^{r_1} h_1 \\ L_f^{r_2} h_2 \\ \vdots \\ L_f^{r_m} h_m \end{bmatrix} + M(x) \begin{bmatrix} u_1 \\ u_2 \\ \vdots \\ u_m \end{bmatrix} \tag{14}$$

Since $M(x_0)$ is nonsingular, then $M(x) \in \Re^{m \times m}$ is nonsingular for each $x \in U$. As a consequence, the control signal vector can be written as:

$$u = -M^{-1}(x) \begin{bmatrix} L_f^{r_1} h_1 \\ L_f^{r_2} h_2 \\ \vdots \\ L_f^{r_m} h_m \end{bmatrix} + M^{-1}(x)v = \alpha_c(x) + \beta_c(x)v \tag{15}$$

yielding the linearized system as:

$$\begin{bmatrix} y_1^{r_1} \\ y_2^{r_2} \\ \vdots \\ y_m^{r_m} \end{bmatrix} = \begin{bmatrix} v_1 \\ v_2 \\ \vdots \\ v_m \end{bmatrix} \tag{16}$$

The states $x$ undergo a change of coordinates given by:

$$x_c = \begin{bmatrix} y_1 & \cdots & L_f^{r_1-1} y_1 & y_2 & \cdots & L_f^{r_2-1} y_2 & \cdots & \cdots & y_m & \cdots & L_f^{r_m-1} y_m \end{bmatrix}^T \tag{17}$$

The nonlinear MIMO system in (11) is linearized to give:

$$\dot{x}_c = A_c x_c + B_c v \tag{18}$$

with $A_c = \begin{bmatrix} A_{c_1} & 0_{r_1 \times r_2} & \cdots & 0_{r_1 \times r_m} \\ 0_{r_2 \times r_1} & A_{c_2} & \cdots & 0_{r_2 \times rm} \\ \vdots & \vdots & \vdots & \vdots \\ 0_{r_m \times r_1} & 0_{r_m \times r_2} & 0_{r_m \times r_3} & A_{c_m} \end{bmatrix}$ and $B_c = \begin{bmatrix} B_{c_1} & 0_{r_1 \times r_2} & \cdots & 0_{r_1 \times r_m} \\ 0_{r_2 \times r_1} & B_{c_2} & \cdots & 0_{r_2 \times r_m} \\ \vdots & \vdots & \vdots & \vdots \\ 0_{r_m \times r_1} & 0_{r_m \times r_2} & 0_{r_m \times r_3} & B_{c_m} \end{bmatrix}$, where each

term individually is given by: $A_{c_i} = \begin{bmatrix} 1 & 0 & \cdots & 0 \\ 0 & 1 & \cdots & 0 \\ \vdots & \vdots & \vdots & \vdots \\ 0 & 0 & 0 & 1 \end{bmatrix}$ and $B_{c_i} = \begin{bmatrix} 0 & 0 & \cdots & 0 & 1 \end{bmatrix}^T$.

In a classical approach, the feedback linearization is achieved through a feedback control law and a state transformation, leading to a linearized system in the form of a chain of integrators (Isidori, 1995). Thus the design of the linear controller is difficult, since the linearized system obtained bears no physical meaning similar to the initial nonlinear system

(Pop *et al.*, 2009). In fact, two nonlinear systems having the same degree will lead to the same feedback linearized system.

## 2.2 Robust feedback linearization

To overcome the disadvantages of classical feedback linearization, the robust feedback linearization is performed in a neighborhood of an operating point, $x_0$. The linearized system would be equal to the tangent linearized system around the chosen operating point. Such system would bear similar physical interpretation as compared to the initial nonlinear system, thus making it more efficient and simple to design a controller (Pop *et al.*, 2009; Pop *et al.*, 2010; Franco, *et al.*, 2006).

The multivariable nonlinear system with disturbance vector $d$, is given in the following equation:

$$\dot{x} = f(x) + g(x)u + p(x)d$$
$$y = h(x) \tag{19}$$

where $x \in \Re^n$ is the state, $u \in \Re^m$ is the control input vector and $y \in \Re^m$ is the output vector. In robust feedback linearization, the purpose is to find a state feedback control law that transforms the nonlinear system (19) in a tangent linearized one around an equilibrium point, $x_0$:

$$\dot{z} = Az + Bw \tag{20}$$

In what follows, we assume the feedback linearization conditions (Isidori, 1995) are satisfied and that the output of the nonlinear system given in (19) can be chosen as: $y(x) = \lambda(x)$, where $\lambda(x) = [\lambda_1(x)....\lambda_m(x)]$ is a vector formed by functions $\lambda_i(x)$, such that the sum of the relative degrees of each function $\lambda_i(x)$ to the input vector is equal to the number of states of (19).

With the $(A,B)$ pair in (20) controllable, we define the matrices $L(m \times n)$, $T(n \times n)$ and $R(m \times m)$ such that (Levine, 1996):

$$T(A - BRL)T^{-1} = A_c$$
$$TBR = B_c \tag{21}$$

with $T$ and $R$ nonsingular.
By taking:

$$v = LT^{-1}x_c + R^{-1}w \tag{22}$$

And using the state transformation:

$$z = T^{-1}x_c \tag{23}$$

the system in (18) is rewritten as:

$$\dot{x}_c = A_c x_c + B_c LT^{-1}x_c + B_c R^{-1}w = \left(A_c + B_c LT^{-1}\right)x_c + B_c R^{-1}w \tag{24}$$

Equation (23) yields:

$$z = T^{-1}x_c \Rightarrow x_c = Tz \tag{25}$$

Replacing (25) into (24) and using (21), gives:

$$
\begin{aligned}
T\dot{z} &= \left(A_c + B_c L T^{-1}\right)Tz + B_c R^{-1}v \Rightarrow \dot{z} = T^{-1}\left(A_c + B_c L T^{-1}\right)Tz + T^{-1}B_c R^{-1}v = \\
&= T^{-1}A_c Tz + T^{-1}B_c L T^{-1}Tz + T^{-1}B_c R^{-1}v \\
\dot{z} &= T^{-1}T\left(A - BRL\right)T^{-1}Tz + T^{-1}TBRLT^{-1}Tz + T^{-1}TBRR^{-1}v = \\
&= \left(A - BRL\right)z + BRLz + Bv = Az + Bv
\end{aligned}
\tag{26}
$$

resulting the liniarized system in (20), with $A = \partial_x f(x_0)$ and $B = g(x_0)$.
The control signal vector is given by:

$$u = a_c(x) + \beta_c(x)w = a_c(x) + \beta_c(x)LT^{-1}x_c + \beta_c(x)R^{-1}v = a(x) + \beta(x)v \tag{27}$$

The $L$, $T$ and $R$ matrices are taken as: $L = -M(x_0)\partial_x a_c(x_0)$, $T = \partial_x x_c(x_0)$, $R = M^{-1}(x_0)$ (Franco et al., 2006; Guillard și Bourles, 2000).
Disturbance rejection in nonlinear systems, based on classical feedback linearization theory, has been tackled firstly by (Daoutidis and Kravaris, 1989). Disturbance rejection in the framework of robust feedback linearization has not been discussed so far.
In what follows, we assume that the relative degrees of the disturbances to the outputs are equal to those of the inputs. Thus, for measurable disturbances, a simple static feedforward structure can be used (Daoutidis and Kravaris, 1989; Daoutidis et al., 1990). The final closed loop control scheme used in robust feedback linearization and feed-forward compensation is given in Figure 1, (Pop et al., 2010).

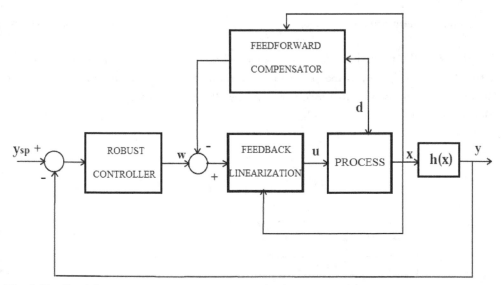

Fig. 1. Feedback linearization closed loop control scheme

or the nonlinear system given in (19), the state feedback/ feed-forward control law is given by:

$$u = a(x) + \beta(x)v - \gamma(x)d \tag{28}$$

with $a(x)$ and $\beta(x)$ as described in (27), and $\gamma(x) = M^{-1}(x)p(x)$.

## 3. Robust H∞ controller design

To ensure stability and performance against modelling errors, the authors choose the method of McFarlane-Glover to design a robust linear controller for the feedback linearized system. The method of loop-shaping is chosen due to its ability to address robust performance and robust stability in two different stages of controller design (McFarlane and Glover, 1990).

The method of loopshaping consists of three steps:

**Step 1. Open loop shaping**

Using a pre-weighting matrix $W_I$ and/or a post-weighting matrix $W_o$, the minimum and maxiumum singular values are modified to shape the response. This step results in an augmented matrix of the process transfer function: $P_s = W_o P W_I$.

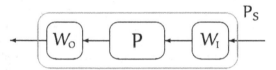

Fig. 2. Augmented matrix of the process transfer function

**Step 2. Robust stability**

The stability margin is computed as $\dfrac{1}{\varepsilon_{\max}} = \displaystyle\inf_{K \ \text{stabilizator}} \left\| \begin{bmatrix} I \\ K \end{bmatrix} (I - P_s K)^{-1} \tilde{M}_s^{-1} \right\|_\infty$, where $P_s = \tilde{M}_s^{-1} \tilde{N}_s$ is the normalized left coprime factorization of the process transfer function matrix. If $\varepsilon_{\max} \ll 1$, the pre and post weighting matrices have to be modified by relaxing the constraints imposed on the open loop shaping. If the value of $\varepsilon_{\max}$ is acceptable, for a value $\varepsilon < \varepsilon_{\max}$ the resulting controller - $K_a$ - is computed in order to sati1sfy the following relation:

$$\left\| \begin{bmatrix} I \\ K_a \end{bmatrix} (I - P_s K_a)^{-1} \tilde{M}_s^{-1} \right\|_\infty \leq \varepsilon \tag{29}$$

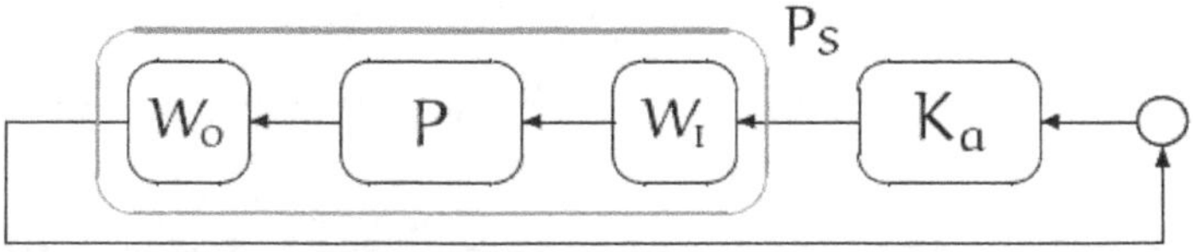

Fig. 3. Robust closed loop control scheme

**Step 3. Final robust controller**

The final resulting controller is given by the sub-optimal controller $K_a$ weighted with the matrices $W_I$ and/or $W_o$ : $K = W_I K_a W_o$ .

Using the McFarlane-Glover method, the loop shaping is done without considering the problem of robust stability, which is explicitily taken into account at the second design step, by imposing a stability margin for the closed loop system. This stability margin $\varepsilon_{max}$ is an indicator of the efficiency of the loopshaping technique.

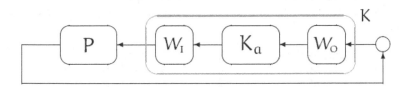

Fig. 4. Optimal controller obtained with the pre and post weighting matrices

The stability of the closed loop nonlinear system using robust stability and loopshaping is proven theoretically using W-stability (Guillard & Bourles, 2000; Franco *et al.*, 2006).

## 4. Case study: Reference tracking and disturbance rejection in an isothermal CSTR

The authors propose as an example, the control of an isothermal CSTR. A complete description of the steps required to obtain the final feedback linearization control scheme - in both approaches – is given. The robustness of the final nonlinear $H_\infty$ controller is demonstrated through simulations concerning reference tracking and disturbance rejection, for the robust feedback linearization case.

### 4.1 The isothermal continuous stirred tank reactor

The application studied is an isothermal continuous stirred tank reactor process with first order reaction:

$$A + B \rightarrow P \tag{30}$$

Different strategies have been proposed for this type of multivariable process (De Oliveira, 1994; Martinsen et al., 2004; Chen et al., 2010). The choice of the CSTR resides in its strong nonlinear character, which makes the application of a nonlinear control strategy based directly on the nonlinear model of the process preferable to classical linearization methods (De Oliveira, 1994).

The schematic representation of the process is given in Figure 5.

The tank reactor is assumed to be a well mixed one. The control system designed for such a process is intended to keep the liquid level in the tank – $x_1$- constant, as well as the $B$ product concentration – $x_2$, extracted at the bottom of the tank. It is also assumed that the output flow rate $F_o$ is determined by the liquid level in the reactor. The final concentration $x_2$ is obtained by mixing two input streams: a concentrated one $u_1$, of concentration $C_{B1}$ and a diluted one $u_2$, of concentration $C_{B2}$. The process is therefore modelled as a multivariable system, having two manipulated variables, $u = [u_1 \, u_2]^T$ and two control outputs: $x = [x_1 \, x_2]^T$.

The process model is then given as:

$$\frac{dx_1}{dt} = u_1 + u_2 - k_1\sqrt{x_1}$$

$$\frac{dx_2}{dt} = \left(C_{B1} - x_2\right)\frac{u_1}{x_1} + \left(C_{B2} - x_2\right)\frac{u_2}{x_1} - \frac{k_2 x_2}{\left(1+x_2\right)^2} \tag{31}$$

with the parameters' nominal values given in table 1. The steady state operating conditions are taken as $x_{1ss}=100$ and $x_{2ss}=7.07$, corresponding to the input flow rates: $u_{1s} =1$ and $u_{2s} =1$. The concentrations of B in the input streams, $C_{B1}$ and $C_{B2}$, are regarded as input disturbances.

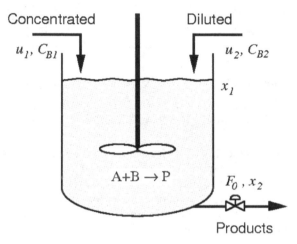

Fig. 5. Continuous stirred tank reactor (De Oliveira, 1994)

| Parameter | Meaning | Nominal Value |
|---|---|---|
| $C_{B1}$ | Concentration of B in the inlet flow $u_1$ | 24.9 |
| $C_{B2}$ | Concentration of B in the inlet flow $u_2$ | 0.1 |
| $k_1$ | Valve constant | 0.2 |
| $k_2$ | Kinetic constant | 1 |

Table 1. CSTR parameters and nominal values

From a feedback linearization point of view the process model given in (31) is rewritten as:

$$\begin{pmatrix} \dot{x}_1 \\ \dot{x}_2 \end{pmatrix} = \begin{pmatrix} -k_1\sqrt{x_1} \\ -\dfrac{k_2 x_2}{\left(1+x_2\right)^2} \end{pmatrix} + \begin{pmatrix} 1 \\ \dfrac{\left(C_{B1} - x_2\right)}{x_1} \end{pmatrix} u_1 + \begin{pmatrix} 1 \\ \dfrac{\left(C_{B2} - x_2\right)}{x_1} \end{pmatrix} u_2 \tag{32}$$

$$y = \begin{bmatrix} x_1 & x_2 \end{bmatrix}^T$$

yielding:

$$\begin{pmatrix} \dot{x}_1 \\ \dot{x}_2 \end{pmatrix} = f(x) + g_1(x)u_1 + g_2(x)u_2$$
$$y_1 = h_1(x) = x_1 \tag{33}$$
$$y_2 = h_2(x) = x_2$$

The relative degrees of each output are obtained based on differentiation:

$$\dot{y}_1 = -k_1\sqrt{x_1} + u_1 + u_2$$
$$\dot{y}_2 = -\frac{k_2 x_2}{(1+x_2)^2} + \frac{(C_{B1} - x_2)}{x_1}u_1 + \frac{(C_{B2} - x_2)}{x_1}u_2 \tag{34}$$

thus yielding $r_1 = 1$ and $r_2 = 1$, respectively, with $r_1 + r_2 = 2$, the number of state variables of the nonlinear system (32). Since this is the case, the linearization will be exact, without any state variables rendered unobservable through feedback linearization.
The decoupling matrix $M(x)$ in (13), will be equal to:

$$M(x) = \begin{bmatrix} L_{g_1}\left(L_f^0 h_1\right) & L_{g_2}\left(L_f^0 h_2\right) \\ L_{g_1}\left(L_f^0 h_1\right) & L_{g_2}\left(L_f^0 h_2\right) \end{bmatrix} = \begin{bmatrix} 1 & 1 \\ \dfrac{(C_{B1} - x_2)}{x_1} & \dfrac{(C_{B1} - x_2)}{x_1} \end{bmatrix} \tag{35}$$

and is non-singular in the equilibrium point $x_0 = [100;\ 7.07]^T$.
The state transformation is given by:

$$x_c = \begin{bmatrix} y_1 & y_2 \end{bmatrix}^T = \begin{bmatrix} x_1 & x_2 \end{bmatrix}^T \tag{36}$$

while the control signal vector is:

$$u = -M^{-1}(x)\begin{bmatrix} L_f^1 h_1 \\ L_f^1 h_2 \end{bmatrix} + M^{-1}(x)v = \alpha_c(x) + \beta_c(x)v \tag{37}$$

with $\alpha_c(x) = -\begin{bmatrix} 1 & 1 \\ \dfrac{(C_{B1} - x_2)}{x_1} & \dfrac{(C_{B1} - x_2)}{x_1} \end{bmatrix}^{-1} \begin{bmatrix} -k_1\sqrt{x_1} \\ -\dfrac{k_2 x_2}{(1+x_2)^2} \end{bmatrix}$ and $\beta_c(x) = \begin{bmatrix} 1 & 1 \\ \dfrac{(C_{B1} - x_2)}{x_1} & \dfrac{(C_{B1} - x_2)}{x_1} \end{bmatrix}^{-1}$.

In the next step, the L, T and R matrices needed for the robust feedback linearization method are computed:

$$L = -M(x_0)\partial_x a_c(x_0) = \begin{pmatrix} -0.1 \cdot 10^{-1} & 0 \\ -0.11 \cdot 10^{-2} & -0.84 \cdot 10^{-2} \end{pmatrix} \tag{38}$$

$$T = \partial_x x_c(x_0) = \begin{pmatrix} 1 & 0 \\ 0 & 1 \end{pmatrix} \tag{39}$$

$$R = M^{-1}(x_0) = \begin{pmatrix} 0.28 & 4.03 \\ 0.72 & -4.03 \end{pmatrix} \tag{40}$$

The control law can be easily obtained based on (27) as:

$$\begin{aligned} a(x) &= a_c(x) + \beta_c(x)LT^{-1}x_c \\ \beta(x) &= \beta_c(x)R^{-1} \end{aligned} \tag{41}$$

while the linearized system is given as:

$$\dot{z} = \begin{pmatrix} -\dfrac{k_1}{2}x_{10}^{-1/2} & 0 \\ 0 & \dfrac{k_2(x_{20}-1)}{(x_{20}+1)^3} \end{pmatrix} z + \begin{pmatrix} 1 & 1 \\ \dfrac{C_{B1}-7.07}{100} & \dfrac{C_{B2}-7.07}{100} \end{pmatrix} w \tag{42}$$

The linear $H_\infty$ controller is designed using the McFarlane-Glover method (McFarlane, et al., 1989; Skogestad, et al., 2007) with loop-shaping that ensures the robust stabilization problem of uncertain linear plants, given by a normalized left co-prime factorization. The loop-shaping $P_s(s) = W(s)P(s)$, with $P(s)$ the matrix transfer function of the linear system given in (41), is done with the weighting matrix, $W$:

$$W = diag\left(\frac{14}{s} \quad \frac{10}{s}\right) \tag{43}$$

The choice of the weighting matrix corresponds to the performance criteria that need to be met. Despite robust stability, achieved by using a robust $H_\infty$ controller, all process outputs need to be maintained at their set-point values. To keep the outputs at the prescribed set-points, the steady state errors have to be reduced. The choice of the integrators in the weighting matrix $W$ above ensure the minimization of the output signals steady state errors. To keep the controller as simple as possible, only a pre-weighting matrix is used (Skogestad, et al., 2007). The resulting robust controller provides for a robustness of 38%, corresponding to a value of $\varepsilon = 2.62$.

The simulation results considering both nominal values as well as modelling uncertainties are given in Figure 6. The results obtained using the designed nonlinear controller show that the closed loop control scheme is robust, the uncertainty range considered being of ±20% for $k_1$ and ±30% for $k_2$.

A different case scenario is considered in Figure 7, in which the input disturbances $C_{B1}$ and $C_{B2}$ have a +20% deviation from the nominal values. The simulation results show that the nonlinear robust controller, apart from its robustness properties, is also able to reject input disturbances.

To test the output disturbance rejection situation, the authors consider an empiric model of a measurable disturbance that has a direct effect on the output vector. To consider a general situation from a feedback linearization perspective, the nonlinear model in (33) is altered to model the disturbance, $d(t)$, as:

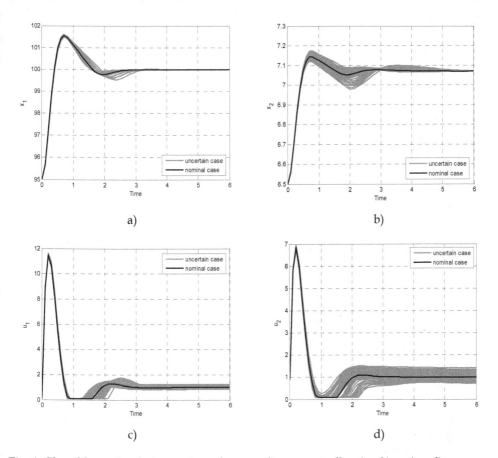

Fig. 6. Closed loop simulations using robust nonlinear controller a) $x_1$ b) $x_2$ c) $u_1$ d) $u_2$

$$\begin{pmatrix} \dot{x}_1 \\ \dot{x}_2 \end{pmatrix} = f(x) + g_1(x)u_1 + g_2(x)u_2 + p(x)d$$
$$y_1 = h_1(x) = x_1 \tag{44}$$
$$y_2 = h_2(x) = x_2$$

with $p(x)$ taken to be dependent on the output vector:

$$p(x) = \begin{pmatrix} x_1 \\ x_2 \end{pmatrix} \tag{45}$$

The relative degrees of the disturbance to the outputs of interest are: $\gamma_1 = 1$ and $\gamma_2 = 1$. Since the relative degrees of the disturbances to the outputs are equal to those of the inputs, a simple static feed-forward structure can be used for output disturbance rejection purposes, with the control law given in (28), with $\alpha(x)$ and $\beta(x)$ determined according to (27) and $\gamma(x)$ being equal to:

$$\gamma(x) = M^{-1}(x)p(x) = \begin{bmatrix} \dfrac{1}{(C_{B1} - x_2)} & \dfrac{1}{(C_{B1} - x_2)} \\ x_1 & x_1 \end{bmatrix}^{-1} \begin{pmatrix} x_1 \\ x_2 \end{pmatrix} \quad (46)$$

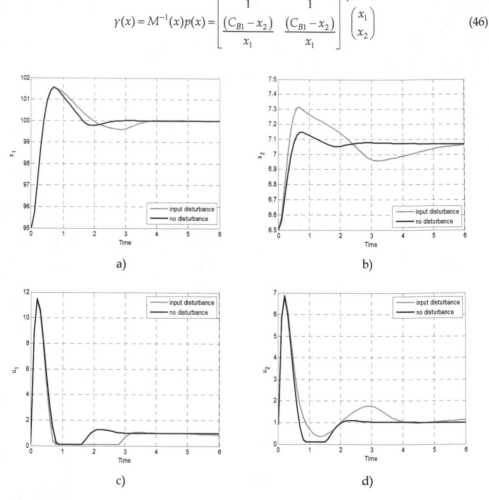

Fig. 7. Input disturbance rejection using robust nonlinear controller a) $x_1$ b) $x_2$ c) $u_1$ d) $u_2$

The simulation results considering a unit disturbance $d$ are given in Figure 8, considering a time delay in the sensor measurements of 1 minute. The results show that the state feedback/feed-forward scheme proposed in the robust feedback linearization framework is able to reject measurable output disturbances. A comparative simulation is given considering the case of no feed-forward scheme. The results show that the use of the feed-forward scheme in the feedback linearization loop reduces the oscillations in the output, with the expense of an increased control effort.

In the unlikely situation of no time delay measurements of the disturbance $d$, the results obtained using feed-forward compensator are highly notable, as compared to the situation without the compensator. The simulation results are given in Figure 9. Both, Figure 8 and Figure 9 show the efficiency of such feed-forward control scheme in output disturbance rejection problems.

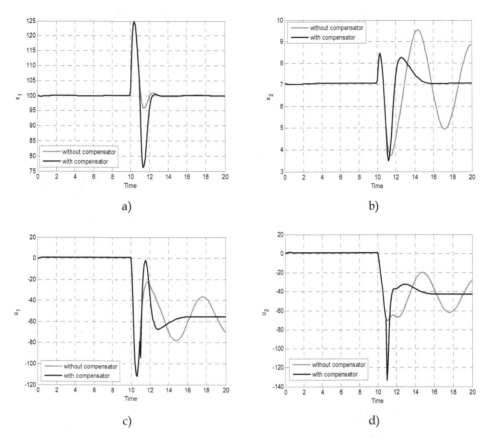

Fig. 8. Output disturbance rejection using robust nonlinear controller and feed-forward compensator considering time delay measurements of the disturbance $d$ a) $x_1$ b) $x_2$ c) $u_1$ d) $u_2$

## 5. Conclusions

As it has been previously demonstrated theoretically through mathematical computations (Guillard, et al., 2000), the results in this paper prove that by combining the robust method of feedback linearization with a robust linear controller, the robustness properties are kept when simulating the closed loop nonlinear uncertain system. Additionally, the design of the loop-shaping controller is significantly simplified as compared to the classical linearization technique, since the final linearized model bears significant information regarding the initial nonlinear model. Finally, the authors show that robust nonlinear controller - designed by combining this new method for feedback linearization (Guillard & Bourles, 2000) with a linear $H_\infty$ controller - offers a simple and efficient solution, both in terms of reference tracking and input disturbance rejection. Moreover, the implementation of the feed-forward control scheme in the state-feedback control structure leads to improved output disturbance rejection.

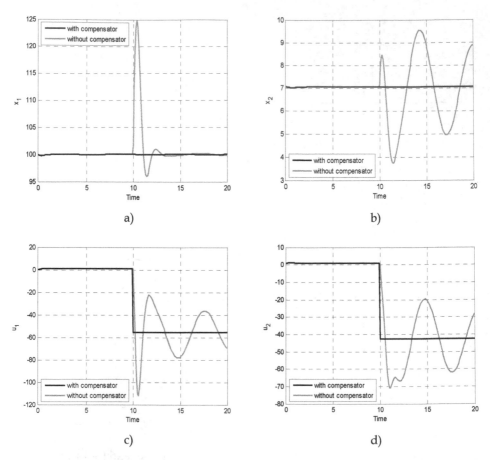

Fig. 9. Output disturbance rejection using robust nonlinear controller and feed-forward compensator considering instant measurements of the disturbance $d$ a) $x_1$ b) $x_2$ c) $u_1$ d) $u_2$

## 6. References

Barkhordari Yazdi, M., & Jahed-Motlagh, M.R. (2009), Stabilization of a CSTR with two arbitrarily switching modes using modal state feedback linearization, In: *Chemical Engineering Journal*, vol. 155, pp. 838-843, ISSN: 1385-8947

Chen, P., Lu, I.-Z., & Chen, Y.-W. (2010), Extremal Optimization Combined with LM Gradient Search for MLP Network Learning, *International Journal of Computational Intelligence Systems*, Vol.3, No. 5, pp. 622-631, ISSN: 1875-6891

Chou, YI-S., & Wu, W. (1995), Robust controller design for uncertain nonlinear systems via feedback linearization, In: *Chemical Engineering Science*, vol. 50, No. 9, pp. 1429-1439, ISSN: 0009-2509

Dabo, M., Langlois, & N., Chafouk, H. (2009), Dynamic feedback linearization applied to asymptotic tracking: Generalization about the turbocharged diesel engine outputs choice, In: *Proceedings of the American Control Conference ACC'09*, ISBN: 978-1-4244-4524-0, pp. 3458 – 3463, St. Louis, Missouri, USA, 10-12 June 2009

Daoutidis, P., & Kravaris, C. (1989), Synthesis of feedforward/state feedback controllers for nonlinear processes, In: *AIChE Journal*, vol. 35, pp.1602–1616, ISSN: 1547-5905

Daoutidis, P., Soruosh, M, & Kravaris, C. (1990), Feedforward-Feedback Control of Multivariable Nonlinear Processes, In: *AIChE Journal*, vol. 36, no.10, pp.1471–1484, ISSN: 1547-5905

Franco, A.L.D., Bourles, H., De Pieri, E.R., & Guillard, H. (2006), Robust nonlinear control associating robust feedback linearization and $H_\infty$ control, In: *IEEE Transactions on Automatic Control*, vol. 51, No. 7, pp. 1200-1207, ISSN: 0018-9286

Franco, A.L.D., Bourles, H., & De Pieri, E.R. (2005), A robust nonlinear controller with application to a magnetic bearing, In: Proceedings of the 44th *IEEE Conference on Decision and Control and The European Control Conference*, ISBN: 0-7803-9567-0, Seville, Spain, 12-15 December 2005

Guillard, H., &Bourles, H. (2000), Robust feedback linearization, In: *Proc. 14 th International Symposium on Mathematical Theory of Networks and Systems*, Perpignan, France, 19-23 June 2000

Isidori, A. (1995), *Nonlinear control systems*, Springer-Verlag, ISBN: 3540199160, New York, USA

Martinesn, F., Biegler, L. T., & Foss, B. A. (2004), A new optimization algorithm with application to nonlinear MPC, *Journal of Process Control*, vol. 14, No. 8, pp. 853-865, ISSN: 0959-1524

McFarlane, D.C, & Glover, K. (1990), Robust controller design using normalized coprime factor plant descriptions, In: *Lecture Notes in Control and Information Sciences*, vol. 138, Springer Verlag, New York, USA, ISSN: 0170-8643

De Oliveira, N. M. C (1994), *Newton type algorithms for nonlinear constrained chemical process control*, PhD thesis, Carnegie Melon University, Pennsylvania

Pop, C.I, Dulf, E., & Festila, Cl. (2009), Nonlinear Robust Control of the 13C Cryogenic Isotope Separation Column, In: *Proceedings of the 17th International Conference on Control Systems and Computer Science*, Vol.2., pp.59-65, ISSN: 2066-4451, Bucharest, Romania, 26-29 May 2009

Pop, C.-I., & Dulf, E.-H. (2010), Control Strategies of the 13C Cryogenic Separation Column, *Control Engineering and Applied Informatics*, Vol. 12, No. 2, pp.36-43, June 2010, ISSN 1454-8658

Pop, C.I., Dulf, E., Festila, Cl., & Muresan, B. (2010), Feedback Linearization Control Design for the 13C Cryogenic Separation Column, In: *International IEEE-TTTC International Conference on Automation, Quality and Testing, Robotics AQTR 2010*, vol. I, pp. 157-163, ISBN: 978-1-4244-6724-2, Cluj-Napoca, Romania, 28-30 May 2010

Robenack, K. (2005), Automatic differentiation and nonlinear controller design by exact linearization, In: *Future Generation Computer Systems*, vol. 21, pp. 1372-1379, ISSN: 0167-739X

Seo, J., Venugopala, & R., Kenne, J.-P. (2007), Feedback linearization based control of a rotational hydraulic drive, In: *Control Engineering Practice*, vol. 15, pp. 1495–1507, ISSN: 0967-0661

Sastry, S. S. (1999), *Nonlinear systems: analysis, stability and control*, Springer Verlag, ISBN: 0-387-98513-1, New York, USA

Henson, M., & Seborg, D. (Eds.),(1997), *Nonlinear process control*, Prentice Hall, ISBN: 978-0136251798, New York, USA

# 3

# Simplified Deployment of Robust Real-Time Systems Using Multiple Model and Process Characteristic Architecture-Based Process Solutions

Ciprian Lupu
*Department of Automatics and Computer Science, University "Politehnica" Bucharest*
*Romania*

## 1. Introduction

A common industrial practice is to find some specific control structures for the nonlinear processes that reduce, as much as possible, the design techniques to classic control approaches. There are a lot of situations when the designing of robust controller leads to complex hardware and software requirements. In international literature there are some interesting solutions (Kuhnen & Janocha, 2001; Dai et al., 2003; Wang & Su, 2006) for solving implementation reduction.

In following sections there will be presented, in the first part, some elements of classic robust design of RST control algorithm and on the second, two alternative solutions based on multiple model and nonlinear compensators structures.

## 2. Some elements about classic RST robust control design

The robustness of the systems is reported mainly to model parameters change or the structural model estimation uncertainties (Landau et al., 1997). A simple frequency analysis shows that the critical Nyquist point (i.e. the point (-1, 0) in the complex plane) plays an important role in assessing the robustness of the system. In this plan, we can trace hodograf (Nyquist place) open-loop system, i.e. the frequency response. The distance from the hodograf critical point system (edge module), i.e. radius centered at the critical point and tangent to hodograf is a measure of the intrinsic robustness of the system. The distance is greater, the system is more robust.

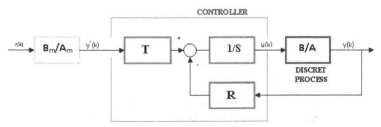

Fig. 1. RST control algorithm structure

For this study we use a RST algorithm. For robustification there are used pole placement procedures (Landau et al., 1997). Fig. 1 presents a RST algorithm.
The R, S, T polynomials are:

$$R\left(q^{-1}\right) = r_0 + r_1 q^{-1} + ... + r_{nr} q^{-nr}$$
$$S\left(q^{-1}\right) = s_0 + s_1 q^{-1} + ... + s_{ns} q^{-ns} \tag{1}$$
$$T\left(q^{-1}\right) = t_0 + t_1 q^{-1} + ... + t_{nt} q^{-nt}$$

The RST control algorithm is:

$$S(q^{-1})u(k) + R(q^{-1})y(k) = T(q^{-1})y^*(k) \tag{2}$$

or:

$$u(k) = \frac{1}{s_0}[-\sum_{i=1}^{n_S} s_i u(k-i) - \sum_{i=0}^{n_R} r_i y(k-i) + \sum_{i=0}^{n_T} t_i y^*(k-i)] \tag{3}$$

where: u(k) - algorithm output, y(k) - process output, y*(k) - trajectory or filtered set point. When necessary, an imposed trajectory can be generated using a trajectory model generator:

$$y^*(k+1) = \frac{B_m(q^{-1})}{A_m(q^{-1})}r(k) \tag{4}$$

with $A_m$ and $B_m$ like:

$$A_m(q^{-1}) = 1 + a_{m1}q^{-1} + ... + a_{mn_{Am}} q^{-n_{Am}}$$
$$B_m(q^{-1}) = b_{m0} + b_{m1}q^{-1} + ... + b_{mn_{Bm}} q^{-n_{Bm}} \tag{5}$$

Algorithm pole placement design procedure is based on the identified process' model.

$$y(k) = \frac{q^{-d}B(q^{-1})}{A(q^{-1})}u(k) \tag{6}$$

where

$$B\left(q^{-1}\right) = b_1 q^{-1} + b_2 q^{-2} + ... + b_{nb}q^{-nb}$$
$$A\left(q^{-1}\right) = 1 + a_1 q^{-1} + ... + a_{na}q^{-na} \tag{7}$$

The identification (Landau & Karimi, 1997; Lainiotis & Magill, 1969; Foulloy et al., 2004) is made in a specific process operating point and can use recursive least square algorithm exemplified in next relations developed in (Landau et al., 1997):

Simplified Deployment of Robust Real-Time Systems Using Multiple Model and Process Characteristic
Architecture-Based Process Solutions

43

$$\hat{\theta}(k+1) = \hat{\theta}(k) + F(k+1)\phi(k)\varepsilon^0(k+1), \forall k \in N$$

$$F(k+1) = F(k) - \frac{F(k)\phi(k)\phi^T(k)F(k)}{1 + \phi^T(k)F(k)\phi(k)}, \forall k \in N \qquad (8)$$

$$\varepsilon^0(k+1) = y(k+1) - \hat{\theta}^T(k)\phi(t), \forall k \in N$$

with the following initial conditions:

$$F(0) = \frac{1}{\delta}I = (GI)I, 0 < \delta < 1 \qquad (9)$$

The estimated $\hat{\theta}(k)$ represents the parameters of the polynomial plant model and $\phi^T(k)$ represents the measures vector.

This approach allows the users to verify, and if necessary, to calibrate the algorithm's robustness (Landau et al., 1997). Next expression and Fig. 2 present "disturbance-output" sensibility function.

$$S_{vy}(e^{j\omega}) \stackrel{def}{=} H_{vy}(e^{j\omega}) =$$

$$= \frac{A(e^{j\omega})S(e^{j\omega})}{A(e^{j\omega})S(e^{j\omega}) + B(e^{j\omega})R(e^{j\omega})}, \quad \forall \omega \in R \qquad (10)$$

In the same time, the negative maximum value of the sensibility function represents the module margin.

$$\Delta M\big|_{dB} = -\max_{\omega \in R}\big|S_{vy}(e^{j\omega})\big|_{dB} \qquad (11)$$

Based on this value, in an "input-output" representation (Landau et al., 1997), process nonlinearity can be bounded inside the "conic" sector, presented in Fig. 3, where $a_1$ and $a_2$ are calculated using the next expression:

$$\frac{1}{1-\Delta M} \ge a_1 \ge a_2 \ge \frac{1}{1+\Delta M} \qquad (12)$$

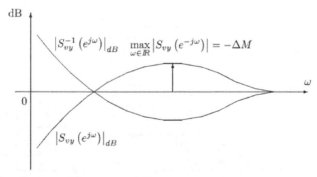

Fig. 2. Sensibility function graphic representation

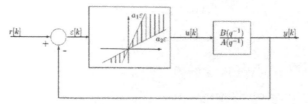

Fig. 3. Robust control design procedure

## 3. Nonlinear compensator control solution

Various papers and researches target the inverse model control approach; a few of these can be mentioned: (Tao & Kokotovic, 1996; Yuan et al., 2007) etc.

In these researches there have been proposed several types of structures based on the inverse model. According to those results, this section comes up with two very simple and efficient structures presented in Figures 4 and 5. Here, the inverse model is reduced to the geometric inversed process (nonlinear) characteristic – reflection from the first leap of static characteristic of the process, as presented in Figure 6(b).

The first solution (parallel structure) considers the addition of two commands: the first "a feedforward command" generated by the inverse model command generator and the second, generated by a classic, simple algorithm (PID, RST ).

The first command, based on the static process characteristic, depends on the set point value and is designed to generate a corresponding value that drives the process' output close to the imposed set point. The second (classic) algorithm generates a command that corrects the difference caused by external disturbances and, according to the set point, by eventual bias errors caused by mismatches between calculated inverse process characteristic and the real process.

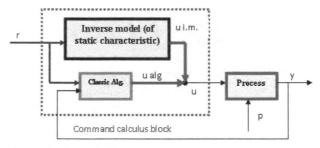

Fig. 4. Proposed scheme for "parallel" structure

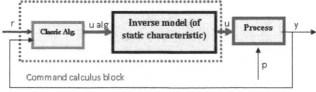

Fig. 5. Proposed scheme for "serial" structure

Simplified Deployment of Robust Real-Time Systems Using Multiple Model and Process Characteristic
Architecture-Based Process Solutions

45

The second solution (serial structure) has the inverse model command generator between the classic algorithm and the process. The inverse model command generator acts as a nonlinear compensator and depends on the command value. The (classic) algorithm generates a command that, filtered by the nonlinearity compensator, controls the real process.

The presented solutions propose treating the inverse model mismatches that "disturb" the classic command as some algorithm's model mismatches. This approach imposes designing the classic algorithm with a sufficient robustness reserve.

In Figure 4 and 5, the blocks and variables are as follows:

- Process – physical system to be controlled;
- Command calculus – unit that computes the process control law;
- Classic Alg. – control algorithm (PID, RST);
- y – outp5t of the process;
- u – output of the Command calculus block;
- u alg. – output of the classic algorithm;
- u i.m. – output of the inverse model block;
- r – system's set point or reference trajectory;
- p – disturbances.

Related to classical control loops, both solutions need addressing some supplementary specific aspects: determination of static characteristic of the process, construction of inverse model, robust control law design. In next sections we will focus on the most important aspects met on designing of the presented structure.

## 3.1 Control design procedure

For the first structure the specific aspects of the control design procedure are:
a.  determination of the process' (static) characteristic,
b.  construction of command generator,
c.  robust control law design of classic algorithm.

The second structure imposes following these steps:
a.  determination of process' characteristic,
b.  construction of nonlinearity compensator,
c.  designing the classic algorithm based on "composed process" which contains the nonlinearity compensator serialized with real process.

These steps are more or less similar for the two structures. For the (a) and (c) steps it is obvious; for (b) the command generator and nonlinearity compensator have different functions but the same design and functioning procedure. Essential aspects for these steps will be presented.

## 3.2 Determination of process characteristic

This operation is based on several experiments of discrete step increasing and decreasing of the command $u(k)$ and measuring the corresponding stabilized process output $y(k)$ (figure 6 (a)). The command $u(k)$ covers all (0 to 100%) possibilities. Because the noise is present, the static characteristics are not identical. The final static characteristic is obtained by meaning of all correspondent positions of these experiments. The graphic between two "mean" points is obtained using extrapolation procedure.

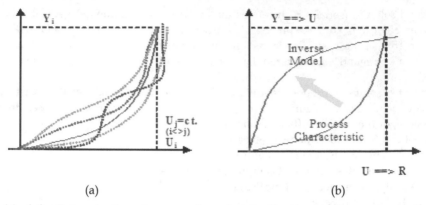

(a)                                                                                        (b)

Fig. 6. (a) - left - Determination of process characteristic. Continuous line represents the final characteristic. (b) - right - Construction of nonlinearity compensator

According to system identification theory, the dispersion of process trajectory can be found using next expression (Ljung & Soderstroom, 1983).

$$\sigma^2[n] \cong \frac{1}{n-1}\sum_{i=1}^{n} y^2[i], \ \forall n \in N^* \setminus \{1\} \tag{13}$$

This can express a measure of superposing of noise onto process, process' nonlinearity etc. and it is very important for the control algorithm robust design.

### 3.3 Construction of nonlinearity compensator (generator)
This step deals with the process's static characteristic „transposition" operation. Figure 6 (b) presents this construction. According to this, $u(k)$ is dependent to $r(k)$. This characteristic is stored in a table; thus we can conclude that, for the nonlinearity compensator based controller, selecting a new set point $r(k)$ will impose finding in this table the corresponding command $u(k)$ that determines a process output $y(k)$ close to the reference value.

### 3.4 Control law design
The control algorithm's duty is to eliminate the disturbances and differences between the nonlinearity compensator computed command and the real process behavior. A large variety of control algorithms can be used: PID, RST, fuzzy etc., but the goal is to have a very simple one. For this study we use a RST algorithm. This is designed using the pole placement procedure (Landau et al., 1997). Figure 7 presents a RST base algorithm structure. Finally, if it is imposed that all nonlinear characteristics be (graphically) bounded by the two gains, or gain limit to be great or equal to the process static maximal distance characteristic $\Delta G \geq mg$, a controller that has sufficient robustness was designed.

### 3.5 Analysis and conclusions for proposed structure
The main advantage consists in using a classic procedure for designing the control algorithm and determining the nonlinearity compensator command block, comparative to robust control design procedures. Well known procedures for identification and law control design are used. All procedures for the inverse characteristic model identification can be included in a real time software application.

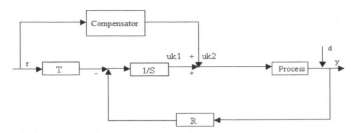

Fig. 7. Parallel RST feedback-feedforward control structure

The system is very stabile due to the global command that contains a "constant" component generated by an inverse static model command block, according to the set point value. This component is not influenced by the noise.

A fuzzy logic bloc that can "contain" human experience about some nonlinear processes can replace the inverse model command generator.

Being not very complex in terms of real time software and hardware implementation, the law control doesn't need important resources.

This structure is very difficult to use for the system that doesn't have a bijective static characteristic and for systems with different functioning regimes.

Another limitation is that this structure can only be used for stabile processes. In the situations where the process is "running", the global command is likely to not have enough flexibility to control it.

The increased number of experiments for the determination of a correct static characteristic can be another disadvantage.

## 4. Multiple model control solution

The essential function of a real-time control system is to preserve the closed-loop performances in case of non-linearity, structural disturbances or process uncertainties. A valuable way to solve these problems is the multiple-models or multicontroller structure. The first papers that mentioned the "multiple-models" structure/system have been reported in the 90s. Balakrishnan and Narendra are among the first authors addressing problems of stability, robustness, switching and designing this type of structures in their papers Narendra & Balakrishnan, 1997).

Research refinement in this field has brought extensions to the multiple-model control concept. Parametric adaptation procedures – Closed-Loop Output Error (Landau & Karimi, 1997), use of Kalman filter representation (Lainiotis & Magill, 1969), the use of neural networks (Balakrishnan, 1996) or the fuzzy systems are some of the important developments.

Related to classical control loops, multiple-model based systems need addressing some supplementary specific aspects:

• Dimension of multiple-model configuration;
• Selection of the best algorithm;
• Control law switching.

From the multiple-models control systems viewpoint, two application oriented problems can be highlighted:

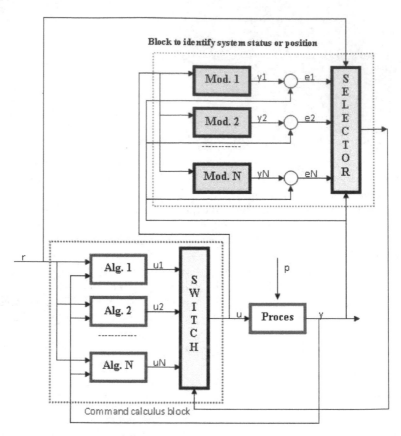

Fig. 8. General scheme for multiple model structure

- Class of systems with nonlinear characteristic, which cannot be controlled by a single algorithm;
- Class of systems with different operating regimes, where different functioning regimes don't allow the use of a unique algorithm or imposes using a very complex one with special problems on implementation.

As function of the process particularity, several multiple-models structures are proposed (Balakrishnan, 1996). One of the most general architectures is presented in Figure 8.

In Fig 8, the blocks and variables are as follows:

- Process – physical system to be controlled;
- Command calculus – unit that computes the process law control ;
- Status or position identification system – component that provide information about the model–control algorithm "best" matching for the current state of the system;
- Mod. 1, Mod. 2, ..., Mod. N - previously identified models of different regimes or operating points;
- Alg. 1, Alg. 2, ..., Alg. N – control algorithms designed for the N models;
- SWITCH – mix or switch between the control laws;

- SELECTOR – based on adequate criteria evaluations, provides information about the most appropriate model for the system's current state;
- y and y1, y2, ..., yN – output of the process and outputs of the N models;
- u – output generate by Command calculus block
- u and u1, u2, uN – output of the Command calculus block and outputs of the N control algorithms, respectively;
- r –set point system or reference trajectory;
- p – disturbances of physical process.

As noted above, depending on the process specifics and the approach used to solve the "control algorithms switching" and/or "the best model choice" problems, the scheme can be adapted on the situation by adding/eliminating some specific blocks. This section focuses on the "switching" problem.

## 4.1 Control algorithms switching

The logic operation of multiple model system structure implies that after finding the best algorithm for the current operating point of the, the next step consists in switching the control algorithm. Two essential conditions must be verified with respect to this operation:

- To be designed so that no bumps in the applications of the control law are encountered;
- To be (very) fast.

Shocks determined by the switching operation cause non-efficient and/or dangerous behaviors. Moreover, a switch determines a slow moving area of action of the control algorithm, which involves at least performance degradation.

These are the main problems to be solved in designing block switching algorithms. From structurally point of view, this block may contain all implementation algorithms or at least the algorithm coefficients.

## 4.1.1 Classic solutions

Present solutions (Landau et al., 1997; Dumitrache, 2005) solve more or less this problem and they are based on maintaining in active state all the control algorithms, also called "warm state". This supposes that every algorithm receives information about the process output $y(k)$ and set the point value (eventually filtered) $r(k)$, but only the control law $u_i(k)$ is applied on the real process, the one chosen by the switching block. This solution does not impose supplementary logic function for the system architecture and, for this reason, the switching time between algorithms is short. The drawback of this approach is that when designing the multi-model structure several supplementary steps are necessary.

These supplementary conditions demand the match of the control algorithm outputs in the neighborhood switching zones. The superposition of models identification zones accomplishes this aspect. That can be seen in Fig. 9. As a result of this superposition, the multi-model structure will have an increased number of models.

Other approaches (Dussud et al., 2000; Pages et al., 2002) propose the mix of two or more algorithms outputs. The "weighting" of each control law depends on the distance from the current process operating point and the action zone of each algorithm. Based on this, the switching from an algorithm to another one is done using weighting functions with a continuous evolution in [0–1] intervals. This technique can be easily implemented using fuzzy approach, An example is presented in Fig. 10. This solution involves solving control gain problems, determined by mixing algorithm outputs.

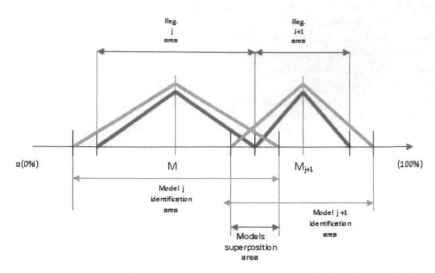

Fig. 9. Superposition of identification zones for two neighbor-models and their corresponding control actions

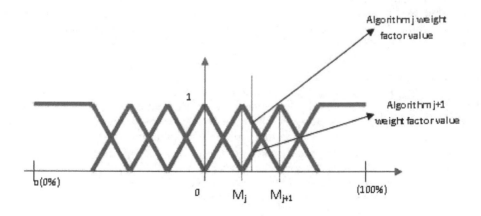

Fig. 10. Algorithms weighting functions for a specified operating position

### 4.1.2 Proposed solution

In this subsection, there is presented a solution that provides very good results for fast processes with nonlinear characteristics. The main idea is that, during the current functioning of multiple-models control systems with N model-algorithm pairs, it is supposed that just one single algorithm is to be maintained active, the good one, and all the other N-1 algorithms rest inactive. The active and inactive states represent automatic, respectively manual, regimes of a law control. The output value of the active algorithm

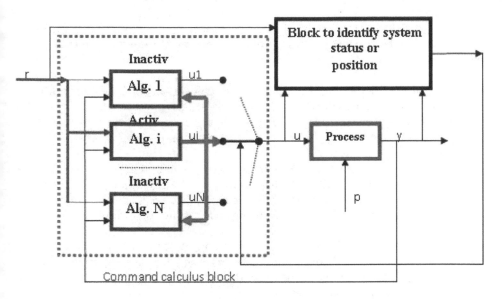

Fig. 11. Proposed multiple model switching solution

corresponds to the manual control for all the other N-1 inactive algorithms., as presented in
Fig. 11. In the switching situation, when a "better" $Aj$ algorithm is found, the actual $Ai$ active
algorithm is commuted in an inactive state, and $Aj$ in active state, respectively. For a
bumpless commutation, the manual–automatic transfer problems must be solved, and the
performance solution to this is proposed in the next section.
The system can be implemented in two variants – first - with all inactive algorithms holding
on manual regime, or – second - just a single operating algorithm (the active one) and
activation of the "new" one after the computation of the currently corresponding manual
regime and switching on automatic regime. Both variants have advantages and
disadvantages. Choosing one of them requires knowledge about the hardware performances
of the structure. After a general view, the first variant seems to be more reasonable.
In all cases, it is considered that the active algorithm output values represent manual
commands for the "new" selected one.

### 4.2 Manual – automatic bumpless transfer

The „key" of proposed multiple model switching solution performances is based on
manual-to-automatc bumpless transfer, so in this section some important elements about are
presented.
The practice implementation highlights important problems like manual-to-automatic
(M→A)/automatic-to-manual (A→M) regime commutations, respectively turning out/in
from the control saturation states; (i.e. manual operation is the situation where the
command is calculated and applied by human operator). Of course, these problems exist in

analogical systems and have specific counteracting procedures, which are not applicable on numerical systems.

In real functioning, M→A transfer is preceded by "driving" the process in the nominal action zone. To avoid command switching "bumps", one must respect the following two conditions:

- Process output must be perfectly matched with the set point value;
- According to the algorithm complexity (function of the degrees of controller polynomials), the complete algorithm memory actualization must be waited for.

Neglecting these conditions leads to "bumps" in the transfer because the control algorithm output value is computed using the actual, but also the past, values of the command, process and set point, respectively.

At the same time, there are situations when the perfect "matching" between process output and set point value is very difficult to obtained and/or needs a very long time. Hence, the application of this procedure becomes impossible in the presence of important disturbances. In the following, these facts will be illustrated using an RST control algorithm (Foulloy et al., 2004), Fig. 1.

In this context, for a inactive algorithm – possible candidate for next active one, since the algorithm output is the manual command set by operator (or active algorithm) and the process output depends on command, the set point remains the only "free" variable in the control algorithm computation. Therefore, the proposed solution consists in the modification of the set point value, according to the existent control algorithm, manual command and process output (Lupu et al., 2006).

Memory updating control algorithm is done similarly as in the automatic regime. For practical implementatio a supplementary memory location for the set point value is necessary. From Eq(3), results the expression for the set point value:

$$y^*(k) = \frac{1}{t_0}[\sum_{i=0}^{n_S} s_i u(k-i) + \sum_{i=0}^{n_R} r_i y(k-i) - \sum_{i=1}^{n_T} t_i y^*(k-i)] \tag{14}$$

When the set point (trajectory) generator Eq(4) exists, keeping all the data in correct chronology must be with respect to the following relation:

$$r(k) = \frac{A_m(q^{-1})}{B_m(q^{-1})} y^*(k) \tag{15}$$

System operation scheme is presented in Fig. 12.

Concluding, this solution proposes the computation of that set point value that determines, according to the algorithm history and process output, a control equal to the manual command applied by the operator (or active algorithm). At the instant time of the M→A switching, there are no gaps in the control algorithm memory that could determine bumps. An eventually mismatching between the set point and process output is considered as a simple change of the set point value. Moreover, this solution can be successfully used in cases of command limitation.

The only inconvenient of this solution is represented by the necessary big computation power when approaching high order systems, which is not, however, a problem nowadays.

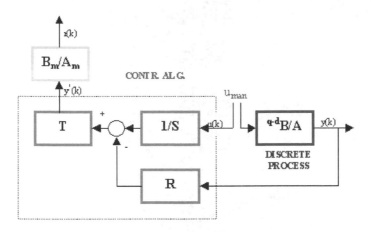

Fig. 12. Computation of the set point value for imposed manual command

## 5. Experimental results

We have evaluated the achieved performances of the multi-model control structure and
nonlinear compensator control using a hardware and software experimental platform,
developed on National Instruments LabWindows/CVI. In figure 13, one can see a
positioning control system. The main goal is the vertical control of the ball position, placed
inside the pipe; here, the actuator is air supply unit connected to cDAQ family data
acqusition module.

The obtained results are compareead to very complex (degree = 8) RST robust algorithm.
Total operations number for robust structure is 24 multiplies and 24 adding or subtraction.

The nonlinear relation between the position Y (%) and actuator command U (%) is presented
in Figure 14. One considers three operating points $P_1$, $P_2$, and P3 on the plant's nonlinear
diagram (Figure 14). Three different models are identified like: $M_1$ (0-21%), $M_2$ (21-52%) and
$M_3$ (52-100%). These will be the zones for corresponding algorithms.

According to the models-algorithms matching zones (Lupu et al., 2008), we have identified
the models $M_1$, $M_2$ and $M_3$, as being appropriated to the following intervals (0-25%), (15-
55%) (48-100%), respectively. For a sampling period $T_e$=0.2 sec, the least-squares
identification method from Adaptech/WinPIM platform (Landau et al., 1997) identifies the
next models:

$$M_1 = \frac{0.35620 - 0.05973q^{-1}}{1 - 0.454010q^{-1} - 0.09607q^{-2}}$$

$$M_2 = \frac{1.23779 - 0.33982q^{-1}}{1 - 0.98066q^{-1} - 0.17887q^{-2}}$$

$$M_3 = \frac{2.309530 - 0.089590q^{-1}}{1 - 0.827430q^{-1} - 0.006590q^{-2}}$$

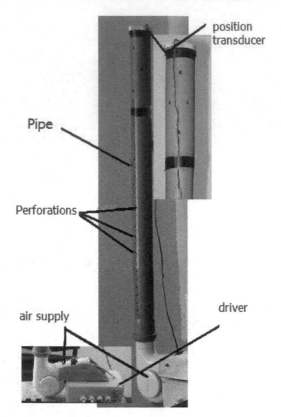

Fig. 13. Process experimental platform

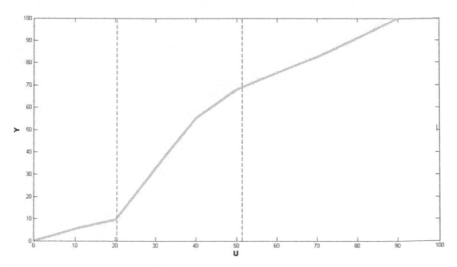

Fig. 14. Nonlinear diagram of the process

In this case, we have computed three corresponding RST algorithms using a pole placement procedure from Adaptech/WinREG platform (Landau et al., 1997). The same nominal performances are imposed to all systems, through a second order system, defined by the dynamics $\omega_0 = 3.0$, $\xi = 2.5$ (tracking performances) and $\omega_0 = 7.5$, $\xi = 0.8$ (disturbance rejection performances) respectively, keeping the same sampling period as for identification.
All of these algorithms control the process in only their corresponding zones.

$$R_1(q^{-1}) = 1.670380 \ -0.407140q^{-1} \ -0.208017q^{-2}$$

$$S_1(q^{-1}) = 1.000000 \ -1.129331q^{-1} \ + \ 0.129331q^{-2}$$

$$T_1(q^{-1}) = 3.373023 \ -3.333734q^{-1} \ + \ 1.015934q^{-2}$$

$$R_2(q^{-1}) = 0.434167 \ \ 0.153665q^{-1} \ -0.239444q^{-2}$$

$$S_2(q^{-1}) = 1.000000 \ -0.545100q^{-1} \ -0.454900q^{-2}$$

$$T_2(q^{-1}) = 1.113623 \ -1.100651q^{-1} \ + \ 0.335417q^{-2}$$

$$R_3(q^{-1}) = 0.231527 \ -0.160386q^{-1} \ -8.790E-04q^{-2}$$

$$S_3(q^{-1}) = 1.000000 \ -0.988050q^{-1} \ -0.011950q^{-2}$$

$$T_3(q^{-1}) = 0.416820 \ -0.533847q^{-1} \ + \ 0.187289q^{-2}$$

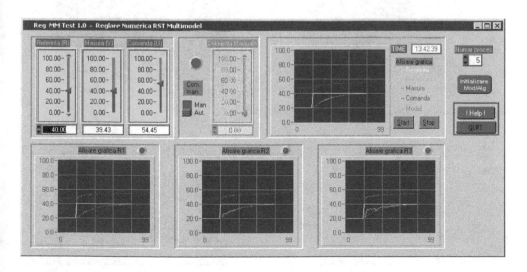

Fig. 15. Multi-model controller real-time software application

To verify the proposed switching algorithm, a multi-model controller real-time software application was designed and implemented, that can be connected to the process. The user interface is presented on Figure 15.

On the top of Figure 15, there are respectively the set point, the output and control values, manual-automatic general switch, general manual command and graphical system evolution display. On the bottom of Figure 15, one can see three graphical evolution displays corresponding to the three controllers ($R_i$, $S_i$, $T_i$, i=1...3). The colors are as follows: yellow – set point value, red – command value, blue – process output value and green – filtered set point value.

Using this application, few tests were done to verify the switching between two algorithms. The switching procedure is determinate by the change of the set point value. These tests are:

a.  from 20% (where algorithm 1 is active) to 40% (where algorithm 2 is active). The effective switching operation is done when the filtered set point (and process output) becomes greater than 21%. Figure 16(a) presents the evolutions.

b.  from 38% (where algorithm 2 is active) to 58% (where algorithm 3 is active). The effective switching operation is done when the filtered set point (and process output) becomes greater than 52%. Figure 16(b) presents the evolutions.

In both tests, one can see that there are no shocks or that there are very small oscillations in the control evolution by applying this approach. Increasing the number of models-algorithms to 4 or 5 could eliminate the small oscillations.

To verify the nonlinear compensator control structure, a second real-time software application was designed and implemented, that can be connected with the process. The

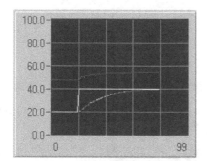 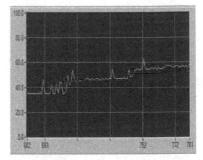

Fig. 16. a) (left) switching test;   b) (right) switching test

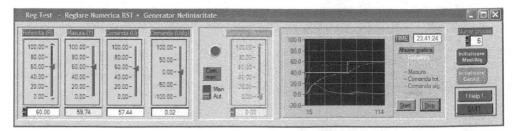

Fig. 17. Nonlinear compensator controller real-time software application

user interface is presented on Figure 17. This application implement the scheme proposed in
Fig 7 and allows the user in a special window, to construct the nonlinear compensator.
Using this application, that contains a simple second order RST algorithm, few tests were
effectuated to verify the structure. These tests are:

a.  Determination of inverse model characteristic. Figure 18(a) presents this evolutions and
    contains the corresponding $r(k)$-$u(k)$ data pairs obtained by dividing the total domain
    (0-100%) in 10 subinterval (0-10, 10-20 etc).
b.  Testing structure stability on different functioning point. Figure 18(b) presents these
    evolutions.

On (a) test one can see the nonlinear process model characteristics identification procedures.
The second one, present that there are no shocks and the system is stable on different
functioning points.

For proposed control structure, presented in Figure 7 was identified a wery simple model:

$$M = \frac{1.541650}{1 - 0.790910q^{-1}}$$

In this case, we have computed the corresponding RST algorithms using a pole placement
procedure from Adaptech/WinREG platform. The nominal performances are imposed,
through a second order system, defined by the dynamics $\omega_0 = 2$, $\xi = 0.95$ (tracking
performances) and $\omega_0 = 1.1$, $\xi = 0.8$ (disturbance rejection performances) respectively,
keeping the same sampling period as for identification.

$$R(q^{-1}) = 0.083200 \ -0.056842q^{-1}$$

$$S(q^{-1}) = 1.000000 \ -1.000000q^{-1}$$

$$T(q^{-1}) = 0.648656 \ -1.078484q^{-1} + \ 0.456187q^{-2}$$

To calculate corresponding command for a single controller presented before, there are used
7 multiplies and 7 adding or subtraction operations.
For the second control structure, in addition to command calculus operation here is the
calculus of direct command. This depends on software implementation. For PLC, particular

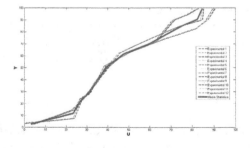
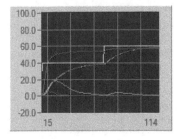

Fig. 18. a) Process static determination test; b) functioning test;

and real time process computer, in general, where (C) code programming can be used, in a solution or other similar implementation:

*// segment determination*
*segment = (int)(floor(rdk/10));*
*// segment gain and difference determination*
*panta = (tab_cp[segment+1] - tab_cp[segment]) \* 0.1;*
*// linear value calculus*
*val_com_tr = uk + 1.00 \* (panta \* (rdk - segment\*10.0) + tab_cp[segment]);*

there are necessary 10 multiplies and 4 adding or subtraction operations (the time and memory addressing effort operation is considered equal to a multiply operation). Total operations number for nonlinear compensator structure is 17 multiplies and 14 adding or subtraction.

Because the multi-models control structure must assure no bump commutations, all of 3 control algorithms work in parallel (Lupu et al., 2008). So, for multiple model structure, to calculate corresponding command for a C1 controller  9 multiplies and 9 adding or subtraction operations are used, for C2 9 multiplies and 9 adding or subtraction operations and for C3 9 multiplies and 9 adding or subtraction operations, total number 27 multiplies and 27 adding or subtractions.

As mentioned before, total operations number for classic robust structure is 24 multiplies and 24 adding or subtraction.

It is visible that nonlinear compensator structure has a less number of multiplies and adding or subtraction comparative to classic multi-model solutions and robust control approach.

In the same time multi-model and robust control solutions have comparative numbers of implemented operations. The choice of solution depends on process features and used hardware.

This means that the system with nonlinear compensator is faster or needs a more simplified hardware and software arquitecture.

## 6. Conclusions

The first proposed method (multiple models) is a more elaborated one and needs a lot of precise operations like data acquisition, models identification, and control algorithms design. For these reasons it allows us to control a large class of nonlinear processes that can contain nonlinear characteristics, different functioning regimes etc.

The second proposed method (inverse model) does not impose complex operations, it is very easy to use, but it is limited from the nonlinearity class point of view. This structure is very difficult to use for the system that doesn't have a bijective static characteristic or have different functioning regimes.

## 7. Acknowledgment

This work was supported by CNCSIS - IDEI Research Program of Romanian Research, Development and Integration National Plan II, Grant no. 1044/2007 and „Automatics, Process Control and Computers" Research Center from University „Politehnica" of Bucharest. (U.P.B. – A.C.P.C.) projects.

# 8. References

Balakrishnan, J., (1996). *Control System Design Using Multiple Models, Switching and Tuning*, Ph. D. Dissertation, University of Yale, USA

Dai, X., He, D., Zhang, T. & Zhang, K., (2003). Generalized inversion for the linearization and decoupling control of nonlinear systems, *Proc. Of IEE Control Theory Application*, pp. 267-277

Dumitrache, I., (2005). *Engineering the automatic (Ingneria Reglarii Automate)*, Politehnica Press, Bucuresti, 2005, ISBN 973-8449-72-3

Dussud, M., Galichet S. & Foulloy L.P., (2000). Application of fuzzy logic control for continuous casting mold level control, *IEEE Trans. on Control Systems Technology*, 6. no. 2, pp. 246-256, ISSN 1063–6536

Foulloy, L., Popescu, D. & Tanguy, G.D., (2004). *Modelisation, Identification et Commande des Systemes*, Editura Academiei Romane, Bucuresti, ISBN 973-27-1086-1

Kuhnen, K. & Janocha, H. (2001). Inverse feedforward controller for complex hysteretic nonlinearities in smart-material systems, *Proc. of the 20th IASTED-Conf. on Modeling, Identification and Control, Insbruck*, pp. 375-380, ISBN 0171-8096

Lainiotis, D. G. & Magill, D.T, (1969). Recursive algorithm for the calculation of the adaptive Kalman filter weighting coefficients, *IEEE Transactions on Automatic Control*, 14(2):215–218, April, *ISSN* 0018-9286

Landau, I. D. & Karimi, A., (1997). Recursive algorithm for identification in closed loop: a unified approach and evaluation, *Automatica*, vol. 33, no. 8, pp. 1499-1523, ISSN 0005-1098

Landau, I. D., Lozano, R. & Saad, M. M', (1997). *Adaptive Control*, Springer Verlag, London, ISBN 3-540-76187-X

Ljung, L. & Soderstroom, T., (1983). *Theory and Practice of Recursive Identification*, MIT Press, Cambridge, Massahusetts, ISBN 10 - 0-262-12095-X.

Lupu C., Popescu D., Ciubotaru, Petrescu C. & Florea G., (2006). Switching Solution for Multiple Models Control Systems, *Proc. of MED'06*, The *14th Mediterranean Conference on Control Automation*, 28-30 June, 2006, Ancona, Italy, pp. 1-6, ISBN: 0-9786720-0-3

Lupu, C., Popescu, D., Petrescu, C., Ticlea, Al., Dimon, C., Udrea, A. & Irimia, B., (2008). Multiple-Model Design and Switching Solution for Nonlinear Processes Control, *Proc. of ISC'08, The 6th Annual Industrial Simulation Conference*, 09-11 June, Lyon, France, pp. 71-76, ISBN 978-90-77381-4-03

Narendra, K. S. & Balakrishnan, J., (1997). Adaptive Control using multiple models, *IEEE Transactions on Automatic Control*, vol. 42, no. 2, pp. 171 – 187, *ISSN* 0018-9286

Pages, O., Mouille P., Odonez, R. & Caron, B., (2002). Control system design by using a multi-controller approach with a real-time experimentation for a robot wrist, *International Journal of Control*, vol. 75 (no. 16 & 17), pp. 1321 – 1334, ISSN: 1366-5820

Tao, G. & Kokotovic, P., (1996). *Adaptive control of systems with actuator and sensor nonlinearities*, Wiley, N.Y., ISBN 0-471-15654-X

Yuan, X., Wang, Y. & Wu, L., (2007). Adaptive inverse control of excitation system with actuator uncertainty, *Wseas Transactions on System and Control*, Issue 8, Vol.2, August 2007, pp. 419-428, ISSN 1991-8763

Wang, Q. & Su, C., (2006). Robust adaptive control of a class of nonlinear systems including actuator hysteresis with Prandtl–Ishlinskii presentations, *Automatica*, vol. 42, 2006, pp. 859 – 867, ISSN 0005-1098

Wang, Q. & Stengel, R., F., (2001). Searching for robust minimal-order compensators, *ASME Journal Dynamic Systems, Measurement and, Control*, vol. 123, no. 2, pp. 233–236, 2001, ISSN 0022-0434

# 4

# Partially Decentralized Design Principle in Large-Scale System Control

Anna Filasová and Dušan Krokavec
*Technical University of Košice*
*Slovakia*

## 1. Introduction

A number of problems that arise in state control can be reduced to a handful of standard convex and quasi-convex problems that involve matrix inequalities. It is known that the optimal solution can be computed by using interior point methods (Nesterov & Nemirovsky (1994)) which converge in polynomial time with respect to the problem size, and efficient interior point algorithms have recently been developed for and further development of algorithms for these standard problems is an area of active research. For this approach, the stability conditions may be expressed in terms of linear matrix inequalities (LMI), which have a notable practical interest due to the existence of powerful numerical solvers. Some progres review in this field can be found e.g. in Boyd et al. (1994), Hermann et al. (2007), Skelton et al. (1998), and the references therein.

Over the past decade, $H_\infty$ norm theory seems to be one of the most sophisticated frameworks for robust control system design. Based on concept of quadratic stability which attempts to find a quadratic Lyapunov function (LF), $H_\infty$ norm computation problem is transferred into a standard LMI optimization task, which includes bounded real lemma (BRL) formulation (Wu et al. (2010)). A number of more or less conservative analysis methods are presented to assess quadratic stability for linear systems using a fixed Lyapunov function. The first version of the BRL presents simple conditions under which a transfer function is contractive on the imaginary axis of the complex variable plain. Using it, it was possible to determine the $H_\infty$ norm of a transfer function, and the BRL became a significant element to shown and prove that the existence of feedback controllers (that results in a closed loop transfer matrix having the $H_\infty$ norm less than a given upper bound) is equivalent to the existence of solutions of certain LMIs. Linear matrix inequality approach based on convex optimization algorithms is extensively applied to solve the above mentioned problem (Jia (2003), Kozáková & Veselý (2009)), Pipeleers et al. (2009).

For time-varying parameters the quadratic stability approach is preferable utilized (see. e.g. Feron et al. (1996)). In this approach a quadratic Lyapunov function is used which is independent of the uncertainty and which guarantees stability for all allowable uncertainty values. Setting Lyapunov function be independent of uncertainties, this approach guarantees uniform asymptotic stability when the parameter is time varying, and, moreover, using a parameter-dependent Lyapunov matrix quadratic stability may be established by LMI tests over the discrete, enumerable and bounded set of the polytope vertices, which define the uncertainty domain. To include these requirements the equivalent LMI representations of

BRL for continuous-time, as well as discrete-time uncertain systems were introduced (e.g. see Wu and Duan (2006), and Xie (2008)). Motivated by the underlying ideas a simple technique for the BRL representation can be extended to state feedback controller design, performing system $H_\infty$ properties of quadratic performance. When used in robust analysis of systems with polytopic uncertainties, they can reduce conservatism inherent in the quadratic methods and the parameter-dependent Lyapunov function approach. Of course, the conservativeness has not been totally eliminated by this approach.

In recent years, modern control methods have found their way into design of interconnected systems leading to a wide variety of new concepts and results. In particular, paradigms of LMIs and $H_\infty$ norm have appeared to be very attractive due to their good promise of handling systems with relative high dimensions, and design of partly decentralized schemes substantially minimized the information exchange between subsystems of a large scale system. With respect to the existing structure of interconnections in a large-scale system it is generally impossible to stabilize all subsystems and the whole system simultaneously by using decentralized controllers, since the stability of interconnected systems is not only dependent on the stability degree of subsystems, but is closely dependent on the interconnections (Jamshidi (1997), Lunze (1992), Mahmoud & Singh (1981)). Including into design step the effects of interconnections, a special view point of decentralized control problem (Filasová & Krokavec (1999), Filasová & Krokavec (2000), Leros (1989)) can be such adapted for large-scale systems with polytopic uncertainties. This approach can be viewed as pairwise-autonomous partially decentralized control of large-scale systems, and gives the possibility establish LMI-based design method as a special problem of pairwise autonomous subsystems control solved by using parameter dependent Lyapunov function method in the frames of equivalent BRL representations.

The chapter is devoted to studying partially decentralized control problems from above given viewpoint and to presenting the effectiveness of parameter-dependent Lyapunov function method for large-scale systems with polytopic uncertainties. Sufficient stability conditions for uncertain continuous-time systems are stated as a set of linear matrix inequalities to enable the determination of parameter independent Lyapunov matrices and to encompass quadratic stability case. Used structures in the presented forms enable potentially to design systems with the reconfigurable controller structures.

The chapter is organized as follows. In section 2 basis preliminaries concerning the $H_\infty$ norm problems are presented along with results on BRL, improved BRLs representations and modifications, as well as with quadratic stability. To generalize properties of non-expansive systems formulated as $H_\infty$ problems in BRL forms, the main motivation of section 3 was to present the most frequently used BRL structures for system quadratic performance analyzes. Starting work with such introduced formalism, in section 4 the principle of memory-less state control design with quadratic performances which performs $H_\infty$ properties of the closed-loop system is formulated as a feasibility problem and expressed over a set of LMIs. In section 5, the BRL based design method is outlined to posse the sufficient conditions for the pairwise decentralized control of one class of large-scale systems, where Lyapunov matrices are separated from the matrix parameters of subsystem pairs. Exploring such free Lyapunov matrices, the parameter-dependent Lyapunov method is adapted for pairwise decentralized controller design method of uncertain large-scale systems in section 6, namely quadratic stability conditions and the state feedback stabilizability problem based on these conditions. Finally, some concluding remarks are given in the end. However, especially in sections 4-6, numerical examples are given to illustrate the feasibility and properties of different equivalent BRL representations.

## 2. Basic preliminaries

### 2.1 System model

The class of the systems considering in this section can be formed as follows

$$\dot{q}(t) = Aq(t) + Bu(t) \tag{1}$$

$$y(t) = Cq(t) + Du(t) \tag{2}$$

where $q(t) \in R^n$, $u(t) \in R^r$, and $y(t) \in R^m$ are vectors of the state, input and measurable output variables, respectively, nominal system matrices $A \in R^{n \times n}$, $B \in R^{n \times r}$, $C \in R^{m \times n}$ and $D \in R^{m \times r}$ are real matrices.

### 2.2 Schur complement

**Proposition 1.** . *Let $Q > 0$, $R > 0$, $S$ are real matrices of appropriate dimensions, then the next inequalities are equivalent*

$$\begin{bmatrix} Q & S \\ S^T & -R \end{bmatrix} < 0 \Leftrightarrow \begin{bmatrix} Q + SR^{-1}S^T & 0 \\ 0 & -R \end{bmatrix} < 0 \Leftrightarrow Q + SR^{-1}S^T < 0, \; R > 0 \tag{3}$$

*Proof.* Let the linear matrix inequality takes the starting form in (3), $\det R \neq 0$ then using Gauss elimination principle it yields

$$\begin{bmatrix} I & SR^{-1} \\ 0 & I \end{bmatrix} \begin{bmatrix} Q & S \\ S^T & -R \end{bmatrix} \begin{bmatrix} I & 0 \\ R^{-1}S^T & I \end{bmatrix} = \begin{bmatrix} Q + SR^{-1}S^T & 0 \\ 0 & -R \end{bmatrix} \tag{4}$$

Since

$$\det \begin{bmatrix} I & SR^{-1} \\ 0 & I \end{bmatrix} = 1 \tag{5}$$

and it is evident that (4) implies (3). This concludes the proof. □

Note that in the next sections the matrix notations $Q, R, S$, can be used in another context, too.

### 2.3 Bounded real lemma

**Proposition 2.** *System (1), (2) is stable with quadratic performance $\|C(sI - A)^{-1}B + D\|_{\infty}^2 \le \gamma$ if there exist a symmetric positive definite matrix $P > 0$, $P \in R^{n \times n}$ and a positive scalar $\gamma > 0$, $\gamma \in R$ such that*

$$i. \quad \begin{bmatrix} A^T P + PA & PB & C^T \\ * & -\gamma I_r & D^T \\ * & * & -I_m \end{bmatrix} < 0$$

$$ii. \quad \begin{bmatrix} PA^T + AP & PC^T & B \\ * & -\gamma I_m & D \\ * & * & -I_r \end{bmatrix} < 0$$

$$iii. \quad \begin{bmatrix} P^{-1}A^T + AP^{-1} & B & P^{-1}C^T \\ * & -\gamma I_r & D^T \\ * & * & -I_m \end{bmatrix} < 0$$

$$iv. \quad \begin{bmatrix} A^T P^{-1} + P^{-1}A & C^T & P^{-1}B \\ * & -\gamma I_m & D \\ * & * & -I_r \end{bmatrix} < 0$$
(6)

*where $I_r \in R^{r \times r}$, $I_m \in R^{m \times m}$ are identity matrices, respectively.*

Hereafter, $*$ denotes the symmetric item in a symmetric matrix.

*Proof. i.* Defining Lyapunov function as follows (Gahinet et al. (1996))

$$v(q(t)) = q^T(t)Pq(t) + \int_0^t (y^T(r)y(r) - \gamma u^T(r)u(r))dr > 0 \tag{7}$$

where $P = P^T > 0$, $P \in R^{n \times n}$, $\gamma > 0 \in R$, and evaluating the derivative of $v(q(t))$ with respect to $t$ along a system trajectory then it yields

$$\dot{v}(q(t)) = \dot{q}^T(t)Pq(t) + q^T(t)P\dot{q}(t) + y^T(t)y(t) - \gamma u^T(t)u(t) < 0 \tag{8}$$

Thus, substituting (1), (2) into (8) gives

$$\dot{v}(q(t)) = (Aq(t) + Bu(t))^T Pq(t) + q^T(t)P(Aq(t) + Bu(t)) - \gamma u^T(t)u(t) + \\ + (Cq(t) + Du(t))^T (Cq(t) + Du(t)) < 0 \tag{9}$$

and with the next notation
$$q_c^T(t) = [q^T(t) \ u^T(t)] \tag{10}$$

it is obtained
$$\dot{v}(q(t)) = q_c^T(t)P_c q_c(t) < 0 \tag{11}$$

where
$$P_c = \begin{bmatrix} A^T P + PA & PB \\ * & -\gamma I_r \end{bmatrix} + \begin{bmatrix} C^T C & C^T D \\ * & D^T D \end{bmatrix} < 0 \tag{12}$$

Since
$$\begin{bmatrix} C^T C & C^T D \\ * & D^T D \end{bmatrix} = \begin{bmatrix} C^T \\ D^T \end{bmatrix} [C \ D] \geq 0 \tag{13}$$

Schur complement property implies

$$\begin{bmatrix} 0 & 0 & C^T \\ * & 0 & D^T \\ * & * & -I_m \end{bmatrix} \geq 0 \tag{14}$$

and using (14) the LMI condition (12) can be written compactly as *i.* of (2).
*ii.* Since $H_\infty$ norm is closed with respect to complex conjugation and matrix transposition (Petersen et al. (2000)), then

$$\|C(sI - A)^{-1}B + D\|_\infty^2 \leq \gamma \quad \Leftrightarrow \quad \|B^T(sI - A^T)^{-1}C^T + D^T\|_\infty^2 \leq \gamma \tag{15}$$

and substituting the dual matrix parameters into *i.* of (2) implies *ii.* of (2).
*iii.* Defining the congruence transform matrix

$$L_1 = \text{diag} \left[ \, P^{-1} \; I_r \; I_m \right] \tag{16}$$

and pre-multiplying left-hand side and right-hand side of *i.* of (2) by (16) subsequently gives *ii.* of (16).

*iii.* Analogously, substituting the matrix parameters of the dual system description form into *iii.* of (2) implies *iv.* of (2). $\qquad\qquad\qquad\qquad\qquad\qquad\qquad\qquad\qquad\qquad\qquad\qquad\quad\Box$

Note, to design the gain matrix of memory-free control law using LMI principle only the condition *ii.* and *iii.* of (2) are suitable.
Preposition 2 is quite attractive giving a representative result of its type to conclude the asymptotic stability of a system which $H_\infty$ norm is less than a real value $\gamma > 0$, and can be employed in the next for comparative purposes. However, its proof is technical, which more or less, can brings about inconvenience in understanding and applying the results. Thus, in this chapter, some modifications are proposed to directly reach applicable solutions.

### 2.4 Improved BRL representation
As soon as the representations (2) of the BRL is given, the proof of improvement BRL representation is rather easy as given in the following.

**Theorem 1.** *System (1), (2) is stable with quadratic performance* $\|C(sI-A)^{-1}B+D\|_\infty^2 \le \gamma$ *if there exist a symmetric positive definite matrix* $P > 0$, $P \in R^{n \times n}$, *matrices* $S_1, S_2 \in R^{n \times n}$, *and a scalar* $\gamma > 0$, $\gamma \in R$ *such that*

$$i. \quad \begin{bmatrix} -S_1A - A^TS_1^T & -S_1B & P+S_1-A^TS_2^T & C^T \\ * & -\gamma I_r & -B^TS_2^T & D^T \\ * & * & S_2+S_2^T & 0 \\ * & * & * & -I_m \end{bmatrix} < 0$$

$$ii. \quad \begin{bmatrix} -S_1A^T - AS_1^T & -S_1C^T & P+S_1-AS_2^T & B \\ * & -\gamma I_m & -CS_2^T & D \\ * & * & S_2+S_2^T & 0 \\ * & * & * & -I_r \end{bmatrix} < 0 \tag{17}$$

*Proof. i.* Since (1) implies

$$\dot{q}(t) - Aq(t) - Bu(t) = 0 \tag{18}$$

then with arbitrary square matrices $S_1, S_2 \in R^{n \times n}$ it yields

$$(q^T(t)S_1 + \dot{q}^T(t)S_2)(\dot{q}(t) - Aq(t) - Bu(t)) = 0 \tag{19}$$

Thus, adding (19), as well as its transposition to (8) and substituting (2) it yields

$$\dot{v}(q(t)) = $$
$$= \dot{q}^T(t)Pq(t) + q^T(t)P\dot{q}(t) - \gamma u^T(t)u(t) + (Cq(t)+Du(t))^T(Cq(t)+Du(t)) +$$
$$+ (q^T(t)S_1 + \dot{q}^T(t)S_2)(\dot{q}(t) - Aq(t) - Bu(t)) +$$
$$+ (\dot{q}^T(t) - q^T(t)A^T - u^T(t)B^T)(S_1^Tq(t) + S_2^T\dot{q}(t)) < 0 \tag{20}$$

and using the notation

$$q_c^T(t) = \left[ q^T(t) \; u^T(t) \; \dot{q}^T(t) \right] \tag{21}$$

it can be obtained

$$\dot{v}(q(t)) = q_c^T(t) P_c^\circ q_c(t) < 0 \tag{22}$$

where

$$P_c^\circ = \begin{bmatrix} C^T C & C^T D & 0 \\ * & D^T D & 0 \\ * & * & 0 \end{bmatrix} + \begin{bmatrix} -S_1 A - A^T S_1^T & -S_1 B & P + S_1 - A^T S_2^T \\ * & -\gamma I_m & -B^T S_2^T \\ * & * & S_2 + S_2^T \end{bmatrix} < 0 \tag{23}$$

Thus, analogously to (13), (14) it then follows the inequality (23) can be written compactly as i. of (17).

ii. Using duality principle, substituting the dual matrix parameters into i. of (17) implies ii. of (17). □

## 2.5 Basic modifications

Obviously, the aforementioned proof for Theorem 1 is rather simple, and connection between Theorem 1 and the existing results of Preposition 2 can be established. To convert it into basic modifications the following theorem yields alternative ways to describe the $H_\infty$-norm.

**Theorem 2.** *System (1), (2) is stable with quadratic performance* $\|C(sI - A)^{-1} B + D\|_\infty^2 \le \gamma$ *if there exist a symmetric positive definite matrix* $P > 0$, $P \in R^{n \times n}$, *a matrix* $S_2 \in R^{n \times n}$, *and a scalar* $\gamma > 0$, $\gamma \in R$ *such that*

$$i. \quad \begin{bmatrix} P^{-1} A^T + A P^{-1} & B & P^{-1} A^T & P^{-1} C^T \\ * & -\gamma I_r & B^T & D^T \\ * & * & -S_2^{-1} - S_2^{-T} & 0 \\ * & * & * & -I_m \end{bmatrix} < 0$$

$$ii. \quad \begin{bmatrix} P A^T + A P & P C^T & A & B \\ * & -\gamma I_m & C & D \\ * & * & -S_2^{-1} - S_2^{-T} & 0 \\ * & * & * & -I_r \end{bmatrix} < 0 \tag{24}$$

*Proof. i.* Since $S_1$, $S_2$ are arbitrary square matrices selection of $S_1$ can now be made in the form $S_1 = -P$, and it can be supposed that $\det(S_2) \ne 0$. Thus, defining the congruence transform matrix

$$L_2 = \text{diag} \left[ P^{-1} \; I_r \; -S_2^{-1} \; I_m \right] \tag{25}$$

and pre-multiplying right-hand side of *i.* of (17) by $L_2$, and left-hand side of *i.* of (17) by $L_2^T$ leads to *i.* of (24).

*ii.* Analogously, selecting $S_1 = -P$, and considering $\det(S_2) \ne 0$ the next congruence transform matrix can be introduced

$$L_3 = \text{diag} \left[ I_n \; I_m \; -S_2^{-1} \; I_n \right] \tag{26}$$

and pre-multiplying right-hand side of *ii.* of (17) by $L_3$, and left-hand side of *ii.* of (17) by $L_3^T$ leads to *ii.* of (24). □

## 2.6 Associate modifications

Since alternate conditions of a similar type are also available, similar to the proof of Theorem 2 the following conclusions can be given.

**Corollary 1.** *Similarly, setting $S_2 = -\delta P$, where $\delta > 0$, $\delta \in R$ the inequality ii. given in (24) reduces to*

$$\begin{bmatrix} PA^T+AP & PC^T & A & B \\ * & -\gamma I_m & C & D \\ * & * & -2\delta^{-1}P^{-1} & 0 \\ * & * & * & -I_r \end{bmatrix} < 0 \tag{27}$$

$$\begin{bmatrix} PA^T+AP & PC^T & AP & B \\ * & -\gamma I_m & CP & D \\ * & * & -2\delta^{-1}P & 0 \\ * & * & * & -I_r \end{bmatrix} < 0 \tag{28}$$

*respectively, and using Schur complement property then (28) can now be rewritten as*

$$\Lambda_1 + 0.5\,\delta\Lambda_2 < 0 \tag{29}$$

*where*

$$\Lambda_1 = \begin{bmatrix} AP+PA^T & PC^T & B \\ * & -\gamma I_m & D \\ * & * & -I_r \end{bmatrix} < 0 \tag{30}$$

$$\Lambda_2 = \begin{bmatrix} AP \\ CP \\ 0 \end{bmatrix} P^{-1} \begin{bmatrix} PA^T & PC^T & 0 \end{bmatrix} = \begin{bmatrix} APA^T & APC^T & 0 \\ CPA^T & CPC^T & 0 \\ 0 & 0 & 0 \end{bmatrix} \tag{31}$$

*Choosing $\delta$ as a sufficiently small scalar, where*

$$0 < \delta < 2\lambda_1/\lambda_2 \tag{32}$$

$$\lambda_1 = \lambda_{max}(-\Lambda_1), \qquad \lambda_2 = \lambda_{min}(\Lambda_2) \tag{33}$$

*(28) be negative definite for a feasible P of ii. of (2).* ∎

**Remark 1.** *Associated with the second statement of the Theorem 2, setting $S_2 = -\delta I_n$, then ii. of (24) implies*

$$\begin{bmatrix} AP+PA^T & PC^T & A & B \\ * & -\gamma I_m & C & D \\ * & * & -2\delta^{-1}I_n & 0 \\ * & * & * & -I_r \end{bmatrix} < 0 \tag{34}$$

*and (34) can be written as (29), with (30) and with*

$$\Lambda_2 = \begin{bmatrix} AA^T & AC^T & 0 \\ CA^T & CC^T & 0 \\ 0 & 0 & 0 \end{bmatrix} \tag{35}$$

*Thus, satisfying (32), (33) then (34) be negative definite for a feasible P of iii. of (2).* ∎

Note, the form (34) is suitable to optimize a solution with respect to both LMI variables $\gamma$, $\delta$ in an LMI structure. Conversely, the form (28) behaves LMI structure only if $\delta$ is a prescribed constant design parameter, and only $\gamma$ can by optimized as an LMI variable if possible, or to formulate design task as BMI problem.

**Corollary 2.** *By the same way, setting $S_2 = -\delta P$, where $\delta > 0$, $\delta \in R$ the inequality i. given in (24) be reduced to*

$$\begin{bmatrix} P^{-1}A^T + AP^{-1} & B & P^{-1}A^T & P^{-1}C^T \\ * & -\gamma I_r & B^T & D^T \\ * & * & -2\delta^{-1}P^{-1} & 0 \\ * & * & * & -I_m \end{bmatrix} < 0 \tag{36}$$

*Then (36) can be written as (29), with*

$$\Lambda_1 = \begin{bmatrix} P^{-1}A^T + AP^{-1} & B & P^{-1}C^T \\ * & -\gamma I_r & D^T \\ * & * & -I_m \end{bmatrix} \tag{37}$$

$$\Lambda_2 = \begin{bmatrix} P^{-1}A^TPAP^{-1} & P^{-1}A^TPB & 0 \\ B^TPAP^{-1} & B^TPB & 0 \\ 0 & 0 & 0 \end{bmatrix} \tag{38}$$

*Thus, satisfying (32), (33) then (36) be negative definite for a feasible $P$ of iii. of (2).* ∎

**Remark 2.** *By a similar procedure, setting $S_2 = -\delta I_n$, where $\delta > 0$, $\delta \in R$ then i. of (24) implies the following*

$$\begin{bmatrix} P^{-1}A^T + AP^{-1} & B & P^{-1}A^T & P^{-1}C^T \\ * & -\gamma I_r & B^T & D^T \\ * & * & -2\delta^{-1}I_n & 0 \\ * & * & * & -I_m \end{bmatrix} < 0 \tag{39}$$

*It is evident that (39) yields with the same $\Lambda_1$ as given in (37) and*

$$\Lambda_2 = \begin{bmatrix} P^{-1}A^TAP^{-1} & P^{-1}A^TB & 0 \\ B^TAP^{-1} & B^TB & 0 \\ 0 & 0 & 0 \end{bmatrix} \tag{40}$$

*Thus, this leads to the equivalent results as presented above, but with possible different interpretation.* ∎

## 3. Control law parameter design

### 3.1 Problem description
Through this section the task is concerned with the computation of a state feedback $u(t)$, which control the linear dynamic system given by (1), (2), i.e.

$$\dot{q}(t) = Aq(t) + Bu(t) \tag{41}$$

$$y(t) = Cq(t) + Du(t) \tag{42}$$

Problem of the interest is to design stable closed-loop system with quadratic performance $\gamma > 0$ using the linear memoryless state feedback controller of the form

$$u(t) = -Kq(t) \tag{43}$$

where matrix $K \in R^{r \times n}$ is a gain matrix.
Then the unforced system, formed by the state controller (43), can be written as

$$\dot{q}(t) = (A - BK)q(t) \tag{44}$$

$$y(t) = (C - DK)q(t) \tag{45}$$

The state-feedback control problem is to find, for an optimized (or prescribed) scalar $\gamma > 0$, the state-feedback gain $K$ such that the control law guarantees an upper bound of $\sqrt{\gamma}$ to $H_\infty$ norm of the closed-loop transfer function. Thus, Theorem 2 can be reformulated to solve this state-feedback control problem for linear continuous time systems.

**Theorem 3.** *Closed-loop system* (44), (45) *is stable with performance* $\|C_c(sI - A_c)^{-1}B\|_\infty^2 \leq \gamma$, $A_c = A - BK$, $C_c = C - DK$ *if there exist regular square matrices* $T, U, V \in R^{n \times n}$, *a matrix* $W \in R^{r \times n}$, *and a scalar* $\gamma > 0$, $\gamma \in R$ *such that*

$$T = T^T > 0, \quad \gamma > 0 \tag{46}$$

$$\begin{bmatrix} VA^T - W^T B^T + AV^T - BW & -B & T - U^T + VA^T - W^T B^T & -VC^T + W^T D^T \\ * & -\gamma I_r & -B^T & D^T \\ * & * & -U - U^T & 0 \\ * & * & * & -I_m \end{bmatrix} < 0 \tag{47}$$

*The control law gain matrix is now given as*

$$K = WV^{-T} \tag{48}$$

*Proof.* Considering that $\det S_1 \neq 0$, $\det S_2 \neq 0$ the congruence transform $L_4$ can be defined as follows

$$L_4 = \text{diag} \begin{bmatrix} S_1^{-1} & I_r & S_2^{-1} & I_m \end{bmatrix} \tag{49}$$

and multiplying left-hand side of *i.* of (17) by $L_4$, and right-hand side of (17) by $L_4^T$ gives

$$\begin{bmatrix} -AS_1^{-T} - S_1^{-1}A^T & -B & S_1^{-1}PS_2^{-T} + S_2^{-T} - S_1^{-1}A^T & S_1^{-1}C^T \\ * & -\gamma I_r & -B^T & D^T \\ * & * & S_2^{-1} + S_2^{-T} & 0 \\ * & * & * & -I_m \end{bmatrix} < 0 \tag{50}$$

Inserting $A \leftarrow A_c$, $C \leftarrow C_c$ into (50) and denoting

$$S_1^{-1}PS_2^{-T} = T, \qquad S_1^{-1} = -V, \qquad S_2^{-1} = -U \tag{51}$$

(50) takes the form

$$\begin{bmatrix} (A - BK)V^T + V(A - BK)^T & -B & T - U^T + V(A - BK)^T & -V(C - DK)^T \\ * & -\gamma I_r & -B^T & D^T \\ * & * & -U - U^T & 0 \\ * & * & * & -I_m \end{bmatrix} < 0 \tag{52}$$

and with

$$W = KV^T \tag{53}$$

(50) implies (47).                                                                                        □

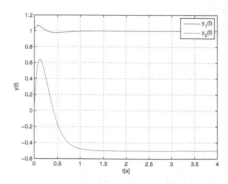
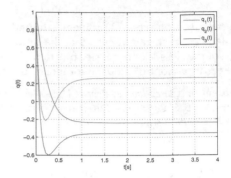

Fig. 1. System output and state response

### 3.2 Basic modification

**Corollary 3.** *Following the same lines of that for Theorem 2 it is immediate by inserting $A \leftarrow A_c$, $C \leftarrow C_c$ into i. of (24) and denoting*

$$P^{-1} = X, \qquad S_2 = Z \qquad (54)$$

*that*

$$\begin{bmatrix} AX+XA^T-BKX-XK^TB^T & B & -XA^T+XK^TB^T & XC^T-XK^TD^T \\ * & -\gamma I_r & -B^T & D^T \\ * & * & -Z-Z^T & 0 \\ * & * & * & -I_m \end{bmatrix} < 0 \qquad (55)$$

*Thus, using Schur complement equivalency, and with*

$$Y = KX \qquad (56)$$

*(58) implies*

$$X = X^T > 0, \qquad \gamma > 0 \qquad (57)$$

$$\begin{bmatrix} AX+XA^T-BY-Y^TB^T & B & XA^T-Y^TB^T & XC^T-Y^TD^T \\ * & -\gamma I_r & B^T & D^T \\ * & * & -Z-Z^T & 0 \\ * & * & * & -I_m \end{bmatrix} < 0 \qquad (58)$$

∎

### Illustrative example

The approach given above is illustrated by an example where the parameters of the (41), (42) are

$$A = \begin{bmatrix} 0 & 1 & 0 \\ 0 & 0 & 1 \\ -5 & -9 & -5 \end{bmatrix}, \quad B = \begin{bmatrix} 1 & 3 \\ 2 & 1 \\ 1 & 5 \end{bmatrix}, \quad C^T = \begin{bmatrix} 1 & 1 \\ 2 & -1 \\ -2 & 0 \end{bmatrix}, \quad D = 0$$

Solving (57), (58) with respect to the next LMI variables $X$, $Y$, $Z$, and $\delta$ using SeDuMi (Self-Dual-Minimization) package for Matlab (Peaucelle et al. (1994)) given task was feasible with

$$X = \begin{bmatrix} 0.6276 & -0.3796 & -0.0923 \\ -0.3796 & 0.7372 & 0.3257 \\ -0.0923 & 0.3257 & 0.9507 \end{bmatrix}, \quad Z = \begin{bmatrix} 5.0040 & 0.1209 & 0.4891 \\ 0.1209 & 4.9512 & 0.4888 \\ 0.4891 & 0.4888 & 5.2859 \end{bmatrix}$$

$$Y = \begin{bmatrix} 0.4917 & 3.2177 & 0.7775 \\ 0.6100 & -1.5418 & -0.3739 \end{bmatrix}, \qquad \gamma = 8.4359$$

and results the control system parameters

$$K = \begin{bmatrix} 5.1969 & 7.6083 & -1.2838 \\ -0.5004 & -2.5381 & 0.4276 \end{bmatrix}, \quad \rho(A_c) = \{-5.5999,\ -8.3141 \pm 1.6528\,i\}$$

The example is shown of the closed-loop system response in the forced mode, where in the Fig. 1 the output response, as well as state variable response are presented, respectively. The desired steady-state output variable values were set as $[y_1\ y_2] = [1\,{-}0.5]$.

### 3.3 Associate modifications

**Remark 3.** *Inserting $A \leftarrow A_c$, $C \leftarrow C_c$ into (39) and setting $X = P^{-1}$, $Y = KX$, $\delta^{-1} = \xi$, as well as inserting the same into (34) and setting $X = P$, $Y = KX$, $\delta^{-1} = \xi$ gives*

$$X = X^T > 0, \quad \gamma > 0, \quad \xi > 0 \tag{59}$$

i.
$$\begin{bmatrix} AX+XA^T-BY-Y^TB^T & B & XA^T-Y^TB^T & XC^T-Y^TD^T \\ * & -\gamma I_r & B^T & D^T \\ * & * & -2\xi I_n & 0 \\ * & * & * & -I_m \end{bmatrix} < 0$$

$$\tag{60}$$

ii.
$$\begin{bmatrix} AX+XA^T-BY-Y^TB^T & XC^T-Y^TD^T & AX-BY & B \\ * & -\gamma I_m & CX-DY & D \\ * & * & -2\xi I_n & 0 \\ * & * & * & -I_r \end{bmatrix} < 0$$

*where feasible $X$, $Y$, $\gamma$, $\xi$ implies the gain matrix (48).*  ∎

### Illustrative example

Considering the same parameters of (41), (42) and desired output values as is given above then solving (59), (59) with respect to LMI variables $X$, $Y$, and $\gamma$ given task was feasible with

i. $\gamma = 8.3659$  
$\xi = 5.7959$

$$X = \begin{bmatrix} 0.6402 & -0.3918 & -0.1075 \\ -0.3918 & 0.7796 & 0.3443 \\ -0.1075 & 0.3443 & 0.9853 \end{bmatrix}$$

$$Y = \begin{bmatrix} 0.5451 & 3.3471 & 0.6650 \\ 0.6113 & -1.6481 & -0.3733 \end{bmatrix}$$

$$K = \begin{bmatrix} 5.2296 & 7.5340 & -1.3870 \\ -0.5590 & -2.6022 & 0.4694 \end{bmatrix}$$

$\rho(A_c) = \{-6.3921,\ -7.7931 \pm 1.8646\,i\}$

ii. $\gamma = 35.7411$  
$\xi = 30.0832$

$$X = \begin{bmatrix} 8.7747 & -4.7218 & -1.2776 \\ -4.7218 & 5.8293 & 0.4784 \\ -1.2776 & 0.4784 & 8.4785 \end{bmatrix}$$

$$Y = \begin{bmatrix} 2.7793 & 14.7257 & 5.1591 \\ 3.3003 & -6.8347 & -1.8016 \end{bmatrix}$$

$$K = \begin{bmatrix} 3.1145 & 4.9836 & 0.7966 \\ -0.4874 & -1.5510 & -0.1984 \end{bmatrix}$$

$\rho(A_c) = \{-2.3005,\ -3.8535,\ -8.7190\}$

The closed-loop system response concerning *ii.* of (60) is in the Fig. 2.

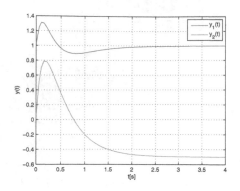
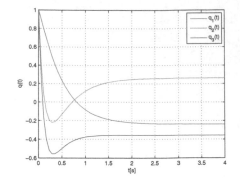

Fig. 2. System output and state response

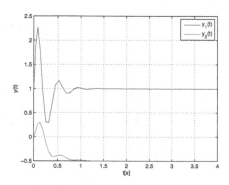
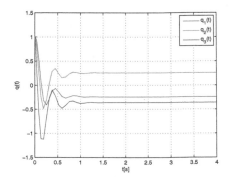

Fig. 3. System output and state response

**Remark 4.** *The closed-loop system (44), (45) is stable with quadratic performance $\gamma > 0$ and the inequalities (15) are true if and only if there exists a symmetric positive definite matrix $X > 0$, $X \in R^{n \times n}$, a matrix $Y \in R^{r \times n}$, and a scalar $\gamma > 0$, $\gamma \in R$ such that*

$$X = X^T > 0, \quad \gamma > 0, \quad \xi > 0 \tag{61}$$

$$i. \quad \begin{bmatrix} AX + XA^T - BY - Y^TB^T & B & XC^T - Y^TD^T \\ * & -\gamma I_r & 0 \\ * & * & -I_m \end{bmatrix} < 0 \tag{62}$$

$$ii. \quad \begin{bmatrix} AX + XA^T - BY - Y^TB^T & XC^T - Y^TD^T & B \\ * & -\gamma I_m & D \\ * & * & -I_r \end{bmatrix} < 0$$

∎

## Illustrative example

Using the same example consideration as are given above then solving (61), (62) with respect to LMI variables $X$, $Y$, and $\gamma$ given task was feasible with

i. $\gamma = 6.8386$                                             ii. $\gamma = 17.6519$

$$X = \begin{bmatrix} 1.1852 & 0.1796 & 0.6494 \\ 0.1796 & 1.4325 & 1.1584 \\ 0.6494 & 1.1584 & 2.1418 \end{bmatrix} \qquad X = \begin{bmatrix} 6.0755 & -0.9364 & 1.0524 \\ -0.9364 & 5.1495 & 2.4320 \\ 1.0524 & 2.4320 & 7.2710 \end{bmatrix}$$

$$Y = \begin{bmatrix} 2.0355 & 3.7878 & -3.2286 \\ 0.6142 & -2.1847 & -3.0636 \end{bmatrix} \qquad Y = \begin{bmatrix} 6.3651 & 9.9547 & -8.7603 \\ 2.2941 & -5.3741 & -6.2975 \end{bmatrix}$$

$$K = \begin{bmatrix} 4.4043 & 7.8029 & -7.0627 \\ 1.5030 & -0.3349 & -1.7049 \end{bmatrix} \qquad K = \begin{bmatrix} 2.0688 & 3.5863 & -2.7038 \\ 0.4033 & -0.6338 & -0.7125 \end{bmatrix}$$

$$\rho(A_c) = \{-4.3952, \ -4.6009 \pm 14.8095\,i\} \qquad \rho(A_c) = \{-2.2682, \ -3.1415 \pm 9.634\,i\}$$

The simulation results are shown in Fig. 3, and are concerning with i. of (62).

It is evident that different design conditions implying from the equivalent, but different, bounded lemma structures results in different numerical solutions.

### 3.4 Dependent modifications

Similar extended LMI characterizations can be derived by formulating LMI in terms of product $\xi P$, where $\xi$ is a prescribed scalar to overcome BMI formulation (Veselý & Rosinová (2009)).

**Theorem 4.** *Closed-loop system (1), (2) is stable with quadratic performance* $\|C_c(sI - A_c)^{-1}B\|_\infty^2 \leq \gamma$, $A_c = A - BK$, $C_c = C - DK$ *if for given* $\xi > 0$ *there exist a symmetric positive definite matrix* $X > 0$, $X \in R^{n \times n}$, *a regular square matrix* $Z \in R^{n \times n}$, *a matrix* $Y \in R^{r \times n}$, *and a scalar* $\gamma > 0$, $\gamma \in R$ *such that*

$$X - X^T > 0, \quad \gamma > 0 \tag{63}$$

i.
$$\begin{bmatrix} AX + XA^T - BY - Y^TB^T & B & XA^T - Y^TB^T & XC^T - Y^TD^T \\ * & -\gamma I_r & B^T & D^T \\ * & * & -2\xi X & 0 \\ * & * & * & -I_m \end{bmatrix} < 0$$

$$\tag{64}$$

ii.
$$\begin{bmatrix} AX + XA^T - BY - Y^TB^T & XC^T - Y^TD^T & AX - BY & B \\ * & -\gamma I_m & CX - DY & D \\ * & * & -2\xi X & 0 \\ * & * & * & -I_r \end{bmatrix} < 0$$

*where $K$ is given in (48).*

*Proof.* i. Inserting $A \leftarrow A_c$, $C \leftarrow C_c$ into (36) and setting $X = P^{-1}$, $Y = KX$, and $\xi = \delta^{-1}$ then (36) implies ii. of (64).

ii. Inserting $A \leftarrow A_c$, $C \leftarrow C_c$ into (28) and setting $X = P$, $Y = KX$, and $\xi = \delta^{-1}$ then (28) implies i. of (64).                                                                                       □

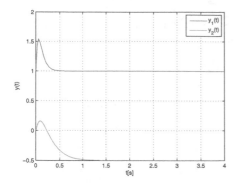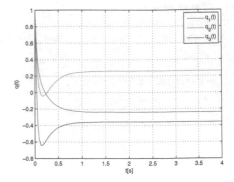

Fig. 4. System output and state response

Note, other nontrivial solutions can be obtained using different setting of $S_l$, $l = 1, 2$.

### Illustrative example

Considering the same system parameters of (1), (2), and the same desired output values as are given above then solving (63), (64) with respect to LMI variables $X$, $Y$, and $\gamma$ with prescribed $\zeta = 10/xi = 30$, respectively, given task was feasible with

*i.* $\gamma = 8.3731$

$\zeta = 10$

$$X = \begin{bmatrix} 0.5203 & -0.2338 & 0.0038 \\ -0.2338 & 0.7293 & 0.2359 \\ 0.0038 & 0.2359 & 0.7728 \end{bmatrix}$$

$$Y = \begin{bmatrix} 0.8689 & 3.2428 & 0.6068 \\ 0.3503 & -1.6271 & -0.1495 \end{bmatrix}$$

$$K = \begin{bmatrix} 4.4898 & 6.2565 & -1.1462 \\ -0.4912 & -2.5815 & 0.5968 \end{bmatrix}$$

$\rho(A_c) = \{-8.3448, \; -5.7203 \pm 3.6354\,i\}$

*ii.* $\gamma = 17.6519$

$\zeta = 30$

$$X = \begin{bmatrix} 0.8926 & -0.2332 & 0.0489 \\ -0.2332 & 1.2228 & 0.3403 \\ 0.0489 & 0.3403 & 1.3969 \end{bmatrix}$$

$$Y = \begin{bmatrix} 3.0546 & 8.8611 & 0.2482 \\ 2.0238 & -2.8097 & 3.0331 \end{bmatrix}$$

$$K = \begin{bmatrix} 5.8920 & 8.9877 & -2.2185 \\ 1.3774 & -2.8170 & 2.8094 \end{bmatrix}$$

$\rho(A_c) = \{-4.6346, \; -12.3015, \; -25.0751\}$

The same simulation study as above was carried out, and the simulation results concerning *ii.* of (64) for the states and output variables of the system are shown in Fig. 4.

It also should be noted, the cost value $\gamma$ will not be a monotonously decreasing function with the decreasing of $\zeta$, if $\delta = \zeta^{-1}$ is chosen.

## 4. Uncertain continuous-time systems

The importance of Theorem 3 is that it separates $T$ from $A$, $B$, $C$, and $D$, i.e. there are no terms containing the product of $T$ and any of them. This enables to derive other forms of bonded real lemma for a system with polytopic uncertainties by using a parameter-dependent Lyapunov function.

## 4.1 Problem description

Assuming that the matrices $A$, $B$, $C$, and $D$ of (1), (2) are not precisely known but belong to a polytopic uncertainty domain $\mathcal{O}$,

$$\mathcal{O} := \left\{ (A, B, C, D)(a) : (A, B, C, D)(a) = \sum_{i=1}^{s} a_i (A_i, B_i, C_i, D_i), \quad a \in \mathcal{Q} \right\} \quad (65)$$

$$\mathcal{Q} = \left\{ (a_1, a_2, \cdots, a_s) : \sum_{i=1}^{s} a_i = 1; \quad a_i > 0, \ i = 1, 2, \ldots, s \right\} \quad (66)$$

where $\mathcal{Q}$ is the unit simplex, $A_i$, $B_i$, $C_i$, and $D_i$ are constant matrices with appropriate dimensions, and $a_i$, $i = 1, 2, \ldots, s$ are time-invariant uncertainties.

Since $a$ is constrained to the unit simplex as (66) the matrices $(A, B, C, D)(a)$ are affine functions of the uncertain parameter vector $a \in R^s$ described by the convex combination of the vertex matrices $(A_i, B_i, C_i, D_i)$, $i = 1, 2, \ldots, s$.

The state-feedback control problem is to find, for a $\gamma > 0$, the state-feedback gain matrix $K$ such that the control law of

$$u(t) = -Kq(t) \quad (67)$$

guarantees an upper bound of $\sqrt{\gamma}$ to $H_\infty$ norm.

By virtue of the property of convex combinations, (48) can be readily used to derive the robust performance criterion.

**Theorem 5.** *Given system (65), (66) the closed-loop $H_\infty$ norm is less than a real value $\sqrt{\gamma} > 0$, if there exist positive matrices $T_i \in R^{n \times n}$, $i = 1, 2, \ldots, s$, real square matrices $U, V \in R^{n \times n}$, and a real matrix $W \in R^{r \times n}$ such that*

$$\gamma > 0 \quad (68)$$

$$\begin{bmatrix} VA_i^T - W^T B_i^T + A_i V^T - B_i W & -B_i & T_i - U^T + VA_i^T - W^T B_i^T & -VC_i^T + W^T D_i^T \\ * & -\gamma I_r & -B_i^T & D_i^T \\ * & * & -U - U^T & 0 \\ * & * & * & -I_m \end{bmatrix} < 0 \quad (69)$$

*If the existence is affirmative, the state-feedback gain $K$ is given by*

$$K = WV^{-T} \quad (70)$$

*Proof.* It is obvious that (47), (48) implies directly (69), (70).  $\square$

**Remark 5.** *Thereby, robust control performance of uncertain continuous-time systems is guaranteed by a parameter-dependent Lyapunov matrix, which is constructed as*

$$T(a) = \sum_{i=1}^{s} a_i T_i \quad (71)$$

## 4.2 Dependent modifications

**Theorem 6.** *Given system (65), (66) the closed-loop $H_\infty$ norm is less than a real value $\sqrt{\gamma} > 0$, if there exist positive symmetric matrices $T_i \in R^{n \times n}$, $i = 1, 2, \ldots, n$, a real square matrices $V \in R^{n \times n}$, a real matrix $W \in R^{r \times n}$, and a positive scalar $\delta > 0$, $\delta \in R$ such that*

$$T_i > 0, \ i = 1, 2, \ldots, n, \quad \gamma > 0 \tag{72}$$

$$i. \begin{bmatrix} VA_i^T + A_i V^T - W^T B_i^T - B_i W & -B_i & T_i - \delta V^T + VA_i^T - W^T B_i^T & -VC_i^T + W^T D_i^T \\ * & -\gamma I_r & -B_i^T & D_i^T \\ * & * & -\delta(V + V^T) & 0 \\ * & * & * & -I_m \end{bmatrix} < 0$$

$$ii. \begin{bmatrix} VA_i^T + A_i V^T - W^T B_i^T - B_i W & VC_i^T - W^T D_i^T & T_i - V^T + \delta A_i V - \delta B_i W & B_i \\ * & -\gamma I_m & \delta C_i V - \delta D_i W & D_i \\ * & * & -\delta(V + V^T) & 0 \\ * & * & * & -I_r \end{bmatrix} < 0 \tag{73}$$

*If the existence is affirmative, the state-feedback gain $K$ is given by*

$$K = WV^{-T} \tag{74}$$

*Proof.* *i.* Setting $U = \delta V$ then (69) implies *i.* of (73).
*ii.* Setting $S_1 = -V$, and $S_2 = -\delta V$ then *ii.* of (17) implies *ii.* of (73).  □

## Illustrative example

The approach given above is illustrated by the numerical example yielding the matrix parameters of the system $D(t) = D = 0$

$$A(t) = \begin{bmatrix} 0 & 1 & 0 \\ 0 & 0 & 1 \\ -5 & -6r(t) & -5r(t) \end{bmatrix}, \quad B(t) = B = \begin{bmatrix} 1 & 3 \\ 2 & 1 \\ 1 & 5 \end{bmatrix}, \quad C^T(t) = C^T = \begin{bmatrix} 1 & 1 \\ 2 & -1 \\ -2 & 0 \end{bmatrix}$$

where the time varying uncertain parameter $r(t)$ lies within the interval $\langle 0.5, 1.5 \rangle$.
In order to represent uncertainty on $r(t)$ it is assumed that the matrix parameters belongs to the polytopic uncertainty domain $\mathcal{O}$,

$$\mathcal{O} := \left\{ (A, B, C, D)(a) : (A, B, C, D)(a) = \sum_{i=1}^{2} a_i (A_i, B_i, C_i, D_i), \quad a \in \mathcal{Q} \right\}$$

$$\mathcal{Q} = \{(a_1, a_2) : a_2 = 1 - a_1; \ 0 < a_1 < 1\}$$

$$A_1 = \begin{bmatrix} 0 & 1 & 0 \\ 0 & 0 & 1 \\ -5 & -3 & -2.5 \end{bmatrix} \quad A_2 = \begin{bmatrix} 0 & 1 & 0 \\ 0 & 0 & 1 \\ -5 & -9 & -7.5 \end{bmatrix}$$

$$B_1 = B_2 = B, \quad C_1^T = C_2^T = C^T, \quad D_1 = D_2 = 0$$

$$A = a_1 A_1 + (1 - a_1) A_2, \quad A_c = A - BK \quad A_{c0} = A_0 - BK$$

Thus, solving (72) and *i.* of (73) with respect to the LMI variables $T_1$, $T_2$, $V$, $W$, and $\delta$ given task was feasible for $a_1 = 0.2$, $\delta = 20$. Subsequently, with

$$\gamma = 10.5304$$

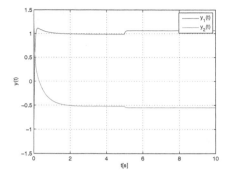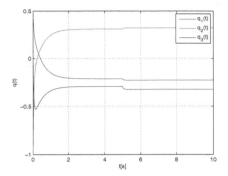

Fig. 5. System output and state response

$$T_1 = \begin{bmatrix} 7.0235 & 2.4579 & 2.6301 \\ 2.4579 & 7.4564 & -0.4037 \\ 2.6301 & -0.4037 & 5.3152 \end{bmatrix}, \quad T_2 = \begin{bmatrix} 6.6651 & 2.6832 & 2.0759 \\ 2.6832 & 7.4909 & -0.2568 \\ 2.0759 & -0.2568 & 6.2386 \end{bmatrix}$$

$$V = \begin{bmatrix} 0.2250 & -0.0758 & -0.0350 \\ 0.0940 & 0.1801 & -0.0241 \\ 0.1473 & 0.0375 & 0.1992 \end{bmatrix}, \quad W = \begin{bmatrix} 0.7191 & 3.0209 & 0.2881 \\ 0.1964 & -0.7401 & 0.7382 \end{bmatrix}$$

the control law parameters were computed as

$$K = \begin{bmatrix} 6.5392 & 12.5891 & -5.7581 \\ 0.2809 & -3.6944 & 4.1922 \end{bmatrix}, \quad \|K\| = 16.3004$$

and including into the state control law the were obtained the closed-loop system matrix eigenvalues set

$$\rho(A_{c0}) = \{-2.0598, \ -22.2541, \ -24.7547\}$$

Solving (72) and *ii.* of (73) with respect to the LMI variables $T_1$, $T_2$, $V$, $W$, and $\delta$ given task was feasible for $a_1 = 0.2$, $\delta = 20$, too, and subsequently, with

$$\gamma = 10.5304$$

$$T_1 = \begin{bmatrix} 239.1234 & 108.9248 & 250.1206 \\ 108.9248 & 307.9712 & 13.8497 \\ 250.1206 & 13.8497 & 397.1333 \end{bmatrix}, \quad T_2 = \begin{bmatrix} 222.8598 & 121.9115 & 251.6458 \\ 121.9115 & 341.0193 & 63.4202 \\ 251.6458 & 63.4202 & 445.9279 \end{bmatrix}$$

$$V = \begin{bmatrix} 6.5513 & -2.0718 & -0.2451 \\ 2.1635 & 2.2173 & 0.1103 \\ 0.2448 & 0.2964 & 0.4568 \end{bmatrix}, \quad W = \begin{bmatrix} 4.6300 & 6.6167 & -2.6780 \\ 1.7874 & -0.7898 & 4.3214 \end{bmatrix}$$

the closed-loop parameters were computed as

$$K = \begin{bmatrix} 1.1296 & 2.2771 & -7.9446 \\ 0.2888 & -1.1375 & 10.0427 \end{bmatrix}, \quad \|K\| = 13.1076$$

$$\rho(A_c) = \{-50.4633, \ -1.1090 \pm 2.1623\,i\}$$

It is evident, that the eigenvalues spectrum $\rho(A_{c0})$ of the closed control loop is stable in both cases. However, taking the same values of $\gamma$, the solutions differ especially in the

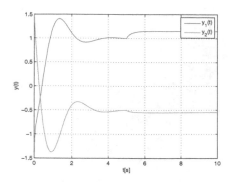 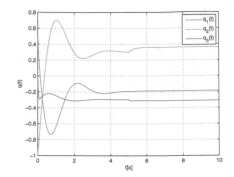

Fig. 6. System output and state response

closed-loop dominant eigenvalues, as well as in the control law gain matrix norm, giving together closed-loop system matrix eigenstructure. To prefer any of them is not as so easy as it seems at the first sight, and the less gain norm may not be the best choice.

Fig. 5 illustrates the simulation results with respect to a solution of *i.* of (73) and (72). The initial state of system state variable was setting as $[q_1 \, q_2 \, q_3]^T = [0.5 \, 1 \, 0]^T$, the desired steady-state output variable values were set as $[y_1 \, y_2]^T = [1 \, -0.5]^T$, and the system matrix parameter change from $p = 1$ to $p = 0.54$ was realized 5 seconds after the state control start-up.

The same simulation study was carried out using the control parameter obtained by solving *ii.* of (73), (72), and the simulation results are shown in Fig. 6. It can be seen that the presented control scheme partly eliminates the effects of parameter uncertainties, and guaranteed the quadratic stability of the closed-loop system.

## 5. Pairwise-autonomous principle in control design

### 5.1 Problem description
Considering the system model of the form (1), (2), i.e.

$$\dot{q}(t) = Aq(t) + Bu(t) \tag{75}$$

$$y(t) = Cq(t) + Du(t) \tag{76}$$

but reordering in such way that

$$A = [A_{i,l}], \quad C = [C_{i,l}], \quad B = \text{diag}[B_i], \quad D = 0 \tag{77}$$

where $i, l = 1, 2, \ldots, p$, and all parameters and variables are with the same dimensions as it is given in Subsection 2.1. Thus, respecting the above give matrix structures it yields

$$\dot{q}_h(t) = A_{hh}q_h(t) + \sum_{l=1, l \neq h}^{p} (A_{hl}q_l(t) + B_h u_h(t)) \tag{78}$$

$$y_h(t) = C_{hh}q_h(t) + \sum_{l=1, l \neq h}^{p} C_{hl}q_l(t) \tag{79}$$

where $q_h(t) \in R^{n_h}$, $u_h(t) \in R^{r_h}$, $y_h(t) \in R^{m_h}$, $A_{hl} \in R^{n_h \times n_l}$, $B_h \in R^{r_h \times n_h}$, and $C_{hl} \in R^{m_h \times n_h}$, respectively, and $n = \sum_{l=1}^{p} n_l$, $r = \sum_{l=1}^{p} r_l$, $m = \sum_{l=1}^{p} m_l$.

Problem of the interest is to design closed-loop system using a linear memoryless state feedback controller of the form

$$u(t) = -Kq(t) \tag{80}$$

in such way that the large-scale system be stable, and

$$K = \begin{bmatrix} K_{11} & K_{12} & \dots & K_{1p} \\ K_{21} & K_{22} & \dots & K_{2p} \\ & & \vdots & \\ K_{p1} & K_{p2} & \dots & K_{pp} \end{bmatrix}, \qquad K_{hh} = \sum_{l=1, l \neq h}^{p} K_h^l \tag{81}$$

$$u_h(t) = -K_{hh} q_h(t) - \sum_{l=1, l \neq h}^{p} K_{hl} q_l(t), \quad h = 1, 2, \dots, p \tag{82}$$

**Lemma 1.** *Unforced (autonomous) system (75)-(77) is stable if there exists a set of symmetric matrices*

$$P_{hk}^{\circ} = \begin{bmatrix} P_h^k & P_{hk} \\ P_{kh} & P_k^h \end{bmatrix} \tag{83}$$

*such that*

$$\sum_{h=1}^{p-1} \sum_{k=h+1}^{p} \left( \dot{q}_{hk}^T(t) \begin{bmatrix} P_h^k & P_{hk} \\ P_{kh} & P_k^h \end{bmatrix} q_{hk}(t) + q_{hk}^T(t) \begin{bmatrix} P_h^k & P_{hk} \\ P_{kh} & P_k^h \end{bmatrix} \dot{q}_{hk}(t) \right) < 0 \tag{84}$$

*where*

$$\dot{q}_{hk}(t) = \begin{bmatrix} A_{hh} & A_{hk} \\ A_{kh} & A_{kk} \end{bmatrix} q_{hk}(t) + \sum_{l=1, l \neq h,k}^{p} \begin{bmatrix} A_{hl} \\ A_{kl} \end{bmatrix} q_l(t) \tag{85}$$

$$q_{hk}^T(t) = [ q_h^T(t) \ q_k^T(t) ] \tag{86}$$

*Proof.* Defining Lyapunov function as follows

$$v(q(t)) = q^T(t) P q(t) > 0 \tag{87}$$

where $P = P^T > 0$, $P \in R^{n \times n}$, then the time rate of change of $v(q(t))$ along a solution of the system (75), (77) is

$$\dot{v}(q(t)) = \dot{q}^T(t) P q(t) + q^T(t) P \dot{q}(t) < 0 \tag{88}$$

Considering the same form of $P$ with respect to $K$, i.e.

$$P = \begin{bmatrix} P_{11} & P_{12} & \dots & P_{1M} \\ P_{21} & P_{22} & \dots & P_{2M} \\ & & \vdots & \\ P_{M1} & P_{M2} & \dots & P_{MM} \end{bmatrix}, \qquad P_{hh} = \sum_{l=1, l \neq h}^{p} P_h^l \tag{89}$$

then the next separation is possible

$$
P = \left(\left(\begin{bmatrix} P_1^2 & P_{12} & 0 & \dots & 0 \\ P_{21} & P_2^1 & 0 & \dots & 0 \\ & & \vdots & & \\ 0 & 0 & 0 & \dots & 0 \end{bmatrix} + \dots + \begin{bmatrix} P_1^p & 0 & \dots & 0 & P_{1p} \\ 0 & 0 & \dots & 0 & 0 \\ & & \vdots & & \\ P_{p1} & 0 & \dots & 0 & P_p^1 \end{bmatrix}\right) + \right.
$$

$$
\left. + \dots + \begin{bmatrix} 0 & \dots & 0 & 0 & 0 \\ & & \vdots & & \\ 0 & \dots & 0 & P_{p-1}^p & P_{p-1,p} \\ 0 & \dots & 0 & P_{p,p-1} & P_p^{p-1} \end{bmatrix}\right). \tag{90}
$$

Writing (78) as

$$
\dot{q}_{hk}(t) = \begin{bmatrix} A_{hh} & A_{hk} \\ A_{kh} & A_{kk} \end{bmatrix} q_{hk}(t) + \sum_{l=1,\, l\neq h,k}^{p} \begin{bmatrix} A_{hl} \\ A_{kl} \end{bmatrix} q_l(t) + \begin{bmatrix} B_h & 0 \\ 0 & B_k \end{bmatrix} \begin{bmatrix} u_h(t) \\ u_k(t) \end{bmatrix} \tag{91}
$$

and considering that for unforced system there are $u_l(t) = 0$, $l=1,\dots p$ then (91) implies (85). Subsequently, with (90), (91) the inequality (88) implies (84). $\qquad\square$

### 5.2 Pairwise system description

Supposing that there exists the partitioned structure of $K$ as is defined in (81), (82) then it yields

$$
u_h(t) = -\sum_{l=1,\, l\neq h}^{p} \begin{bmatrix} K_h^l & K_{hl} \end{bmatrix} \begin{bmatrix} q_h(t) \\ q_l(t) \end{bmatrix} =
$$

$$
= -\begin{bmatrix} K_h^k & K_{hk} \end{bmatrix} \begin{bmatrix} q_h(t) \\ q_k(t) \end{bmatrix} - \sum_{l=1,\, l\neq h,k}^{p} \begin{bmatrix} K_h^l & K_{hl} \end{bmatrix} \begin{bmatrix} q_h(t) \\ q_l(t) \end{bmatrix} = u_h^k(t) + \sum_{l=1,\, l\neq h,k}^{p} u_h^l(t) \tag{92}
$$

where for $l = 1, 2, \dots, p,\ i \neq h, k$

$$
u_h^l(t) = -\begin{bmatrix} K_h^l & K_{hl} \end{bmatrix} \begin{bmatrix} q_h(t) \\ q_l(t) \end{bmatrix} \tag{93}
$$

Defining with $h = 1, 2 \dots, p-1,\ k = h+1, h+2 \dots, p$

$$
\begin{bmatrix} u_h^k(t) \\ u_k^h(t) \end{bmatrix} = -\begin{bmatrix} K_h^k & K_{hk} \\ K_{kh} & K_k^h \end{bmatrix} \begin{bmatrix} q_h(t) \\ q_k(t) \end{bmatrix} = -K_{hk}^{\circ} \begin{bmatrix} q_h(t) \\ q_k(t) \end{bmatrix} \tag{94}
$$

$$
K_{hk}^{\circ} = \begin{bmatrix} K_h^k & K_{hk} \\ K_{kh} & K_k^h \end{bmatrix} \tag{95}
$$

and combining (92) for $h$ and $k$ it is obtained

$$
\begin{bmatrix} u_h(t) \\ u_k(t) \end{bmatrix} = -\begin{bmatrix} K_h^k & K_{kh} \\ K_{hk} & K_k^h \end{bmatrix} \begin{bmatrix} q_h(t) \\ q_k(t) \end{bmatrix} - \begin{bmatrix} \sum_{l=1,\, l\neq h,k}^{p} \begin{bmatrix} K_h^l & K_{hl} \end{bmatrix} \begin{bmatrix} q_h(t) \\ q_l(t) \end{bmatrix} \\ \sum_{l=1,\, l\neq h,k}^{p} \begin{bmatrix} K_k^l & K_{kl} \end{bmatrix} \begin{bmatrix} q_k(t) \\ q_l(t) \end{bmatrix} \end{bmatrix} \tag{96}
$$

$$\begin{bmatrix} u_h(t) \\ u_k(t) \end{bmatrix} = \begin{bmatrix} u_h^k(t) \\ u_k^h(t) \end{bmatrix} + \sum_{l=1, l \neq h,k}^{p} \begin{bmatrix} u_h^l(t) \\ u_k^l(t) \end{bmatrix} \tag{97}$$

respectively. Then substituting (97) in (91) gives

$$\dot{q}_{hk}(t) =$$

$$= \left[ \begin{bmatrix} A_{hh} & A_{hk} \\ A_{kh} & A_{kk} \end{bmatrix} - \begin{bmatrix} B_h & 0 \\ 0 & B_k \end{bmatrix} \begin{bmatrix} K_h^k & K_{hk} \\ K_{kh} & K_k^h \end{bmatrix} \right] q_{hk}(t) + \sum_{l=1, l \neq h,k}^{p} \begin{bmatrix} B_h u_h^l(t) + A_{hl} q_l(t) \\ B_k u_k^l(t) + A_{kl} q_l(t) \end{bmatrix} \tag{98}$$

Using the next notations

$$A_{hkc}^{\circ} = \begin{bmatrix} A_{hh} & A_{hk} \\ A_{kh} & A_{kk} \end{bmatrix} - \begin{bmatrix} B_h & 0 \\ 0 & B_k \end{bmatrix} \begin{bmatrix} K_h^k & K_{hk} \\ K_{kh} & K_k^h \end{bmatrix} = A_{hk}^{\circ} - B_{hk}^{\circ} K_{hk}^{\circ} \tag{99}$$

$$w_{hk}^{\circ}(t) = \sum_{l=1, l \neq h,k}^{p} \begin{bmatrix} B_h u_h^l(t) + A_{hl} q_l(t) \\ B_k u_k^l(t) + A_{kl} q_l(t) \end{bmatrix} = \sum_{l=1, l \neq h,k}^{p} \left( B_{hk}^{\circ} \begin{bmatrix} u_h^l(t) \\ u_k^l(t) \end{bmatrix} + \begin{bmatrix} A_{hl} \\ A_{kl} \end{bmatrix} q_l(t) \right) =$$

$$\tag{100}$$

$$= B_{hk}^{\circ} w_{hk}(t) + \sum_{l=1, l \neq h,k}^{p} A_{hk}^{lo} q_l(t)$$

where

$$w_{hk}(t) = \sum_{l=1, l \neq h,k}^{p} \begin{bmatrix} u_h^l(t) \\ u_k^l(t) \end{bmatrix}, \qquad A_{hk}^{lo} = \begin{bmatrix} A_{hl} \\ A_{kl} \end{bmatrix} \tag{101}$$

$$A_{hk}^{\circ} = \begin{bmatrix} A_{hh} & A_{hk} \\ A_{kh} & A_{kk} \end{bmatrix}, \quad B_{hk}^{\circ} = \begin{bmatrix} B_h & 0 \\ 0 & B_k \end{bmatrix}, \quad K_{hk}^{\circ} = \begin{bmatrix} K_h^k & K_{hk} \\ K_{kh} & K_k^h \end{bmatrix} \tag{102}$$

(98) can be written as

$$\dot{q}_{hk}(t) = A_{hkc}^{\circ} q_{hk}(t) + \sum_{l=1, l \neq h,k}^{p} A_{hk}^{lo} q_l(t) + B_{hk}^{\circ} w_{hk}(t) \tag{103}$$

where $w_{hk}(t)$ can be considered as a generalized auxiliary disturbance acting on the pair $h, k$ of the subsystems.
On the other hand, if

$$C_{hh} = \sum_{l=1, l \neq h}^{p} C_h^l, \quad C_{hk}^{\circ} = \begin{bmatrix} C_h^k & C_{hk} \\ C_{kh} & C_k^h \end{bmatrix}, \quad C_{hk}^{lo} = \begin{bmatrix} C_{hl} \\ C_{kl} \end{bmatrix} \tag{104}$$

then

$$y(t) = \sum_{h=1}^{p-1} \sum_{k=h+1}^{p} \left( C_{hk}^{\circ} q_{hk}(t) + \sum_{l=1, l \neq h}^{p} C_h^l q_l(t) \right) \tag{105}$$

$$y_{hk}(t) = C_{hk}^{\circ} q_{hk}(t) + \sum_{l=1, l \neq h}^{p} C_{hk}^{lo} q_l(t) + 0 \, w_{hk}(t) \tag{106}$$

Now, taking (103), (106) considered pair of controlled subsystems is fully described as

$$\dot{q}_{hk}(t) = A_{hkc}^{\circ} q_{hk}(t) + \sum_{l=1, l \neq h,k}^{p} A_{hk}^{lo} q_l(t) + B_{hk}^{\circ} w_{hk}(t) \tag{107}$$

$$y_{hk}(t) = C_{hk}^{\circ} q_{hk}(t) + \sum_{l=1, l \neq h}^{p} C_{hk}^{lo} q_l(t) + 0 \, w_{hk}(t) \tag{108}$$

## 5.3 Controller parameter design

**Theorem 7.** *Subsystem pair (91) in system (75), (77), controlled by control law (97) is stable with quadratic performances* $\|C_{hk}^\circ(sI - A_{hkc}^\circ)^{-1}B_{hk}^\circ\|_\infty^2 \le \gamma_{hk}$, $\|C_{hk}^{l\circ}(sI - A_{hkc}^\circ)^{-1}B_{hk}^{l\circ}\|_\infty^2 \le \varepsilon_{hkl}$ *if for* $h = 1,2\ldots,p-1,\ k = h+1,h+2\ldots,p,\ l = 1,2\ldots,p,\ l \ne h,k$, *there exist a symmetric positive definite matrix* $X_{hk}^\circ \in R^{(n_h+n_k)\times(n_h+n_k)}$, *matrices* $Z_{hk}^\circ \in R^{(n_h+n_k)\times(n_h+n_k)}$, $Y_{hk}^\circ \in R^{(r_h+r_k)\times(n_h+n_k)}$, *and positive scalars* $\gamma_{hk}$, $\varepsilon_{hkl} \in R$ *such that*

$$X_{hk}^\circ = X_{hk}^{\circ T} > 0, \quad \varepsilon_{hkl} > 0, \quad \gamma_{hk} > 0, \quad h,l = 1,\ldots,p,\ l \ne h,k,\ h < k \le p \tag{109}$$

$$\begin{bmatrix} \Phi_{hk}^\circ & A_{hk}^{1\circ} & \cdots & A_{hk}^{p\circ} & B_{hk}^\circ & X_{hk}^\circ A_{hk}^{\circ T} - Y_{hk}^{\circ T}B_{hk}^{\circ T} & X_{hk}^\circ C_{hk}^{\circ T} \\ * & -\varepsilon_{hk1}I_{n_1} & \cdots & 0 & 0 & A_{hk}^{1\circ T} & C_{hk}^{1\circ T} \\ \vdots & \vdots & \ddots & \vdots & \vdots & \vdots & \vdots \\ * & * & \cdots & -\varepsilon_{hkp}I_{n_p} & 0 & A_{hk}^{p\circ T} & C_{hk}^{p\circ T} \\ * & * & \cdots & * & -\gamma_{hk}I_{(r_h+r_k)} & B_{hk}^{\circ T} & 0 \\ * & * & \cdots & * & * & -Z_{hk}^\circ - Z_{hk}^{\circ T} & 0 \\ * & * & \cdots & * & * & * & -I_{(m_h+m_k)} \end{bmatrix} < 0 \tag{110}$$

*where* $A_{hk}^\circ$, $B_{hk}^\circ$, $A_{hk}^{l\circ}$, $C_{hk}^\circ$, $C_{hk}^{l\circ}$ *are defined in (99), (101), (104), respectively,*

$$\Phi_{hk}^\circ = X_{hk}^\circ A_{hk}^{\circ T} + A_{hk}^\circ X_{hk}^\circ - B_{hk}^\circ Y_{hk}^\circ - Y_{hk}^{\circ T}B_{hk}^{\circ T} \tag{111}$$

*and where* $A_{hk}^{h\circ}$, $A_{hk}^{k\circ}$, *as well as* $C_{hk}^{h\circ}$, $C_{hk}^{k\circ}$ *are not included into the structure of (110). Then* $K_{hk}^\circ$ *is given as*

$$K_{hk}^\circ = Y_{hk}^\circ X_{hk}^{\circ-1} \tag{112}$$

Note, using the above given principle based on the the pairwise decentralized design of control, the global system be stable. The proof can be find in Filasová & Krokavec (2011).

*Proof.* Considering $\omega_{hk}^\circ(t)$ given in (100) as an generalized input into the subsystem pair (107), (108) then using (83) - (86), and (107) it can be written

$$\sum_{h=1}^{p-1}\sum_{k=h+1}^{p}(\dot{q}_{hk}^T(t)P_{hk}^\circ q_{hk}(t) + q_{hk}^T(t)P_{hk}^\circ \dot{q}_{hk}(t)) < 0 \tag{113}$$

$$\sum_{h=1}^{p-1}\sum_{k=h+1}^{p}\left( \begin{array}{l} \left(A_{hkc}^\circ q_{hk}(t) + \sum_{l=1,\,l\ne h,k}^{p} A_{hk}^{l\circ}q_l(t) + B_{hk}^\circ \omega_{hk}(t)\right)^T P_{hk}^\circ q_{hk}(t) + \\ + q_{hk}^T(t)P_{hk}^\circ \left(A_{hkc}^\circ q_{hk}(t) + \sum_{l=1,\,l\ne h,k}^{p} A_{hk}^{l\circ}q_l(t) + B_{hk}^\circ \omega_{hk}(t)\right) \end{array} \right) < 0 \tag{114}$$

respectively. Introducing the next notations

$$B_{hk}^{l\circ} = \left[\ \{A_{hk}^{l\circ}\}_{l=1,\,l\ne h,k}^{p}\quad B_{hk}^\circ\ \right], \qquad \omega_{hk}^{l\circ T} = \left[\ \{q_l^T\}_{l=1,\,l\ne h,k}^{p}\quad \omega_{hk}^T(t)\ \right] \tag{115}$$

(114) can be written as

$$\sum_{h=1}^{p-1}\sum_{k=h+1}^{p}((A_{hkc}^\circ q_{hk}(t) + B_{hk}^{l\circ}\omega_{hk}^{l\circ})^T P_{hk}^\circ q_{hk}(t) + q_{hk}^T(t)P_{hk}^\circ(A_{hkc}^\circ q_{hk}(t) + B_{hk}^{l\circ}\omega_{hk}^{l\circ})) < 0 \tag{116}$$

Analogously, (106) can be rewritten as

$$y_{hk}(t) = C_{hk}^{\circ} q_{hk}(t) + \sum_{l=1, l\neq h}^{p} C_{hk}^{l\circ} q_l(t) + 0\, \omega_{hk}(t) = C_{hk}^{\circ} q_{hk}(t) + D_{hk}^{l\circ} \omega_{hk}^{l\circ} \qquad (117)$$

where

$$D_{hk}^{l\circ} = \left[\, \{C_{hk}\}_{l=1,\, l\neq h,k}^{p}\ \ 0 \,\right] \qquad (118)$$

Therefore, defining

$$\Gamma_{hk}^{\circ} = \mathrm{diag}\left[\, \{\varepsilon_{hkl} I_{n_l}\}_{l=1,\, l\neq h,k}^{p}\ \ \gamma_{hk} I_{(r_h+r_k)} \,\right] \qquad (119)$$

and inserting appropriate into (57), (58) then (109), (110) be obtained.  □

**Illustrative example**
To demonstrate properties of this approach a simple system with four-inputs and four-outputs is used in the example. The parameters of (75)-(77) are

$$A = \begin{bmatrix} 3 & 1 & 2 & -1 \\ -1 & 2 & 0 & 1 \\ 1 & -1 & 1 & 3 \\ 1 & -2 & -2 & 2 \end{bmatrix},\ C = \begin{bmatrix} 3 & 1 & 2 & 1 \\ 0 & 6 & 1 & 0 \\ 2 & -1 & 3 & 0 \\ 0 & 0 & 1 & 3 \end{bmatrix},\ B = \mathrm{diag}\begin{bmatrix} 1 & 1 & 1 & 1 \end{bmatrix},$$

To solve this problem the next separations were done

$$B_{hk} = \begin{bmatrix} 1 & 0 \\ 0 & 1 \end{bmatrix},\ h = 1,2,3,\ k = 2,3,4,\ h < k$$

$$A_{12}^{\circ} = \begin{bmatrix} 3 & 1 \\ -1 & 2 \end{bmatrix},\ A_{12}^{3\circ} = \begin{bmatrix} 2 \\ 0 \end{bmatrix},\ A_{12}^{4\circ} = \begin{bmatrix} -1 \\ 1 \end{bmatrix},\ C_{12}^{\circ} = \begin{bmatrix} 1 & 1 \\ 0 & 2 \end{bmatrix},\ C_{12}^{3\circ} = \begin{bmatrix} 2 \\ 1 \end{bmatrix},\ C_{12}^{4\circ} = \begin{bmatrix} 1 \\ 0 \end{bmatrix}$$

$$A_{13}^{\circ} = \begin{bmatrix} 3 & 2 \\ 1 & 1 \end{bmatrix},\ A_{13}^{2\circ} = \begin{bmatrix} 1 \\ -1 \end{bmatrix},\ A_{13}^{4\circ} = \begin{bmatrix} -1 \\ 3 \end{bmatrix},\ C_{13}^{\circ} = \begin{bmatrix} 1 & 2 \\ 2 & 1 \end{bmatrix},\ C_{13}^{2\circ} = \begin{bmatrix} 1 \\ -1 \end{bmatrix},\ C_{13}^{4\circ} = \begin{bmatrix} 1 \\ 0 \end{bmatrix}$$

$$A_{14}^{\circ} = \begin{bmatrix} 3 & -1 \\ 1 & 2 \end{bmatrix},\ A_{14}^{2\circ} = \begin{bmatrix} 1 \\ -2 \end{bmatrix},\ A_{14}^{3\circ} = \begin{bmatrix} 2 \\ -2 \end{bmatrix},\ C_{14}^{\circ} = \begin{bmatrix} 1 & 1 \\ 0 & 1 \end{bmatrix},\ C_{14}^{2\circ} = \begin{bmatrix} 1 \\ 0 \end{bmatrix},\ C_{14}^{3\circ} = \begin{bmatrix} 2 \\ 1 \end{bmatrix}$$

$$A_{23}^{\circ} = \begin{bmatrix} 2 & 0 \\ -1 & 1 \end{bmatrix},\ A_{23}^{1\circ} = \begin{bmatrix} -1 \\ 1 \end{bmatrix},\ A_{23}^{4\circ} = \begin{bmatrix} 1 \\ 3 \end{bmatrix},\ C_{23}^{\circ} = \begin{bmatrix} 2 & 1 \\ -1 & 1 \end{bmatrix},\ C_{23}^{1\circ} = \begin{bmatrix} 0 \\ 2 \end{bmatrix},\ C_{23}^{4\circ} = \begin{bmatrix} 0 \\ 0 \end{bmatrix}$$

$$A_{24}^{\circ} = \begin{bmatrix} 2 & 1 \\ -2 & 2 \end{bmatrix},\ A_{24}^{1\circ} = \begin{bmatrix} -1 \\ 1 \end{bmatrix},\ A_{24}^{3\circ} = \begin{bmatrix} 0 \\ -2 \end{bmatrix},\ C_{24}^{\circ} = \begin{bmatrix} 2 & 0 \\ 0 & 1 \end{bmatrix},\ C_{24}^{1\circ} = \begin{bmatrix} 0 \\ 0 \end{bmatrix},\ C_{24}^{3\circ} = \begin{bmatrix} 1 \\ 1 \end{bmatrix}$$

$$A_{34}^{\circ} = \begin{bmatrix} 1 & 3 \\ -2 & 2 \end{bmatrix},\ A_{34}^{1\circ} = \begin{bmatrix} 1 \\ 1 \end{bmatrix},\ A_{34}^{2\circ} = \begin{bmatrix} -1 \\ -2 \end{bmatrix},\ C_{34}^{\circ} = \begin{bmatrix} 1 & 0 \\ 1 & 1 \end{bmatrix},\ C_{34}^{1\circ} = \begin{bmatrix} 2 \\ 0 \end{bmatrix},\ C_{34}^{2\circ} = \begin{bmatrix} -1 \\ 0 \end{bmatrix}$$

Solving e.g. with respect to $X_{23}^{\circ}$, $Y_{23}^{\circ}$, $Z_{23}^{\circ}$, $\varepsilon_{231}$, $\varepsilon_{234}$ $\delta_{23}$ it means to rewrite (109)-(111) as

$$X_{23}^{\circ} = X_{23}^{\circ T} > 0, \quad \varepsilon_{231} > 0, \quad \varepsilon_{234} > 0, \quad \gamma_{23} > 0$$

$$\begin{bmatrix} \Phi_{23}^{\circ} & A_{23}^{1\circ} & A_{23}^{4\circ} & B_{23}^{\circ} & X_{23}^{\circ}A_{23}^{\circ T} - Y_{23}^{\circ T}B_{23}^{T} & X_{23}^{\circ}C_{23}^{\circ T} \\ * & -\varepsilon_{231} & 0 & 0 & A_{23}^{1\circ T} & C_{23}^{1\circ T} \\ * & * & -\varepsilon_{234} & 0 & A_{23}^{4\circ T} & C_{23}^{4\circ T} \\ * & * & * & -\gamma_{23}I_2 & B_{23}^{\circ T} & 0 \\ * & * & * & * & -Z_{23}^{\circ} - Z_{23}^{\circ T} & 0 \\ * & * & * & * & * & -I_2 \end{bmatrix} < 0$$

$$\Phi_{23}^{\circ} = X_{23}^{\circ} A_{23}^{\circ T} + A_{23}^{\circ} X_{23}^{\circ} - B_{23}^{\circ} Y_{23}^{\circ} - Y_{23}^{\circ T} B_{23}^{\circ T}$$

Using SeDuMi package for Matlab given task was feasible with

$$\varepsilon_{231} = 9.3761, \qquad \varepsilon_{234} = 6.7928, \qquad \gamma_{23} = 6.2252$$

$$X_{23}^{\circ} = \begin{bmatrix} 0.5383 & -0.0046 \\ -0.0046 & 0.8150 \end{bmatrix}, \ Y_{23}^{\circ} = \begin{bmatrix} 4.8075 & -0.0364 \\ -0.4196 & 5.1783 \end{bmatrix}, \ Z_{23}^{\circ} = \begin{bmatrix} 4.2756 & 0.1221 \\ 0.1221 & 4.5297 \end{bmatrix}$$

$$K_{23}^{\circ} = \begin{bmatrix} 1.1255 & -0.0384 \\ -0.1309 & 1.1467 \end{bmatrix}$$

By the same way computing the rest gain matrices the gain matrix set is

$$K_{12}^{\circ} = \begin{bmatrix} 7.3113 & 3.8869 \\ 1.4002 & 10.0216 \end{bmatrix}, \ K_{13}^{\circ} = \begin{bmatrix} 7.9272 & 4.0712 \\ 4.2434 & 8.8245 \end{bmatrix}, \ K_{14}^{\circ} = \begin{bmatrix} 7.4529 & 1.5651 \\ 1.6990 & 5.6584 \end{bmatrix}$$

$$K_{24}^{\circ} = \begin{bmatrix} 7.2561 & 0.7243 \\ -2.7951 & 4.4839 \end{bmatrix}, \qquad K_{34}^{\circ} = \begin{bmatrix} 6.3680 & 4.1515 \\ 0.8099 & 5.2661 \end{bmatrix}$$

Note, the control laws are realized in the partly-autonomous structure (94), (95), where every subsystem pair is stable, and the large-scale system be stable, too. To compare, an equivalent gain matrix (81) to centralized control can be constructed

$$K = \begin{bmatrix} 22.6914 & 3.8869 & 4.0712 & 1.5651 \\ 1.4002 & 18.4032 & -0.0384 & 0.7243 \\ 4.2434 & -0.1309 & 16.3393 & 4.1515 \\ 1.6990 & -2.7951 & 0.8099 & 15.4084 \end{bmatrix}$$

Thus, the resulting closed-loop eigenvalue spectrum is

$$\rho(A - BK) = \{-13.0595 \pm 0.4024\,i \ -16.2717 \ -22.4515\}$$

Matrix $K$ structure implies evidently that the control gain is diagonally dominant.

## 6. Pairwise decentralized design of control for uncertain systems

Consider for the simplicity that only the system matrix blocks are uncertain, and one or none uncertain function is associated with a system matrix block. Then the structure of the pairwise system description implies

$$A_{hk}r(t) \in \begin{cases} A_{hk}^{\circ} \cup \{A_{lh}^{k\circ}\}_{l=1}^{h-1} \cup \{A_{hl}^{k\circ}\}_{l=h+1}^{p} \ ; \text{upper triagonal blocks } (h<k) \\ \{A_{lh}^{\circ}\}_{l=1}^{h-1} \cup \{A_{hl}^{\circ}\}_{l=h}^{p} \qquad ; \text{diagonal blocks } (h=k) \\ A_{kh}^{\circ} \cup \{A_{lk}^{h\circ}\}_{l=1}^{k-1} \cup \{A_{kl}^{h\circ}\}_{l=k+1}^{p} \ ; \text{lower triagonal blocks } (h>k) \end{cases} \tag{120}$$

Analogously it can be obtained equivalent expressions with respect to $B_{hk}r(t)$, $C_{hk}r(t)$, respectively. Thus, it is evident already in this simple case that a single uncertainty affects $p-1$ from $q = \binom{p}{2}$ linear matrix inequalities which have to be included into design. Generally, the next theorem can be formulated.

**Theorem 8.** *Uncertain subsystem pair (91) in system (75), (77), controlled by control law (97) is stable with quadratic performances* $\|C_{hk}^\circ(sI - A_{hkc}^\circ)^{-1}B_{hk}^\circ\|_\infty^2 \le \gamma_{hk}$, $\|C_{hk}^{l\circ}(sI - A_{hkc}^\circ)^{-1}B_{hk}^{l\circ}\|_\infty^2 \le \varepsilon_{hkl}$ *if for* $\delta > 0$, $\delta \in R$, $h = 1,2\ldots,p-1$, $k = h+1,h+2\ldots,p$, $l = 1,2\ldots,p$, $l \ne h,k$, *there exist symmetric positive definite matrices* $T_{hki}^\circ \in R^{(n_h+n_k)\times(n_h+n_k)}$, *matrices* $V_{hk}^\circ \in R^{(n_h+n_k)\times(n_h+n_k)}$, $W_{hk}^\circ \in R^{(r_h+r_k)\times(n_h+n_k)}$, *and positive scalars* $\gamma_{hk}$, $\varepsilon_{hkl} \in R$ *such that for* $i = 1,2\ldots,s$

$$T_{hki}^\circ = T_{hki}^{\circ T} > 0, \ \varepsilon_{hkl} > 0, \ \gamma_{hk} > 0, \ h,l = 1,\ldots,p, \ l \ne h,k, \ h < k \le p, \ i = 1,2,\ldots,s \quad (121)$$

$$
\begin{bmatrix}
\Phi_{hki}^\circ & A_{hki}^{1\circ} & \cdots & A_{hki}^{p\circ} & B_{hki}^\circ & T_{hki}^\circ - \delta V_{hk}^{\circ T} + V_{hk}^\circ A_{hki}^{\circ T} - W_{hk}^{\circ T} B_{hki}^{\circ T} & V_{hk}^\circ C_{hki}^{\circ T} \\
* & -\varepsilon_{hk1} I_{n_1} & \cdots & 0 & 0 & A_{hki}^{1\circ T} & C_{hki}^{1\circ T} \\
\vdots & \vdots & \ddots & \vdots & \vdots & \vdots & \vdots \\
* & * & \cdots & -\varepsilon_{hkp} I_{n_p} & 0 & A_{hki}^{p\circ T} & C_{hki}^{p\circ T} \\
* & * & \cdots & * & -\gamma_{hk} I_{(r_h+r_k)} & B_{hki}^{\circ T} & 0 \\
* & * & \cdots & * & * & -\delta(V_{hk}^\circ + V_{hk}^{\circ T}) & 0 \\
* & * & \cdots & * & * & * & -I_{(m_h+m_k)}
\end{bmatrix} < 0 \quad (122)
$$

*where* $A_{hk}^\circ$, $B_{hk}^\circ$, $A_{hk}^{l\circ}$, $C_{hk}^\circ$, $C_{hk}^{l\circ}$ *are equivalently defined as in (99), (101), (104), respectively,*

$$\Phi_{hki}^\circ = V_{hk}^\circ A_{hki}^{\circ T} + A_{hki}^\circ V_{hk}^{\circ T} - B_{hki}^\circ W_{hk}^\circ - W_{hk}^{\circ T} B_{hki}^{\circ T} \quad (123)$$

*and where* $A_{hki}^{h\circ}$, $A_{hki}^{k\circ}$, *as well as* $C_{hki}^{h\circ}$, $C_{hki}^{k\circ}$ *are not included into the structure of (122). Then* $K_{hk}^\circ$ *is given as*

$$K_{hk}^\circ = W_{hk}^\circ V_{hk}^{\circ T-1} \quad (124)$$

*Proof.* Considering (109)-(112) and inserting these appropriate into (72), $i$ of(73), and (74) then (121)-(124) be obtained. □

### Illustrative example

Considering the same system parameters as were those given in the example presented in Subsection 5.3 but with $A_{34}r(t)$, and $r(t)$ lies within the interval $\langle 0.8, 1.2 \rangle$ then the next matrix parameter have to be included into solution

$$A_{131}^{4\circ} = \begin{bmatrix} -1 \\ 2.4 \end{bmatrix}, \ A_{132}^{4\circ} = \begin{bmatrix} -1 \\ 3.6 \end{bmatrix}, \ A_{231}^{4\circ} = \begin{bmatrix} 1 \\ 2.4 \end{bmatrix}, \ A_{23}^{4\circ} = \begin{bmatrix} 1 \\ 3.6 \end{bmatrix}$$

$$A_{341}^\circ = \begin{bmatrix} 1 & 2.4 \\ -2 & 2 \end{bmatrix}, \ A_{342}^\circ = \begin{bmatrix} 1 & 3.6 \\ -2 & 2 \end{bmatrix},$$

i.e. a solution be associated with $T_{13i}^\circ$, $T_{23i}^\circ$, and $T_{34i}^\circ$, $i = 1,2$, and in other cases only one matrix inequality be computed ($T_{12}^\circ$, $T_{14}^\circ$, $T_{24}^\circ$).
The task is feasible, the Lyapunov matrices are computed as follows

$$T_{131}^\circ = \begin{bmatrix} 5.7244 & -0.3591 \\ 0.1748 & 5.6673 \end{bmatrix}, \ T_{132}^\circ = \begin{bmatrix} 5.0484 & 0.0232 \\ 0.0232 & 5.0349 \end{bmatrix}, \ T_{12}^\circ = \begin{bmatrix} 6.3809 & 0.5280 \\ -0.6811 & 6.3946 \end{bmatrix}$$

$$T_{231}^\circ = \begin{bmatrix} 6.1360 & 0.0841 \\ 0.0090 & 6.2377 \end{bmatrix}, \ T_{232}^\circ = \begin{bmatrix} 5.5035 & 0.0258 \\ 0.0258 & 5.5252 \end{bmatrix}, \ T_{14}^\circ = \begin{bmatrix} 7.2453 & 0.9196 \\ -1.0352 & 7.5124 \end{bmatrix}$$

$$T_{341}^{\circ} = \begin{bmatrix} 2.4585 & 3.9935 \\ -3.7569 & 1.5487 \end{bmatrix}, \; T_{342}^{\circ} = \begin{bmatrix} 5.7297 & \\ & 5.7249 \end{bmatrix}, \; T_{24}^{\circ} = \begin{bmatrix} 2.5560 & 2.1220 \\ -1.9076 & 2.9055 \end{bmatrix}$$

the control law matrices takes form

$$K_{12}^{\circ} = \begin{bmatrix} 13.2095 & 0.7495 \\ 2.2753 & 14.1033 \end{bmatrix}, \; K_{13}^{\circ} = \begin{bmatrix} 14.2051 & 4.4679 \\ 1.9440 & 13.4616 \end{bmatrix}, \; K_{14}^{\circ} = \begin{bmatrix} 12.6360 & -1.6407 \\ 2.9881 & 10.6109 \end{bmatrix}$$

$$K_{23}^{\circ} = \begin{bmatrix} 14.3977 & -0.4237 \\ -1.0494 & 12.3509 \end{bmatrix}, \; K_{24}^{\circ} = \begin{bmatrix} -2.9867 & 5.9950 \\ -6.8459 & -2.6627 \end{bmatrix}, \; K_{34}^{\circ} = \begin{bmatrix} 5.3699 & 2.7480 \\ -0.6542 & 6.1362 \end{bmatrix}$$

and with the common $\delta = 10$ the subsystem interaction transfer functions $H_\infty$-norm upper-bound squares are

$$\varepsilon_{123} = 10.9960, \; \varepsilon_{124} = 7.6712, \; \gamma_{12} = 7.1988, \; \varepsilon_{132} = 7.7242, \; \varepsilon_{134} = 8.7654, \; \gamma_{13} = 6.4988$$
$$\varepsilon_{142} = 8.9286, \; \varepsilon_{143} = 12.1338, \; \gamma_{14} = 8.1536, \; \varepsilon_{231} = 10.3916, \; \varepsilon_{234} = 8.2081, \; \gamma_{23} = 7.0939$$
$$\varepsilon_{241} = 5.3798, \; \varepsilon_{243} = 6.6286, \; \gamma_{24} = 5.4780, \; \varepsilon_{341} = 16.1618, \; \varepsilon_{342} = 15.0874, \; \gamma_{34} = 9.0965$$

In the same sense as given above, the control laws are realized in the partly-autonomous structure (94), (95), too, and as every subsystem pair as the large-scale system be stable.

Only for comparison reason, the composed gain matrix (defined as in (81)), and the resulting closed-loop system matrix eigenvalue spectrum, realized using the nominal system matrix parameter $A_n$ and the robust and the nominal equivalent gain matrices $K$, $A_n$, respectively, were constructed using the set of gain matrices $K_{hk}$, $k = 1, 2, 3$, $h = 2, 3, 4$, $h \neq k$. As it can see

$$K = \begin{bmatrix} 40.0507 & 0.7495 & 4.4679 & -1.6407 \\ 2.2753 & 25.5144 & -0.4237 & 5.9950 \\ 1.9440 & -1.0494 & 31.1824 & 2.7480 \\ 2.9881 & -6.8459 & -0.6542 & 14.0844 \end{bmatrix}, \; \rho(A_n - BK) = \begin{bmatrix} -15.0336 \\ -20.6661 \\ -29.8475 \\ -37.2846 \end{bmatrix}$$

$$K_n = \begin{bmatrix} 39.6876 & 0.7495 & 4.2372 & -1.6407 \\ 2.2753 & 24.8764 & -0.4500 & 5.9950 \\ 2.3218 & -1.0008 & 30.3905 & 3.2206 \\ 2.9881 & -6.8459 & -0.6666 & 14.0725 \end{bmatrix}, \; \rho(A_n - BK_n) = \begin{bmatrix} -15.3818 \\ -19.6260 \\ -29.0274 \\ -36.9918 \end{bmatrix}$$

and the resulted structures of both gain matrices imply that by considering parameter uncertainties in design step the control gain matrix $K$ is diagonally more dominant then $K_n$ reflecting only the system nominal parameters.                                                                          ∎

It is evident that Lyapunov matrices $T_{hki}^{\circ}$ are separated from $A_{hki}^{\circ}$, $A_{hki}^{l\circ}$, $B_{hki}^{\circ}$, $C_{hki}^{\circ}$, and $C_{hki}^{l\circ}$ $h = 1, 2 \ldots, p-1, k = h+1, h+2 \ldots, p, l = 1, 2 \ldots, p, l \neq h, k$, i.e. there are no terms containing the product of $T_{hki}^{\circ}$ and any of them. By introducing a new variable $V_{hk}^{\circ}$, the products of type $P_{hki}^{\circ} A_{hki}^{\circ}$ and $A_{hki}^{\circ T} P_{hki}^{\circ}$ are relaxed to new products $A_{hki}^{\circ} V_{hk}^{\circ T}$ and $V_{hk}^{\circ} A_{hki}^{\circ T}$ where $V_{hk}^{\circ}$ needs not be symmetric and positive definite. This enables a robust BRL can be obtained for a system with polytopic uncertainties by using a parameter-dependent Lyapunov function, and to deal with linear systems with parametric uncertainties.

Although no common Lyapunov matrices are required the method generally leads to a larger number of linear matrix inequalities, and so more computational effort be needed to provide robust stability. However, used conditions are less restrictive than those obtained via a quadratic stability analysis (i.e. using a parameter-independent Lyapunov function), and are more close to necessity conditions. It is a very useful extension to control performance synthesis problems.

## 7. Concluding remarks

The main difficulty of solving the decentralized control problem comes from the fact that the feedback gain is subject to structural constraints. At the beginning study of large scale system theory, some people thought that a large scale system is decentrally stabilizable under controllability condition by strengthening the stability degree of subsystems, but because of the existence of decentralized fixed modes, some large scale systems can not be decentrally stabilized at all. In this chapter the idea to stabilize all subsystems and the whole system simultaneously by using decentralized controllers is replaced by another one, to stabilize all subsystems pairs and the whole system simultaneously by using partly decentralized control. In this sense the final scope of this chapter are quadratic performances of one class of uncertain continuous-time large-scale systems with polytopic convex uncertainty domain. It is shown how to expand the Lyapunov condition for pairwise control by using additive matrix variables in LMIs based on equivalent BRL formulations. As mentioned above, such matrix inequalities are linear with respect to the subsystem variables, and does not involve any product of the Lyapunov matrices and the subsystem ones. This enables to derive a sufficient condition for quadratic performances, and provides one way for determination of parameter-dependent Lyapunov functions by solving LMI problems. Numerical examples demonstrate the principle effectiveness, although some computational complexity is increased.

## 8. Acknowledgments

The work presented in this paper was supported by VEGA, Grant Agency of Ministry of Education and Academy of Sciences of Slovak Republic under Grant No. 1/0256/11, as well as by Research & Development Operational Programme Grant No. 26220120030 realized in Development of Center of Information and Communication Technologies for Knowledge Systems. These supports are very gratefully acknowledged.

## 9. References

Boyd, D.; El Ghaoui, L.; Peron, F. & Balakrishnan, V. (1994). *Linear Matrix Inequalities in System and Control Theory*. SIAM, ISBN 0-89871-334-X, Philadelphia.

Duan, Z.; Wang, J.Z. & Huang, L. (1994). Special decentralized control problems and effectiveness of parameter-dependent Lyapunov function method. In *Proceedings of the American Control Conference 2005*, pp. 1697-1702, Portland, June 2005.

Feron, E.; Apkarian, P. & Gahinet, P. (1996). Analysis and synthesis of robust control systems via parameter-dependent Lyapunov functions, *IEEE Transactions on Automatic Control*, Vol. 41, No. 7, 1996, 1041-1046, ISSN 0018-9286

Filasová, A. & Krokavec, D. (1999). Pair-wise decentralized control of large-scale systems. *Journal of Electrical Engineering* Vol. 50, No. 3-4, 1999, 1-10, ISSN 1335-3632

Filasová, A. & Krokavec, D. (2000). Pair-wise partially decentralized Kalman estimator. In *Control Systems Design (CSD 2000): A Proceedings Volume from IFAC Conference*, Kozák, Š., Huba, M. (Ed.), pp. 125-130, ISBN 00-08-043546-7, Bratislava, June, 2000, Elsevier, Oxford.

Filasová, A. & Krokavec, D. (2011). Pairwise control principle in large-scale systems. *Archives of Control Sciences*, 21, 2011 (in print).

Gahinet, P.; Nemirovski, A.; Laub, A.J. & Chilali, M. (1995). *LMI Control Toolbox User's Guide*. The MathWorks, Inc., Natick, 1995.

Gahinet, P.; Apkarian, P. & Mahmoud Chilali, M. (1996)    Affine parameter-dependent Lyapunov functions and real parametric uncertainty, *IEEE Transactions on Automatic Control*, Vol. 41, No. 3, 1996, 436-442, ISSN 0018-9286

Herrmann, G.; Turner, M.C. & Postlethwaite, I. (2007). Linear matrix inequalities in control, In *Mathematical Methods for Robust and Nonlinear Control. EPRSC Summer School.*, Turner, M.C., Bates, D.G. (Ed.), pp. 123-142, Springer–Verlag, ISBN 978-1-84800-024-7, Berlin.

Jamshidi, M. (1997). *Large-Scale Systems: Modeling, Control and Fuzzy Logic*, Prentice Hall, ISBN 0-13-125683-1, Upper Saddle River.

Jia, Y. (2003). Alternative proofs for improved LMI representations for the analysis and the design of continuous-time systems with poolytopic type uncertainty: A predictive approach, *IEEE Transactions on Automatic Control*, Vol. 48, No. 8, 2003, 1413-1416, ISSN 0018-9286

Kozáková, A. & V. Veselý, V. (2009). Design of robust decentralized controllers using the $M - \Delta$ structures. Robust stability conditions. *International Journal of System Science*, Vol. 40, No. 5, 2009, 497-505, ISSN 0020-7721

Krokavec, D. & Filasová, A. (2008). *Discrete-Time Systems*, Elfa, ISBN 978-80-8086-101-8, Košice. (in Slovak)

Leros, A.P. (1989).    LSS linear regulator problem. A partially decentralized approach. *International Journal of Control*, Vol. 49, No. 4, 1989, 1377-1399, ISSN 0020-7179

Lunze, J. (1992). *Feedback Control of Large-Scale Systems*, Prentice Hall, ISBN 0-13-318353-X, London.

Mahmoud, M.S. & Singh, M.G. (1981). *Large-Scale Systems Modelling*, Pergamon Press, ISBN 00-08-027313-0, Oxford.

Nesterov, Y. & Nemirovsky, A. (1994). *Interior Point Polynomial Methods in Convex Programming. Theory and Applications.* SIAM, ISBN 0-89871-319-6, Philadelphia.

Peaucelle, D.; Henrion, D.; Labit, Y. & Taitz, K. (1994). *User's Guide for SeDuMi Interface 1.04*, LAAS-CNRS, Toulouse.

Petersen, I.R.; Ugrinovskii, V.A. & Savkin A.V. (2000). *Robust Control Design Using $H_\infty$ Methods*, Springer-Verlag, ISBN 1-85233-171-2, London.

Pipeleers, G.; Demeulenaerea, B.; Sweversa, J. & Vandenbergheb, L. (2009). Extended LMI characterizations for stability and performance of linear systems, *Systems & Control Letters*, Vol.58, 2009, 510-518, ISSN 0167-6911

Skelton, E.E.; Iwasaki, T. & Grigoriadis, K. (1998). *A Unified Algebraic Approach to Linear Control Design*, Taylor & Francis, ISBN 0-7484-0592-5, London.

Veselý, V. & Rosinová, D. (2009). Robust output model predictive control design. BMI approach, *International Journal of Innovative Computing, Information and Control*, Vol. 5, No. 4, 2009, 1115-1123, ISBN 1751-648X

Wang, Q.G. (2003). *Decoupling Control*, Springer-Verlag, ISBN 978-3-54044-128-1, Berlin.

Wu, A.I. & Duan, G.R. (2006). Enhanced LMI representations for $H_2$ performance of polytopic uncertain systems: Continuous-time case, *International Journal of Automation and Computing*, Vol. 3, 2006, 304-308, ISSN 1476-8186

Wu, M.; He, Y. & She, J.H. (2010). *Stability Analysis and Robust Control of Time-Delay Systems*, Springer–Verlag, ISBN 3-64203-036-X, Berlin.

Xie, W. (2008). An equivalent LMI representation of bounded real lemma for continous-time systems, *Journal of Inequalities and Applications*, Vol. 5, 2010, ISSN 1025-5834

Zhou, K.; Doyle, J.C. & Glover, K. (1995). *Robust and Optimal Control*, Prentice Hall, ISBN 0-13-456567-3, Englewood Cliffs

# 5

# Synthesis of Variable Gain Robust Controllers for a Class of Uncertain Dynamical Systems

Hidetoshi Oya[1] and Kojiro Hagino[2]
[1]*The University of Tokushima*
[2]*The University of Electro-Communications*
*Japan*

## 1. Introduction

Robustness of control systems to uncertainties has always been the central issue in feedback control and therefore for dynamical systems with unknown parameters, a large number of robust controller design methods have been presented (e.g. (3; 37)). Also, many robust state feedback controllers achieving some robust performances such as quadratic cost function(28; 31), $\mathcal{H}^\infty$-disturbance attenuation(6) and so on have been suggested. It is well-known that most of these problems are reduced to standard convex optimization problems involving linear matrix inequalities (LMIs) which can be solved numerically very efficiently. Furthermore, in the case that the full state of systems cannot be measured, the control strategies via observer-based robust controllers (e.g. (12; 19; 27)) or robust output feedback one (e.g. (9; 11)) have also been well studied. However, most of the resulting controllers derived in the existing results have fixed structure, and these methods result in worst-case design. Therefore these controllers become cautious when the perturbation region of the uncertainties has been estimated larger than the proper region, because the robust controller designed by the existing results only has a fixed gain.

From these viewpoints, it is important to derive robust controllers with adjustable parameters which are tuned by using available information. Thus some researchers have proposed robust controllers with adjustable parameters(18; 33). In the work of Ushida et al.(33), a quadratically stabilizing state feedback controller based on the parametrization of $\mathcal{H}^\infty$ controllers is derived. Maki and Hagino(18) have introduced a robust controller with adaptation mechanism for linear systems with time-varying parameter uncertainties and the controller gain in their work is tuned on-line based on the information about parameter uncertainties. On the other hand, we have proposed a robust controller with adaptive compensation input for a class of uncertain linear systems(19; 21; 22). The adaptive compensation input is tuned by adjustable parameters based on the error information between the plant trajectory and the desired one. These adaptive robust controllers achieve good control performance and these approaches are very simple due to the application of the linear quadratic control problem. Besides these design methods reduce the cautiousness in a robust controller with a fixed gain, because utilizing the error signal between the real response of the uncertain system and the desired one is equivalent to giving consideration to the effect of the uncertainties as on-line information.

In this chapter, for a class of uncertain linear systems, variable gain robust controllers which achieve not only asymptotical stability but also improving transient behavior of the resulting closed-loop system have been shown(23; 24; 26). The variable gain robust controllers, which consist of fixed gain controllers and variable gain one, are tuned on-line based on the information about parameter uncertainties. In this chapter, firstly, a design method of variable gain state feedback controllers for linear systems with matched uncertainties has been shown and next the variable gain state feedback controller is extended to output feedback controllers. Finally, on the basis of the concept of piecewise Lyapunov functions (PLFs), an LMI-based variable gain robust controller synthesis for linear systems with matched uncertainties and unmatched one has been presented.

The contents of this chapter are as follows, where the item numbers in the list accord with the section numbers.

2. Variable Gain Robust State Feedback Controllers

3. Variable Gain Robust Output Feedback Controllers

4. Variable Gain Robust Controllers based on Piecewise Lyapunov Functions

5. Conclusions and Future Works

Basic symbols are listed bellow.

$$
\begin{aligned}
&\mathbb{Z}^+ && : \text{the set of positive integers}\\
&\mathbb{R} && : \text{the set of real numbers}\\
&\mathbb{R}^n && : \text{the set of } n\text{-dimensional vectors}\\
&\mathbb{R}^{n\times m} && : \text{the set of } n \times m\text{-dimensional matrices}\\
&I_n && : n\text{-dimensional identity matrix}
\end{aligned}
$$

Other than the above, we use the following notation and terms. For a matrix $\mathcal{A}$, the transpose of matrix $\mathcal{A}$ and the inverse of one are denoted by $\mathcal{A}^T$ and $\mathcal{A}^{-1}$ respectively and rank $\{\mathcal{A}\}$ represents the rank of the matrix $\mathcal{A}$. Also, $I_n$ represents $n$-dimensional identity matrix. For real symmetric matrices $\mathcal{A}$ and $\mathcal{B}$, $\mathcal{A} > \mathcal{B}$ (resp. $\mathcal{A} \geq \mathcal{B}$) means that $\mathcal{A} - \mathcal{B}$ is positive (resp. nonnegative) definite matrix. For a vector $\alpha \in \mathbb{R}^n$, $||\alpha||$ denotes standard Euclidian norm and for a matrix $\mathcal{A}$, $||\mathcal{A}||$ represents its induced norm. Besides, a vector $\alpha \in \mathbb{R}^n$, $||\alpha||_1$ denotes 1-norm, i.e. $||\alpha||_1$ is defined as $||\alpha||_1 \overset{\triangle}{=} \sum_{j=1}^{n} |\alpha_j|$. The intersection of two sets $\Gamma$ and $Y$ are denoted by $\Gamma \cap Y$ and the symbols "$\overset{\triangle}{=}$" and "$\star$" mean equality by definition and symmetric blocks in matrix inequalities, respectively. Besides, for a symmetric matrix $\mathcal{P}$, $\lambda_{\max} \{\mathcal{P}\}$ (resp. $\lambda_{\min} \{\mathcal{P}\}$) represents the maximal eigenvalue (resp. minimal eigenvalue).

Furthermore, the following usefule lemmas are used in this paper.

**Lemma 1.** *For arbitrary vectors $\lambda$ and $\xi$ and the matrices $\mathcal{G}$ and $\mathcal{H}$ which have appropriate dimensions, the following relation holds.*

$$
2\lambda^T \mathcal{G} \Delta(t) \mathcal{H} \xi \leq 2 \left\| \mathcal{G}^T \lambda \right\| \left\| \Delta(t) \mathcal{H} \xi \right\|
$$
$$
\leq 2 \left\| \mathcal{G}^T \lambda \right\| \left\| \mathcal{H} \xi \right\|
$$

*where $\Delta(t) \in \mathbb{R}^{p\times q}$ is a time-varying unknown matrix satisfying $\left\| \Delta(t) \right\| \leq 1$.*

*Proof.* The above relation can be easily obtained by Schwartz's inequality (see (8)). $\qquad\square$

**Lemma 2.** *(Schur complement) For a given constant real symmetric matrix $\Xi$, the following arguments are equivalent.*

*(i).* $\Xi = \begin{pmatrix} \Xi_{11} & \Xi_{12} \\ \Xi_{12}^T & \Xi_{22} \end{pmatrix} > 0$

*(ii).* $\Xi_{11} > 0$ *and* $\Xi_{22} - \Xi_{12}^T \Xi_{11}^{-1} \Xi_{12} > 0$

*(iii).* $\Xi_{22} > 0$ *and* $\Xi_{11} - \Xi_{12} \Xi_{22}^{-1} \Xi_{12}^T > 0$

*Proof.* See Boyd et al.(4) □

**Lemma 3.** *( Barbalat's lemma ) Let $\phi : \mathbb{R} \to \mathbb{R}$ be a uniformly continuous function on $[0, \infty)$. Suppose that $\lim_{t \to \infty} \int_0^t \phi(\tau)d\tau$ exists and is finite. Then*

$$\phi(t) \to 0 \text{ as } t \to \infty$$

*Proof.* See Khalil(13). □

**Lemma 4.** *(S-procedure) Let $\mathcal{F}(x)$ and $\mathcal{G}(x)$ be two arbitrary quadratic forms over $\mathbb{R}^n$. Then $\mathcal{F}(x) < 0$ for $\forall x \in \mathbb{R}^n$ satisfying $\mathcal{G}(x) \leq 0$ if and only if there exist a nonnegative scalar $\tau$ such that*

$$\mathcal{F}(x) - \tau\mathcal{G}(x) \leq 0 \text{ for } \forall x \in \mathbb{R}^n$$

*Proof.* See Boyd et al.(4). □

## 2. Variable gain robust state feedback controllers

In this section, we propose a variable gain robust state feedback controller for a class of uncertain linear systems. The uncertainties under consideration are supposed to satisfy the matching condition(3) and the variable gain robust state feedback controller under consideration consists of a state feedback with a fixed gain matrix and a compensation input with variable one. In this section, we show a design method of the variable gain robust state feedback controller.

### 2.1 Problem formulation
Consider the uncertain linear system described by the following state equation.

$$\frac{d}{dt}x(t) = (A + B\Delta(t)E)\,x(t) + Bu(t) \qquad (2.1)$$

where $x(t) \in \mathbb{R}^n$ and $u(t) \in \mathbb{R}^m$ are the vectors of the state (assumed to be available for feedback) and the control input, respectively. In (2.1) the matrices $A$ and $B$ denote the nominal values of the system, and the pair $(A, B)$ is stabilizable and the matrix $\Delta(t) \in \mathbb{R}^{m \times q}$ denotes unknown time-varying parameters which satisfy $\|\Delta(t)\| \leq 1$. Namely, the uncertain parameter satisfies the matching condition (See e.g. (3) and references therein).
The nominal system, ignoring the unknown parameter $\Delta(t)$ in (2.1), is given by

$$\frac{d}{dt}\bar{x}(t) = A\bar{x}(t) + B\bar{u}(t) \qquad (2.2)$$

where $\bar{x}(t) \in \mathbb{R}^n$ and $\bar{u}(t) \in \mathbb{R}^m$ are the vectors of the state and the control input for the nominal system respectively.

First of all, in order to generate the desirable transient behavior in time response for the uncertain system (2.1) systematically, we adopt the standard linear quadratic control problem (LQ control theory) for the nominal system (2.2). Note that some other design method so as to generate the desired response for the controlled system can also be used (e.g. pole assignment). It is well-known that the optimal control input for the nominal system (2.2) can be obtained as $\bar{u}(t) = -K\bar{x}(t)$ and the closed-loop system

$$\frac{d}{dt}\bar{x}(t) = (A + BK)\,\bar{x}(t)$$

$$= A_K\bar{x}(t) \tag{2.3}$$

is asymptotically stable*.

Now in order to obtain on-line information on the parameter uncertainty, we introduce an error signal $e(t) \overset{\triangle}{=} x(t) - \bar{x}(t)$, and for the uncertain system (2.1), we consider the following control input.

$$u(t) \overset{\triangle}{=} Kx(t) + \psi(x, e, \mathcal{L}, t) \tag{2.4}$$

where $\psi(x, e, \mathcal{L}, t) \in \mathbb{R}^m$ is a compensation input(21) to correct the effect of uncertainties, and it is supposed to have the following structure.

$$\psi(x, e, \mathcal{L}, t) \overset{\triangle}{=} \mathcal{F}e(t) + \mathcal{L}(x, e, t)e(t) \tag{2.5}$$

In (2.4), $\mathcal{F} \in \mathbb{R}^{\mathbb{R}^{m \times n}}$ and $\mathcal{L}(t) \in \mathbb{R}^{m \times n}$ are a fixed gain matrix and an adjustable time-varying matrix, respectively. Thus from (2.1), (2.3) – (2.5), the error system can be written as

$$\frac{d}{dt}e(t) = (A + B\Delta(t)E)\,x(t) + B\,(Kx(t) + \mathcal{F}e(t) + \mathcal{L}(x, e, t)x(t)) - A_K\bar{x}(t)$$

$$= A_{\mathcal{F}}e(t) + B\Delta(t)Ex(t) + \mathcal{L}(x, e, t)e(t) \tag{2.6}$$

In (2.6), $A_{\mathcal{F}}$ is the matrix expressed as

$$A_{\mathcal{F}} = A_K + B\mathcal{F} \tag{2.7}$$

Note that from the definition of the error signal, the uncertain system (2.1) is ensured to be stable, because the nominal system is asymptotically stable.

From the above, our control objective in this section is to derive the fixed gain matrix $\mathcal{F} \in \mathbb{R}^{m \times n}$ and the variable gain matrix $\mathcal{L}(x, e, t) \in \mathbb{R}^{m \times n}$ which stabilize the uncertain error system (2.6).

---

* Using the unique solution of the algebraic Riccati equation $A^T\mathcal{X} + \mathcal{X}A - \mathcal{X}B\mathcal{R}^{-1}B^T\mathcal{X} + \mathcal{Q} = 0$, the gain matrix $K \in \mathbb{R}^{m \times n}$ is determined as $K = -\mathcal{R}^{-1}B^T\mathcal{X}$ where $\mathcal{Q}$ and $\mathcal{R}$ are nonnegative and positive definite matrices, respectively. Besides, $\mathcal{Q}$ is selected such that the pair $(A, \mathcal{C})$ is detectable, where $\mathcal{C}$ is any matrix satisfying $\mathcal{Q} = \mathcal{C}\mathcal{C}^T$, and then the matrix $A_K \overset{\triangle}{=} A + BK$ is stable.

## 2.2 Synthesis of variable gain robust state feedback controllers

In this subsection, we consider designing the variable matrix $\mathcal{L}(x, e, t) \in \mathbb{R}^{m \times n}$ and the fixed gain matrix $\mathcal{F} \in \mathbb{R}^{m \times n}$ such that the error system (2.6) with unknown parameters is asymptotically stable. The following theorem gives a design method of the proposed adaptive robust controller.

**Theorem 1.** *Consider the uncertain error system (2.6) with variable gain matrix $\mathcal{L}(x, e, t) \in \mathbb{R}^{m \times n}$ and the fixed gain matrix $\mathcal{F} \in \mathbb{R}^{m \times n}$.*
*By using the LQ control theory, the fixed gain matrix $\mathcal{F} \in \mathbb{R}^{m \times n}$ is designed as $\mathcal{F} = -\mathcal{R}_e^{-1} B^T \mathcal{P}$ where $\mathcal{P} \in \mathbb{R}^{n \times n}$ is unique solution of the following algebraic Riccati equation.*

$$A_K^T \mathcal{P} + \mathcal{P} A_K - \mathcal{P} B \mathcal{R}_e^{-1} B^T \mathcal{P} + \mathcal{Q}_e = 0 \tag{2.8}$$

*where $\mathcal{Q}_e \in \mathbb{R}^{n \times n}$ and $\mathcal{R}_e \in \mathbb{R}^{m \times m}$ are positive definite matrices which are selected by designers. Besides, the variable gain matrix $\mathcal{L}(x, e, t) \in \mathbb{R}^{m \times n}$ is determined as*

$$\mathcal{L}(x, e, t) = -\frac{\|Ex(t)\|^2}{\|B^T \mathcal{P}e(t)\| \, \|Ex(t)\| + \sigma(t)} B^T \mathcal{P} \tag{2.9}$$

*In (2.9), $\sigma(t) \in \mathbb{R}^+$ is any positive uniform continuous and bounded function which satisfies*

$$\int_{t_0}^t \sigma(\tau) d\tau \leq \sigma^* < \infty \tag{2.10}$$

*where $\sigma^*$ is any positive constant and $t_0$ denotes an initial time. Then the uncertain error system (2.6) is bounded and*

$$\lim_{t \to \infty} e(t; t_0, e(t_0)) = 0 \tag{2.11}$$

*Namely, asymptotical stability of the uncertain error system (2.6) is ensured.*

*Proof.* Using symmetric positive definite matrix $\mathcal{P} \in \mathbb{R}^{n \times n}$ which satisfies (2.8), we introduce the following quadratic function

$$\mathcal{V}(e, t) \overset{\triangle}{=} e^T(t) \mathcal{P} e(t) \tag{2.12}$$

Let's $e(t)$ be the solution of (2.6) for $t \geq t_0$. Then the time derivative of the function $\mathcal{V}(e, t)$ along the trajectory of (2.6) can be written as

$$\frac{d}{dt} \mathcal{V}(e, t) = e^T(t) \left( A_{\mathcal{F}}^T \mathcal{P} + \mathcal{P} A_{\mathcal{F}} \right) e(t)$$
$$+ 2e^T(t) \mathcal{P} B \Delta(t) Ex(t) + 2e^T(t) \mathcal{P} B \mathcal{L}(x, e, t) e(t) \tag{2.13}$$

Now, one can see from (2.13) and **Lemma 1** that the following inequality for the function $\mathcal{V}(e, t)$ holds.

$$\frac{d}{dt} \mathcal{V}(e, t) = e^T(t) \left( A_{\mathcal{F}}^T \mathcal{P} + \mathcal{P} A_{\mathcal{F}} \right) e(t) + 2 \|B^T \mathcal{P}e(t)\| \, \|\Delta(t) Ex(t)\|$$
$$+ 2e^T(t) \mathcal{P} B \mathcal{L}(x, e, t) e(t)$$
$$\leq e^T(t) \left( A_{\mathcal{F}}^T \mathcal{P} + \mathcal{P} A_{\mathcal{F}} \right) e(t) + 2 \|B^T \mathcal{P}e(t)\| \, \|Ex(t)\|$$
$$+ 2e^T(t) \mathcal{P} B \mathcal{L}(x, e, t) e(t) \tag{2.14}$$

Additionally, using the relation (2.8), substituting (2.9) into (2.14) and some trivial manipulations give the inequality

$$
\begin{aligned}
\frac{d}{dt}\mathcal{V}(e,t) \leq & e^T(t)\left(A_{\mathcal{F}}^T \mathcal{P} + \mathcal{P}A_{\mathcal{F}}\right)e(t) + 2\left\|B^T\mathcal{P}e(t)\right\|\left\|Ex(t)\right\| \\
& + 2e^T(t)\mathcal{P}B\left(-\frac{\left\|Ex(t)\right\|^2}{\left\|B^T\mathcal{P}e(t)\right\|\left\|Ex(t)\right\| + \sigma(t)}B^T\mathcal{P}\right)e(t) \\
\leq & e^T(t)\left(A_{\mathcal{F}}^T \mathcal{P} + \mathcal{P}A_{\mathcal{F}}\right)e(t) + 2\frac{\left\|B^T\mathcal{P}e(t)\right\|\left\|Ex(t)\right\|}{\left\|B^T\mathcal{P}e(t)\right\|\left\|Ex(t)\right\| + \sigma(t)}\sigma(t) \\
= & -e^T(t)\left\{\mathcal{Q}_e + \mathcal{P}B\mathcal{R}_e^{-1}B^T\mathcal{P}\right\}e(t) + 2\frac{\left\|B^T\mathcal{P}e(t)\right\|\left\|Ex(t)\right\|}{\left\|B^T\mathcal{P}e(t)\right\|\left\|Ex(t)\right\| + \sigma(t)}\sigma(t) \quad (2.15)
\end{aligned}
$$

Notice the fact that for $\forall \alpha, \beta > 0$

$$
0 \leq \frac{\alpha\beta}{\alpha + \beta} \leq \alpha \tag{2.16}
$$

Then we can further obtain that for any $t > t_0$

$$
\frac{d}{dt}\mathcal{V}(e,t) \leq -e(t)\Omega e(t) + \sigma(t) \tag{2.17}
$$

where $\Omega \in \mathbb{R}^{n \times n}$ is the symmetric positive definite matrix given by

$$
\Omega = \mathcal{Q}_e + \mathcal{P}B\mathcal{R}_e^{-1}B^T\mathcal{P} \tag{2.18}
$$

Besides, letting $\zeta \stackrel{\triangle}{=} \lambda_{\min}(\Omega)$, we have

$$
\frac{d}{dt}\mathcal{V}(e,t) \leq -\zeta \left\|e(t)\right\|^2 + \sigma(t) \tag{2.19}
$$

On the other hand, from the definition of the quadratic function $\mathcal{V}(e,t)$, there always exist two positive constants $\xi^-$ and $\xi^+$ such that for any $t \geq t_0$,

$$
\xi^-\left(\left\|e(t)\right\|\right) \leq \mathcal{V}(e,t) \leq \xi^+\left(\left\|e(t)\right\|\right) \tag{2.20}
$$

where $\xi^-\left(\left\|e(t)\right\|\right)$ and $\xi^+\left(\left\|e(t)\right\|\right)$ are given by

$$
\begin{aligned}
\xi^-\left(\left\|e(t)\right\|\right) &\stackrel{\triangle}{=} \xi^- \left\|e(t)\right\|^2 \\
\xi^+\left(\left\|e(t)\right\|\right) &\stackrel{\triangle}{=} \xi^+ \left\|e(t)\right\|^2
\end{aligned} \tag{2.21}
$$

From the above, we want to show that the solution $e(t)$ is uniformly bounded, and that the error signal $e(t)$ converges asymptotically to zero.

By continuity of the error system (2.6), it is obvious that any solution $e(t; t_0, e(t_0))$ of the error system is continuous. Namely, $e(t)$ is also continuous, because the state $\bar{x}(t)$ for the nominal system is continuous. In addition, it follows from (2.19) and (2.20), that for any $t \geq t_0$, we have

$$0 \leq \xi^- \left( \|e(t)\| \right) \leq \mathcal{V}(e,t) = \mathcal{V}(e,t_0) + \int_{t_0}^{t} \frac{d}{dt} V(e,\tau)d\tau \tag{2.22}$$

$$\mathcal{V}(e,t) \leq \xi^+ \left( \|e(t_0)\| \right) - \int_{t_0}^{t} \xi^* \left( \|e(\tau)\| \right) d\tau + \int_{t_0}^{t} \sigma(\tau)d\tau \tag{2.23}$$

In (2.23), $\xi^* \left( \|e(t)\| \right)$ is defined as

$$\xi^* \left( \|e(t)\| \right) \triangleq \zeta \|e(t)\|^2 \tag{2.24}$$

Therefore, from (2.22) and (2.23) we can obtain the following two results. Firstly, taking the limit as $t$ approaches infinity on both sides of inequality (2.23), we have the following relation.

$$0 \leq \xi^+ \left( \|e(t_0)\| \right) - \lim_{t \to \infty} \int_{t_0}^{t} \xi^* \left( \|e(\tau)\| \right) d\tau + \lim_{t \to \infty} \int_{t_0}^{t} \sigma(\tau)d\tau \tag{2.25}$$

Thus one can see from (2.10) and (2.25) that

$$\lim_{t \to \infty} \int_{t_0}^{t} \xi^* \left( \|e(\tau)\| \right) d\tau \leq \xi^+ \left( \|e(t_0)\| \right) + \sigma^* \tag{2.26}$$

On the other hand, from (2.22) and (2.23), we obtain

$$0 \leq \xi^- \left( \|e(t)\| \right) \leq \xi^+ \left( \|e(t_0)\| \right) + \int_{t_0}^{t} \sigma(\tau)d\tau \tag{2.27}$$

Note that for any $t \geq t_0$,

$$\sup_{t \in [t_0,\infty)} \int_{t_0}^{t} \sigma(\tau)d\tau \leq \sigma^* \tag{2.28}$$

It follows from (2.27) and (2.28) that

$$0 \leq \xi^- \left( \|e(t)\| \right) \leq \xi^+ \left( \|e(t_0)\| \right) + \sigma^* \tag{2.29}$$

The relation (2.29) implies that $e(t)$ is uniformly bounded. Since $e(t)$ has been shown to be continuous, it follows that $e(t)$ is uniformly continuous. Therefore that $e(t)$ is uniformly continuous and one can see from the definition that the function $\xi^* \left( \|e(t)\| \right)$ also uniformly continuous. Applying the **Lemma 2** ( Barbalat's lemma ) to (2.26) yields

$$\lim_{t \to \infty} \xi^* \left( \|e(t)\| \right) = 0 \tag{2.30}$$

Besides, since $\xi^* \left( \|e(t)\| \right)$ is a positive definite scalar function, it is obvious that the following equation holds.

$$\lim_{t \to \infty} \|e(t)\| = 0 \tag{2.31}$$

Namely, asymptotical stability of the uncertain error system (2.6) is ensured. Therefore the uncertain system (2.1) is also asymptotically stable, because the nominal system (2.2) is stable. It follows that the result of the theorem is true. Thus the proof of **Theorem 1** is completed.  □

**Remark 1.** *Though, the variable gain controllers in the existing results(19; 21) can also be good transient performance, these controllers may cause serious chattering, because the adjustment parameters in the existing results(19; 21) are adjusted on the boundary surface of the allowable parameter space (see. (26) for details). On the other hand, since the variable gain matrix (2.9) of the proposed robust controller is continuous, chattering phenomenon can be avoided.*

## 2.3 Illustrative examples

In order to demonstrate the efficiency of the proposed control scheme, we have run a simple example.

Consider the following linear system with unknown parameter, i.e. the unknown parameter $\Delta(t) \in \mathbb{R}^1$.

$$\frac{d}{dt}x(t) = \begin{pmatrix} 1 & 1 \\ 0 & -2 \end{pmatrix} x(t) + \begin{pmatrix} 0 \\ 1 \end{pmatrix} \Delta(t) \left( 5 \ 4 \right) + \begin{pmatrix} 0 \\ 1 \end{pmatrix} u(t) \tag{2.32}$$

Now we select the weighting matrices $Q$ and $\mathcal{R}$ such as $Q = 1.0I_2$ and $\mathcal{R} = 4.0$ for the standard linear quadratic control problem for the nominal system, respectively. Then solving the algebraic Riccati equation, we obtain the following optimal gain matrix

$$K = \left( -6.20233 \ -2.08101 \right) \tag{2.33}$$

In addition, setting the design parameters $Q_e$ and $\mathcal{R}_e$ such as $Q_e = 9.0I_2$ and $\mathcal{R}_e = 1.0$, respectively, we have

$$\mathcal{F} = \left( -2.37665 \times 10^2 \ -9.83494 \times 10^1 \right) \tag{2.34}$$

Besides for the variable gain matrix $\mathcal{L}(x, e, t) \in \mathbb{R}^{m \times n}$, we select the following parameter.

$$\sigma(t) = 50 \exp\left(-0.75t\right) \tag{2.35}$$

In this example, we consider the following two cases for the unknown parameter $\Delta(t)$.

- Case 1) :

$$\Delta(t) = \sin(\pi t)$$

- Case 2) :

$$\Delta(t) = -1.0 : 0 \leq t \leq 1.0$$
$$\Delta(t) = 1.0 \quad : 1.0 < t \leq 2.0$$
$$\Delta(t) = -1.0 : t > 2.0$$

Besides, for numerical simulations, the initial values of the uncertain system (2.32) and the nominal system are selected as $x(0) = \bar{x}(0) = \left( 1.0 \ -1.0 \right)^T$.

| | $\mathcal{J}^1(e, t)$ | $\mathcal{J}^2(e, t)$ |
|---|---|---|
| Case 1) | $1.05685 \times 10^{-4}$ | $1.41469 \times 10^{-3}$ |
| Case 2) | $2.11708 \times 10^{-4}$ | $2.79415 \times 10^{-3}$ |

Table 1. The values of the performance indecies

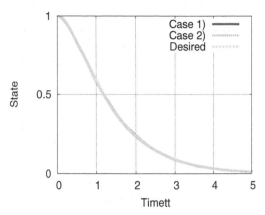

Fig. 1. Time histories of the state $x_1(t)$

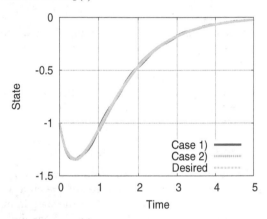

Fig. 2. Time histories of the state $x_2(t)$

The results of the simulation of this example are depicted in Figures 1–3 and Table 1. In these Figures, "Case 1)" and "Case 2)" represent the time-histories of the state variables $x_1(t)$ and $x_2(t)$ and the control input $u(t)$ generated by the proposed controller, and "Desired" shows the desired time-response and the desired control input generated by the nominal system. Additionally $\mathcal{J}^k(e,t)$ $(k=1,2)$ in Table 1 represent the following performance indecies.

$$\mathcal{J}^1(e,t) \overset{\triangle}{=} \int_0^\infty e^T(t)e(t)dt$$
$$\mathcal{J}^2(e,t) \overset{\triangle}{=} \sup_t \|e(t)\|_1$$

(2.36)

From Figures 1–3, we find that the proposed variable gain robust state feedback controller stabilizes the uncertain system (2.32) in spite of uncertainties. Besides one can also see from Figures 1 and 2 and Table 1 that the proposed variable gain robust state feedback controller achieves the good transient performance and can avoid serious chattering.

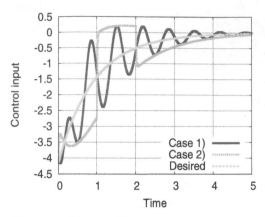

Fig. 3. Time histories of the control input $u(t)$

## 2.4 Summary
In this section, a design method of a variable gain robust state feedback controller for a class of uncertain linear systems has been presented and, by numerical simulations, the effectiveness of the proposed controller has been presented.

Since the proposed state feedback controller can easily be obtained by solving the standard algebraic Riccati equation, the proposed design approach is very simple. The proposed variable gain robust state feedback controller can be extended to robust servo systems and robust tracking control systems.

## 3. Variable gain robust output feedback controllers

In section 2, it is assumed that all the state are measurable and the procedure specifies the current control input as a function of the current value of the state vector. However it is physically and economically impractical to measure all of the state in many practical control systems. Therefore, it is necessary that the control input from the measurable signal is constructed to achieve satisfactory control performance. In this section, for a class of uncertain linear systems, we extend the result derived in section 2 to a variable gain robust output feedback controller.

### 3.1 Problem formulation
Consider the uncertain linear system described by the following state equation.

$$\frac{d}{dt}x(t) = (A + B\Delta(t)E)x(t) + Bu(t)$$
$$y(t) = Cx(t) \tag{3.1}$$

where $x(t) \in \mathbb{R}^n$, $u(t) \in \mathbb{R}^m$ and $y(t) \in \mathbb{R}^l$ are the vectors of the state, the control input and the measured output, respectively. In (3.1), the matrices $A$, $B$ and $C$ are the nominal values of system parameters and the matrix $\Delta(t) \in \mathbb{R}^{p \times q}$ denotes unknown time-varying parameters which satisfy $\|\Delta(t)\| \leq 1$. In this paper, we introduce the following assumption for the system parameters(25).

$$B^T = \mathcal{T}C \tag{3.2}$$

where $T \in \mathbb{R}^{m \times l}$ is a known constant matrix.

The nominal system, ignoring unknown parameters in (3.1), is given by

$$\frac{d}{dt}\bar{x}(t) = A\bar{x}(t) + B\bar{u}(t)$$
$$\bar{y}(t) = C\bar{x}(t) \tag{3.3}$$

In this paper, the nominal system (3.3) is supposed to be stabilizable via static output feedback control. Namely, there exists an output feedback control $\bar{u}(t) = K\bar{y}(t)$ (i.e. a fixed gain matrix $K \in \mathbb{R}^{m \times l}$). In other words, since the nominal system is stabilizable via static output feedback control, the matrix $A_K \stackrel{\triangle}{=} A + BKC$ is asymptotically stable. Note that the feedback gain matrix $K \in \mathbb{R}^{m \times l}$ is designed by using the existing results (e.g. (2; 16)).

Now on the basis of the work of (25), we introduce the error vectors $e(t) \stackrel{\triangle}{=} x(t) - \bar{x}(t)$ and $e_y(t) \stackrel{\triangle}{=} y(t) - \bar{y}(t)$. Beside, using the fixed gain matrix $K \in \mathbb{R}^{m \times l}$, we consider the following control input for the uncertain linear system (3.1).

$$u(t) \stackrel{\triangle}{=} Ky(t) + \psi(e_y, \mathcal{L}, t) \tag{3.4}$$

where $\psi(e_y, \mathcal{L}, t) \in \mathbb{R}^m$ is a compensation input (e.g. (25)) and has the following form.

$$\psi(e_y, \mathcal{L}, t) \stackrel{\triangle}{=} \mathcal{L}(e_y, t)e_y(t) \tag{3.5}$$

In (3.5), $\mathcal{L}(e_y, t) \in \mathbb{R}^{m \times l}$ is a variable gain matrix. Then one can see from (3.1) and (3.3) – (3.5) that the following uncertain error system can be derived.

$$\frac{d}{dt}e(t) = A_K e(t) + B\Delta(t)Ex(t) + B\mathcal{L}(e_y, t)e_y(t)$$
$$e_y(t) = Ce(t) \tag{3.6}$$

From the above, our control objective is to design the variable gain robust output feedback controller which stabilizes the uncertain error system (3.6). That is to derive the variable gain matrix $\mathcal{L}(e_y, t) \in \mathbb{R}^{m \times l}$ which stabilizes the uncertain error system (3.6).

### 3.2 Synthesis of variable gain robust output feedback controllers

In this subsection, an LMI-based design method of the variable gain robust output feedback controller for the uncertain linear system (3.1) is presented. The following theorem gives an LMI-based design method of a variable gain robust output feedback controller.

**Theorem 2.** *Consider the uncertain error system (3.6) with the variable gain matrix $\mathcal{L}(e_y, t) \in \mathbb{R}^{m \times l}$. Suppose there exist the positive definite matrices $S \in \mathbb{R}^{n \times n}$, $\Theta \in \mathbb{R}^{l \times l}$ and $\Psi \in \mathbb{R}^{l \times l}$ and the positive constants $\gamma_1$ and $\gamma_2$ satisfying the following LMIs.*

$$SA_K + A_K^T S + \gamma_1 E^T E \leq -Q$$
$$-C^T \Theta C + SC^T T^T TC + C^T T^T TCS \leq 0$$
$$\begin{pmatrix} -C^T \Psi C & SC^T T & SC^T T \\ \star & -\gamma_1 I_m & 0 \\ \star & \star & -\gamma_2 I_m \end{pmatrix} \leq 0 \tag{3.7}$$

*Using the positive definite matrices $\Theta \in \mathbb{R}^{l \times l}$ and $\Psi \in \mathbb{R}^{l \times l}$, we consider the following variable gain matrix.*

$$\mathcal{L}(e_y, t) = -\frac{\left(\left\|\Psi^{1/2}Ce(t)\right\|^2 + \gamma_2 \left\|E\bar{x}(t)\right\|^2\right)^2}{\left\|\Theta^{1/2}Ce(t)\right\|^2 \left(\left\|\Psi^{1/2}Ce(t)\right\|^2 + \gamma_2 \left\|E\bar{x}(t)\right\|^2 + \sigma(t)\right)}\mathcal{T} \tag{3.8}$$

*In (3.7), $\mathcal{Q} \in \mathbb{R}^{n \times n}$ is a symmetric positive definite matrix selected by designers and $\sigma(t) \in \mathbb{R}^1$ in (3.8) is any positive uniform continuous and bounded function which satisfies*

$$\int_{t_0}^{t} \sigma(\tau)d\tau \leq \sigma^* < \infty \tag{3.9}$$

*where $t_0$ and $\sigma^*$ are an initial time and any positive constant, respectively.*
*Then asymptotical stability of the uncertain error system (3.6) is guaranteed.*

**Proof.** Firstly, we introduce the quadratic function $\mathcal{V}(e,t) \stackrel{\triangle}{=} e^T(t)\mathcal{S}e(t)$. The time derivative of the quadratic function $\mathcal{V}(e,t)$ can be written as

$$\frac{d}{dt}\mathcal{V}(e,t) = e^T(t)\left(\mathcal{S}A_K + A_K^T\mathcal{S}\right)e(t) + 2e^T(t)\mathcal{S}B\Delta(t)Ex(t) + 2e^T(t)\mathcal{S}B\mathcal{L}(e_y,t)e_y(t) \tag{3.10}$$

Now, using **Lemma 1** and the assumption (3.2) we can obtain

$$\frac{d}{dt}\mathcal{V}(e,t) \leq e^T(t)\left(\mathcal{S}A_K + A_K^T\mathcal{S}\right)e(t) + 2e^T(t)\mathcal{S}B\Delta(t)E\left(e(t) + \bar{x}(t)\right) + 2e^T(t)\mathcal{S}B\mathcal{L}(e_y,t)e_y(t)$$

$$\leq e^T(t)\left(\mathcal{S}A_K + A_K^T\mathcal{S} + \gamma_1 E^T E\right)e(t) + 2e^T(t)\mathcal{S}C^T\mathcal{T}^T\mathcal{L}(e_y,t)e_y(t)$$

$$+ \frac{1}{\gamma_1}e^T(t)\mathcal{S}C^T\mathcal{T}^T\mathcal{T}C\mathcal{S}e(t) + \frac{1}{\gamma_2}e^T(t)\mathcal{S}C^T\mathcal{T}^T\mathcal{T}C\mathcal{S}e(t) + \gamma_2\bar{x}^T(t)E^T E\bar{x}(t) \tag{3.11}$$

Here we have used the well-known following relation.

$$2a^T b \leq \mu a^T a + \frac{1}{\mu}b^T b \tag{3.12}$$

where $a$ and $b$ are any vectors with appropriate dimensions and $\mu$ is any positive constant. Besides, we have the following inequality for the time derivative of the quadratic function $\mathcal{V}(e,t)$.

$$\frac{d}{dt}\mathcal{V}(e,t) \leq e^T(t)\left(\mathcal{S}A_K + A_K^T\mathcal{S} + \gamma_1 E^T E\right)e(t) + e^T(t)C^T\Psi Ce(t) + \gamma_2\bar{x}^T(t)E^T E\bar{x}(t)$$

$$+ 2e^T(t)\mathcal{S}C^T\mathcal{T}^T\mathcal{L}(e_y,t)e_y(t) \tag{3.13}$$

because by using **Lemma 2** (Schur complement) the third LMI of (3.7) can be written as

$$-C^T\Psi C + \frac{1}{\gamma_1}\mathcal{S}C^T\mathcal{T}^T\mathcal{T}C\mathcal{S} + \frac{1}{\gamma_2}\mathcal{S}C^T\mathcal{T}^T\mathcal{T}C\mathcal{S} \leq 0 \tag{3.14}$$

Furthermore using the variable gain matrix (3.8), the LMIs (3.7) and the well-known inequality for any positive constants $\alpha$ and $\beta$

$$0 \leq \frac{\alpha\beta}{\alpha + \beta} \leq \alpha \quad \forall \alpha, \beta > 0 \tag{3.15}$$

and some trivial manipulations give the following relation.

$$\frac{d}{dt}\mathcal{V}(e,t) \leq -e^T(t)\mathcal{Q}e(t) + \sigma(t) \tag{3.16}$$

In addition, by letting $\zeta \overset{\triangle}{=} \min\{\lambda_{\min}\{\mathcal{Q}\}\}$, we obtain the following inequality.

$$\frac{d}{dt}\mathcal{V}(e,t) \leq -\zeta\|e(t)\|^2 + \sigma(t) \tag{3.17}$$

On the other hand, one can see from the definition of the quadratic function $\mathcal{V}(e,t)$ that there always exist two positive constants $\delta_{\min}$ and $\delta_{\max}$ such that for any $t \geq t_0$,

$$\xi^-(\|e(t)\|) \leq \mathcal{V}(e,t) \leq \xi^+(\|e(t)\|) \tag{3.18}$$

where $\xi^-(\|e(t)\|)$ and $\xi^+(\|e(t)\|)$ are given by

$$\begin{aligned} \xi^-(\|e(t)\|) &\overset{\triangle}{=} \delta_{\min}\|e(t)\|^2 \\ \xi^+(\|e(t)\|) &\overset{\triangle}{=} \delta_{\max}\|e(t)\|^2 \end{aligned} \tag{3.19}$$

It is obvious that any solution $e(t; t_0, e(t_0))$ of the uncertain error system (3.6) is continuous. In addition, it follows from (3.17) and (3.18), that for any $t \geq t_0$, we have

$$\begin{aligned} 0 \leq \xi^-(\|e(t)\|) &\leq \mathcal{V}(e,t) = \mathcal{V}(e,t_0) + \int_{t_0}^t \frac{d}{dt}\mathcal{V}(e,\tau)d\tau \\ \mathcal{V}(e,t_0) + \int_{t_0}^t \frac{d}{dt}\mathcal{V}(e,\tau)d\tau &\leq \xi^+(\|e(t_0)\|) - \int_{t_0}^t \zeta(\|e(\tau)\|)\,d\tau + \int_{t_0}^t \sigma(\tau)d\tau \end{aligned} \tag{3.20}$$

In (3.20), $\xi^*(\|e(t)\|)$ is defined as

$$\xi^*(\|e(t)\|) \overset{\triangle}{=} \zeta\|e(t)\|^2 \tag{3.21}$$

Therefore, from (3.20) we can obtain the following two results. Firstly, taking the limit as $t$ approaches infinity on both sides of the inequality (3.20), we have

$$0 \leq \xi^+(\|e(t_0)\|) - \lim_{t \to \infty}\int_{t_0}^t \xi^*(\|e(\tau)\|)\,d\tau + \lim_{t \to \infty}\int_{t_0}^t \sigma(\tau)d\tau \tag{3.22}$$

Thus one can see from (3.9) and (3.22) that

$$\lim_{t \to \infty}\int_{t_0}^t \xi^*(\|e(\tau)\|)\,d\tau \leq \xi^+(\|e(t_0)\|) + \sigma^* \tag{3.23}$$

On the other hand, from (3.20), we obtain

$$0 \leq \xi^-(\|e(t)\|) \leq \xi^+(\|e(t_0)\|) + \int_{t_0}^t \sigma(\tau)d\tau \tag{3.24}$$

It follows from (3.9) and (3.24) that

$$0 \leq \xi^- \left( \|e(t)\| \right) \leq \xi^+ \left( \|e(t_0)\| \right) + \sigma^* \tag{3.25}$$

The relation (3.25) implies that $e(t)$ is uniformly bounded. Since $e(t)$ has been shown to be continuous, it follows that $e(t)$ is uniformly continuous. Therefore, one can see from the definition that $\xi^* \left( \|e(t)\| \right)$ is also uniformly continuous. Thus applying **Lemma 3** (Barbalat's lemma) to (3.23) yields

$$\lim_{t \to \infty} \xi^* \left( \|e(t)\| \right) = \lim_{t \to \infty} \zeta \|e(t)\|^2 = 0 \tag{3.26}$$

Namely, asymptotical stability of the uncertain error system (3.6) is ensured. Thus the uncertain linear system (3.1) is also stable.

It follows that the result of the theorem is true. Thus the proof of **Theorem 2** is completed. $\square$

**Theorem 2** provides a sufficient condition for the existence of a variable gain robust output feedback controller for the uncertain linear system (3.1). Next, we consider a special case. In this case, we consider the uncertain linear system described by

$$\frac{d}{dt} x(t) = (A + B\Delta(t)C) x(t) + Bu(t)$$
$$y(t) = Cx(t) \tag{3.27}$$

Thus one can see from (3.3) – (3.5) and (3.27) that we have the following uncertain error system.

$$\frac{d}{dt} e(t) = A_K e(t) + B\Delta(t)Cx(t) + BL(e_y, t)e_y(t)$$
$$e_y(t) = Ce(t) \tag{3.28}$$

Next theorem gives an LMI-based design method of a variable gain robust output feedback controller for this case.

**Theorem 3.** *Consider the uncertain error system (3.28) with the variable gain matrix $\mathcal{L}(e_y, t) \in \mathbb{R}^{m \times l}$.*

*Suppose there exist the symmetric positive definite matrices $\mathcal{X} > 0, \mathcal{Y} > 0$ and matrices $\mathcal{S} \in \mathbb{R}^{n \times n}$, $\Theta \in \mathbb{R}^{l \times l}$ and $\Psi \in \mathbb{R}^{l \times l}$ and the positive constant $\gamma$ satisfying the LMIs.*

$$\mathcal{S}A_K + A_K^T \mathcal{S} \leq -\mathcal{Q} \quad (\mathcal{Q} = \mathcal{Q}^T > 0)$$
$$-C^T \Theta C + \mathcal{S}C^T \mathcal{T}^T \mathcal{T} C + C^T \mathcal{T}^T \mathcal{T} C \mathcal{S} \leq 0$$
$$\begin{pmatrix} -C^T \Psi C & \mathcal{S}C^T \mathcal{T} \\ \star & -\gamma I_m \end{pmatrix} \leq 0 \tag{3.29}$$

*Using positive definite matrices $\Psi \in \mathbb{R}^{l \times l}$ and $\Theta \in \mathbb{R}^{l \times l}$ and the positive scalars $\gamma$ satisfying the LMIs (3.29), we consider the variable gain matrix*

$$\mathcal{L}(e_y, t) = -\frac{\left( \|\Psi^{1/2} e_y(t)\|^2 + \gamma \|y(t)\|^2 \right)^2}{\|\Theta^{1/2} Ce(t)\|^2 \left( \|\Psi^{1/2} e_y(t)\|^2 + \gamma \|y(t)\|^2 + \sigma(t) \right)} \mathcal{T} \tag{3.30}$$

*where $\sigma(t) \in \mathbb{R}^1$ is any positive uniform continuous and bounded function satisfying (3.9). Then asymptotical stability of the uncertain error system (3.28) is guaranteed.*

*Proof.* By using the symmetric positive definite matrix $S \in \mathbb{R}^{n \times n}$, we consider the quadratic function $V(e, t) \overset{\triangle}{=} e^T(t) S e(t)$. Then using the assumption (3.2) we have

$$\frac{d}{dt} V(e, t) = e^T(t) \left( S A_K + A_K^T S \right) e(t) + 2e^T(t) S C^T T^T \Delta(t) C x(t)$$
$$+ 2e^T(t) S C^T T^T \mathcal{L}(e_y, t) e_y(t) \tag{3.31}$$

Additionally, applying the inequality (3.12) to the second term on the right hand side of (3.31) we obtain

$$\frac{d}{dt} V(e, t) \leq e^T(t) \left( S A_K + A_K^T S \right) e(t) + \frac{1}{\gamma} e^T(t) S C^T T^T T C S e(t) + \gamma y^T(t) y(t)$$
$$+ 2e^T(t) S C^T T^T \mathcal{L}(e_y, t) e_y(t) \tag{3.32}$$

Now by using the LMIs (3.29), the variable gain matrix (3.30) and the inequality (3.15), we have

$$\frac{d}{dt} V(e, t) \leq -e^T(t) \mathcal{Q} e(t) + \sigma(t)$$
$$\leq -\zeta \|e(t)\|^2 + \sigma(t) \tag{3.33}$$

where $\zeta$ is a positive scalar given by $\zeta = \lambda_{\max}\{\mathcal{Q}\}$.
Therefore, one can see from the definition of the quadratic function $V(e, t)$ and **Proof 1** that the rest of proof of **Theorem 2** is straightforward. $\qquad\square$

### 3.3 Illustrative examples
Consider the uncertain linear system described by

$$\frac{d}{dt} x(t) = \begin{pmatrix} -2.0 & 0.0 & -6.0 \\ 0.0 & 1.0 & 1.0 \\ 3.0 & 0.0 & -7.0 \end{pmatrix} x(t) + \begin{pmatrix} 2.0 \\ 1.0 \\ 0.0 \end{pmatrix} \Delta(t) \begin{pmatrix} 1.0 & 0.0 & 1.0 \\ 0.0 & 3.0 & 1.0 \end{pmatrix} x(t) + \begin{pmatrix} 2.0 \\ 1.0 \\ 0.0 \end{pmatrix} u(t)$$
$$y(t) = \begin{pmatrix} 1.0 & 0.0 & 0.0 \\ 0.0 & 1.0 & 0.0 \end{pmatrix} x(t) \tag{3.34}$$

Namely, the matrix $T \in \mathbb{R}^{1 \times 2}$ in the assumption (3.2) can be expressed as $T = (2.0 \ \ 1.0)$. Firstly, we design an output feedback gain matrix $K \in \mathbb{R}^{1 \times 2}$ for the nominal system. By selecting the design parameter $\alpha$ such as $\alpha = 4.5$ and applying the LMI-based design algorithm (see. (2) and Appendix in (25)), we obtain the following output feedback gain matrix $K \in \mathbb{R}^{1 \times 2}$.

$$K = (3.17745 \times 10^{-1} \ \ -1.20809 \times 10^{1}) \tag{3.35}$$

Finally, we use **Theorem 1** to design the proposed variable gain robust output feedback controller, i.e. we solve the LMIs (3.7). By selecting the symmetric positive definite matrix $\mathcal{Q} \in \mathbb{R}^{3 \times 3}$ such as $\mathcal{Q} = 0.1 \times I_3$, we have

$$S = \begin{pmatrix} 7.18316 & 1.10208 & 3.02244 \times 10^{-1} \\ \star & 5.54796 & -6.10321 \times 10^{-2} \\ \star & \star & 4.74128 \end{pmatrix}$$
$$\gamma_1 = 2.01669 \times 10^3, \ \ \gamma_2 = 6.34316 \times 10^2, \tag{3.36}$$
$$\Theta = \begin{pmatrix} 3.14338 \times 10^1 & 1.54786 \times 10^1 \\ \star & 8.20347 \end{pmatrix}, \ \Psi = \begin{pmatrix} 6.73050 & 6.45459 \\ \star & 6.57618 \end{pmatrix}$$

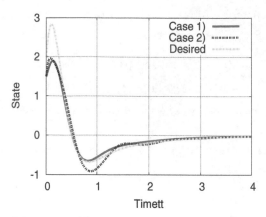

Fig. 4. Time histories of the state $x_1(t)$

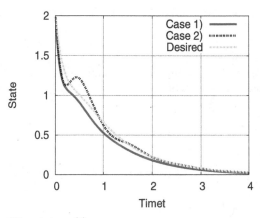

Fig. 5. Time histories of the state $x_2(t)$

In this example, we consider the following two cases for the unknown parameter $\Delta(t) \in \mathbb{R}^{1 \times 2}$.

- Case 1) : $\Delta(t) = \begin{pmatrix} 7.30192 & -5.00436 \end{pmatrix} \times 10^{-1}$

- Case 2) : $\Delta(t) = \begin{pmatrix} \sin(5\pi t) & \cos(5\pi t) \end{pmatrix}$

Furthermore, initial values for the uncertain system (3.24) and the nominal system are selected as $x(0) = \begin{pmatrix} 1.5 & 2.0 & -4.5 \end{pmatrix}^T$ and $\bar{x}(0) = \begin{pmatrix} 2.0 & 2.0 & -5.0 \end{pmatrix}^T$, respectively. Besides, we choose $\sigma(t) \in \mathbb{R}^+$ in (3.8) as $\sigma(t) = 5.0 \times 10^{12} \times \exp\left(-1.0 \times 10^{-4}t\right)$.

The results of the simulation of this example are depicted in Figures 4–7. In these figures, "Case 1)" and "Case 2)" represent the time-histories of the state variables $x_1(t)$ and $x_2(t)$ and the control input $u(t)$ generated by the proposed variable gain robust output feedback controller, and "Desired" shows the desired time-response and the desired control input generated by the nominal system. From Figures 4–6, we find that the proposed variable gain robust output feedback controller stabilize the uncertain linear system (3.34) in spite of plant uncertainties and achieves good transient performance.

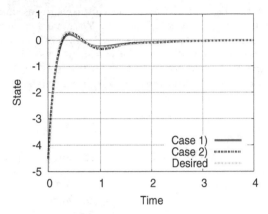

Fig. 6. Time histories of the state $x_3(t)$

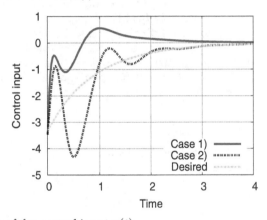

Fig. 7. Time histories of the control input $u(t)$

### 3.4 Summary
In this section, we have proposed a variable gain robust output feedback controller for a class of uncertain linear systems. Besides, by numerical simulations, the effectiveness of the proposed controller has been presented.

The proposed controller design method is easy to design a robust output feedback controller. Additionally, the proposed control scheme is adaptable when some assumptions are satisfied, and in cases where only the output signal of the controlled system is available, the proposed method can be used widely. In addition, the proposed controller is more effective for systems with larger uncertainties. Namely, for the upper bound on the perturbation region of the unknown parameter $\Delta(t)$ is larger than 1, the proposed variable gain output feedback controller can easily be extended.

## 4. Variable gain robust controllers based on piecewise Lyapunov functions

The quadratic stability approach is popularly used for robust stability analysis of uncertain linear systems. This approach, however, may lead to conservative results. Alternatively, non-quadratic Lyapunov functions have been used to improve the estimate of robust stability and to design robust stabilizing controllers(7; 30; 34). We have also proposed variable gain controllers and adaptive gain controllers based on Piecewise Lyapunov functions (PLFs) for a class of uncertain linear systems(23; 24). However, the resulting variable gain robust controllers may occur the chattering phenomenon. In this section, we propose a variable gain robust state feedback controller avoiding chattering phenomenon for a class of uncertain linear systems via PLFs and show that sufficient conditions for the existence of the proposed variable gain robust state feedback controller.

## 4.1 Problem formulation

Consider a class of linear systems with non-linear perturbations represented by the following state equation (see **Remark 2**).

$$\frac{d}{dt}x(t) = (A + \mathcal{D}\Delta(t)\mathcal{E})\,x(t) + Bu(t) \tag{4.1}$$

where $x(t) \in \mathbb{R}^n$ and $u(t) \in \mathbb{R}^m$ are the vectors of the state (assumed to be available for feedback) and the control input, respectively. In (4.1), the matrices $A$ and $B$ denote the nominal values of the system, and the matrix $B$ has full column rank. The matrices $\mathcal{D}$ and $\mathcal{E}$ which have appropriate dimensions represent the structure of uncertainties. The matrix $\Delta(t) \in \mathbb{R}^{p \times q}$ represents unknown time-varying parameters and satisfies the relation $\|\Delta(t)\| \leq 1$. Note that the uncertain term $\mathcal{D}\Delta(t)\mathcal{E}$ consists of matched part and unmatched one. Additionally, introducing the integer $\mathcal{N} \in \mathbb{Z}^+$ defined as

$$\mathcal{N} \triangleq \arg \min_{\mathcal{Z} \in \mathbb{Z}^+} \{\mathcal{Z} \mid (\mathcal{Z}m - n) \geq 0\} \tag{4.2}$$

we assume that there exist symmetric positive definite matrices $\mathcal{S}_k \in \mathbb{R}^{n \times n}$ $(k = 1, \cdots, \mathcal{N})$ which satisfies the following relation(23; 24).

$$\bigcap_{k=1}^{\mathcal{N}} \Omega_{\mathcal{S}_k} = \{0\} \tag{4.3}$$

where $\Omega_{\mathcal{S}_k}$ represents a subspace defined as

$$\Omega_{\mathcal{S}_k} \triangleq \left\{ x \in \mathbb{R}^n \mid B^T \mathcal{S}_k x = 0 \right\} \tag{4.4}$$

The nominal system, ignoring the unknown parameter in (4.1), is given by

$$\frac{d}{dt}\bar{x}(t) = A\bar{x}(t) + B\bar{u}(t) \tag{4.5}$$

where $\bar{x}(t) \in \mathbb{R}^n$ and $\bar{u}(t) \in \mathbb{R}^m$ are the vectors of the state and the control input, respectively. First of all, we adopt the standard linear quadratic LQ control theory for the nominal system (4.5) in order to generate the desirable transient response for the plant systematically, i.e. the control input is given by $\bar{u}(t) = K\bar{x}(t)$. Note that some other design method so as to generate the desired response for the controlled system can also be used (e.g. pole assignment). Thus the feedback gain matrix $K \in \mathbb{R}^{m \times n}$ is derived as $K = -\mathcal{R}^{-1}B^T\mathcal{P}$ where $\mathcal{P} \in \mathbb{R}^{n \times n}$ is unique solution of the algebraic Riccati equation

$$A^T\mathcal{P} + \mathcal{P}A - \mathcal{P}B\mathcal{R}^{-1}B^T\mathcal{P} + \mathcal{Q} = 0 \tag{4.6}$$

In (4.6), the matrices $\mathcal{Q} \in \mathbb{R}^{n \times n}$ and $\mathcal{R} \in \mathbb{R}^{m \times m}$ are design parameters and $\mathcal{Q}$ is selected such that the pair $(A, \mathcal{C})$ is detectable, where $\mathcal{C}$ is any matrix satisfying $\mathcal{Q} = \mathcal{C}\mathcal{C}^T$, and then the matrix $A_K \overset{\triangle}{=} A + BK$ is stable.

Now on the basis of the works of Oya et al.(21; 22), in order to obtain on-line information on the parameter uncertainty, we introduce the error vector $e(t) \overset{\triangle}{=} x(t) - \bar{x}(t)$. Beside, using the optimal gain matrix $K \in \mathbb{R}^{m \times n}$ for the nominal system (4.5), we consider the following control input.

$$u(t) \overset{\triangle}{=} Kx(t) + \psi(x, e, \mathcal{L}, t) \tag{4.7}$$

where $\psi(x, e, \mathcal{L}, t) \in \mathbb{R}^m$ is a compensation input so as to reduce the effect of uncertainties and nonlinear perturbations, and it is supposed to have the following structure.

$$\psi(x, e, \mathcal{L}, t) \overset{\triangle}{=} \mathcal{F}e(t) + \mathcal{L}(x, e, t)e(t) \tag{4.8}$$

where $\mathcal{F} \in \mathbb{R}^{m \times n}$ is a fixed gain matrix and $\mathcal{L}(x, e, t) \in \mathbb{R}^{m \times n}$ is an adjustable time-varying matrix. From (4.1), (4.5), (4.7) and (4.8), we have

$$\begin{aligned} \frac{d}{dt}e(t) &= (A + \mathcal{D}\Delta(t)\mathcal{E})\,x(t) + B\,\{Kx(t) + \psi(x, e, \mathcal{L}, t)\} \\ &= A_{\mathcal{F}}e(t) + \mathcal{D}\Delta(t)\mathcal{E}x(t) + B\mathcal{L}(x, e, t)e(t) \end{aligned} \tag{4.9}$$

In (4.9), $A_{\mathcal{F}} \in \mathbb{R}^{n \times n}$ is a matrix given by $A_{\mathcal{F}} \overset{\triangle}{=} A_K + B\mathcal{F}$. Note that if asymptotical stability of the uncertain error system (4.9) is ensured, then the uncertain system (4.1) is robustly stable, because $e(t) \overset{\triangle}{=} x(t) - \bar{x}(t)$. Here, the fixed gain matrix $\mathcal{F} \in \mathbb{R}^{m \times n}$ is determined by using LQ control theory for the nominal error system. Namely $\mathcal{F} = -\mathcal{R}_{\mathcal{F}}B^T\mathcal{X}_{\mathcal{F}}$ and $\mathcal{X}_{\mathcal{F}} \in \mathbb{R}^{n \times n}$ is unique solution of the algebraic Riccati equation

$$A_K^T\mathcal{X}_{\mathcal{F}} + \mathcal{X}_{\mathcal{F}}A_K - \mathcal{X}_{\mathcal{F}}B\mathcal{R}_{\mathcal{F}}^{-1}B^T\mathcal{X}_{\mathcal{F}} + \mathcal{Q}_{\mathcal{F}} = 0 \tag{4.10}$$

where $\mathcal{Q}_{\mathcal{F}} \in \mathbb{R}^{n \times n}$ and $\mathcal{R}_{\mathcal{F}} \in \mathbb{R}^{m \times m}$ are design parameters and symmetric positive definite matrices. A decision method of the time-varying matrix $\mathcal{L}(x, e, t) \in \mathbb{R}^{m \times n}$ will be stated in the next subsection.

From the above discussion, our control objective in this section is to design the robust stabilizing controller for the uncertain error system (4.9). That is to design the variable gain matrix $\mathcal{L}(x, e, t) \in \mathbb{R}^{m \times n}$ that the error system with uncertainties (4.9) is asymptotically stable.

### 4.2 Synthesis of variable gain robust state feedback controllers via PLFs

The following theorem gives sufficient conditions for the existence of the proposed controller.

**Theorem 4.** *Consider the uncertain error system (4.9) and the control input (4.7) and (4.8). Suppose that the matrices $S_k \overset{\triangle}{=} \mathcal{P}_1 + \mathcal{P}_2 + \cdots + \mathcal{P}_N + \mathcal{P}_k BB^T \mathcal{P}_k \,(k = 1, \cdots, N)$ satisfy the relation (4.3), where $\mathcal{P}_k \in \mathbb{R}^{n \times n}$ are symmetric positive definite matrices[†] satisfying the matrix inequalities*

$$\left(\mathcal{P}_1 + \mathcal{P}_2 + \cdots + \mathcal{P}_N + \mathcal{P}_k BB^T \mathcal{P}_k\right) A_{\mathcal{F}} + A_{\mathcal{F}}^T \left(\mathcal{P}_1 + \mathcal{P}_2 + \cdots + \mathcal{P}_N + \mathcal{P}_k BB^T \mathcal{P}_k\right)$$
$$+ \sum_{j=1}^{N-1} \gamma_j^{(k)} \mathcal{P}_k BB^T \mathcal{P}_k + \mathcal{Q}_k < 0 \quad (k = 1, \cdots, N) \tag{4.11}$$

---

[†] i.e. $S_k \in \mathbb{R}^{n \times n}$ are symmetric positive definite matrices.

In (4.11), $\gamma_j^{(k)}$ $(k = 1, \cdots, \mathcal{N}, j = 1, \cdots, \mathcal{N} - 1)$ are positive scalars and $\mathcal{Q}_k \in \mathbb{R}^{n \times n}$ are symmetric positive definite matrices.

By using the matrices $\mathcal{S}_k \in \mathbb{R}^{n \times n}$, $\mathcal{L}(x, e, t) \in \mathbb{R}^{m \times n}$ is determined as

$$\mathcal{L}(x, e, t) = -\frac{\left(\left\|\mathcal{D}^T \mathcal{S}_k e(t)\right\| \left\|\mathcal{E}x(t)\right\|\right)^2}{\left(\sigma(t) + \left\|\mathcal{D}^T \mathcal{S}_k e(t)\right\| \left\|\mathcal{E}x(t)\right\|\right) \left\|B^T \mathcal{S}_k e(t)\right\|^2} B^T \mathcal{S}_k$$

$$\text{for} \quad k = \arg\max_k \left\{e^T(t) \mathcal{P}_k BB^T \mathcal{P}_k e(t)\right\} \tag{4.12}$$

In (4.12), $\sigma(t) \in \mathbb{R}^1$ is any positive uniform continuous and bounded function which satisfies

$$\int_{t_0}^t \sigma(\tau) d\tau \leq \sigma^* < \infty \tag{4.13}$$

where $\sigma^*$ is any positive constant and $t_0$ denotes an initial time. Then the uncertain error system (4.9) are bounded and

$$\lim_{t \to \infty} e(t; t_0, e(t_0)) = 0 \tag{4.14}$$

Namely, asymptotical stability of the uncertain error system (4.9) is ensured.

Proof. Using symmetric positive definite matrices $\mathcal{P}_k \in \mathbb{R}^{n \times n}$ $(k = 1, \cdots, \mathcal{N})$ which satisfy (4.11), we introduce the following piecewise quadratic function.

$$\mathcal{V}(e, t) = e^T(t) \mathcal{S}_k e(t) \quad \text{for} \quad k = \arg\max_k \left\{e^T(t) \mathcal{P}_k BB^T \mathcal{P}_k e(t)\right\} \quad \text{and} \quad k = 1, \cdots, \mathcal{N}$$

$$= \max_k \left\{e^T(t) \mathcal{S}_k e(t)\right\} \tag{4.15}$$

Note that the piecewise quadratic function $\mathcal{V}(e, t)$ is continuous and its level set is closed. The time derivative of the piecewise quadratic function $\mathcal{V}(e, t)$ can be written as

$$\frac{d}{dt}\mathcal{V}(e, t) = e^T(t)\left(\mathcal{S}_k A_{\mathcal{F}} + A_{\mathcal{F}}^T \mathcal{S}_k\right) e(t) + 2e^T(t) \mathcal{S}_k \mathcal{D}\Delta(t) \mathcal{E}x(t) + 2e^T(t) \mathcal{S}_k B\mathcal{L}(x, e, t)e(t)$$

$$\text{for} \quad k = \arg\max_k \left\{e^T(t) \mathcal{P}_k BB^T \mathcal{P}_k e(t)\right\} \tag{4.16}$$

Now, using **Lemma 1**, we can obtain

$$\frac{d}{dt}\mathcal{V}(e, t) \leq e^T(t)\left(\mathcal{S}_k A_{\mathcal{F}} + A_{\mathcal{F}}^T \mathcal{S}_k\right) e(t) + 2\left\|\mathcal{D}^T \mathcal{S}_k e(t)\right\| \left\|\mathcal{E}x(t)\right\|$$

$$+ 2e^T(t) \mathcal{S}_k B\mathcal{L}(x, e, t)e(t) \quad \text{for} \quad k = \arg\max_k \left\{e^T(t) \mathcal{P}_k BB^T \mathcal{P}_k e(t)\right\} \tag{4.17}$$

Also, using the time-varying gain matrix (4.12) and the relation (4.17) and some trivial manipulations give the following relation for the time derivative of the piecewise quadratic function $V(e,t)$.

$$\frac{d}{dt}V(e,t) \le e^T(t)\left(S_k A_{\mathcal{F}} + A_{\mathcal{F}}^T S\right)e(t) + 2\left\|D^T S_k e(t)\right\|\left\|\mathcal{E}x(t)\right\|$$

$$+ 2e^T(t)S_k B\left\{ -\frac{\left(\left\|D^T S_k e(t)\right\|\left\|\mathcal{E}x(t)\right\|\right)^2}{\left(\sigma(t) + \left\|D^T S_k e(t)\right\|\left\|\mathcal{E}x(t)\right\|\right)\left\|B^T S_k e(t)\right\|^2}B^T S_k\right\}e(t)$$

$$\text{for} \quad k = \arg\max_k\left\{e^T(t)\mathcal{P}_k BB^T \mathcal{P}_k e(t)\right\}$$

$$\le e^T(t)\left(S_k A_{\mathcal{F}} + A_{\mathcal{F}}^T S\right)e(t) + \sigma(t) \quad \text{for} \quad k = \arg\max_k\left\{e^T(t)\mathcal{P}_k BB^T \mathcal{P}_k e(t)\right\}$$

$$(4.18)$$

Now we consider the following inequality.

$$e^T(t)\left(S_k A_{\mathcal{F}} + A_{\mathcal{F}}^T S_k\right)e(t) < 0 \quad \text{for} \quad k = \arg\max_k\left\{e^T(t)\mathcal{P}_k BB^T \mathcal{P}_k e(t)\right\} \quad (4.19)$$

By using **Lemma 4** ($S$-procedure), the inequality (4.19) is satisfied if and only if there exist $S_k > 0$ and $\gamma_j^{(k)} \ge 0$ $(j = 1, \cdots, \mathcal{N}-1, \; k = 1, \cdots, \mathcal{N})$ satisfying

$$S_1 A_{\mathcal{F}} + A_{\mathcal{F}}^T S_1 + \sum_{j=1}^{\mathcal{N}-1}\gamma_j^{(1)}\mathcal{P}_1 BB^T \mathcal{P}_1 - \gamma_1^{(1)}\mathcal{P}_2 BB^T \mathcal{P}_2 - \cdots - \gamma_{\mathcal{N}-1}^{(1)}\mathcal{P}_{\mathcal{N}}BB^T \mathcal{P}_{\mathcal{N}} < 0$$

$$\vdots$$

$$S_{\mathcal{N}} A_{\mathcal{F}} + A_{\mathcal{F}}^T S_{\mathcal{N}} + \sum_{j=1}^{\mathcal{N}-1}\gamma_j^{(\mathcal{N})}\mathcal{P}_{\mathcal{N}}BB^T \mathcal{P}_{\mathcal{N}} - \gamma_1^{(\mathcal{N})}\mathcal{P}_2 BB^T \mathcal{P}_2 - \cdots - \gamma_{\mathcal{N}-1}^{(\mathcal{N})}\mathcal{P}_{\mathcal{N}-1}BB^T \mathcal{P}_{\mathcal{N}-1} < 0$$

$$(4.20)$$

Noting that since the condition (4.11) is a sufficient condition for the matrix inequalities (4.20), if the inequalities (4.11) are satisfied, then the condition (4.20) is also satisfied. Therefore, we have the following relation.

$$e^l(t)\left(S_k A_{\mathcal{F}} + A_{\mathcal{F}}^T S_k\right)e(t) < -e^T(t)\mathcal{Q}_k e(t) \quad (4.21)$$

Besides, by letting $\zeta_k \stackrel{\triangle}{=} \min_k\left\{\lambda_{\min}\left\{\mathcal{Q}_k\right\}\right\}$, we obtain

$$\frac{d}{dt}V(e,t) \le -\zeta_k\left\|e(t)\right\|^2 + \sigma(t) \quad \text{for} \quad k = \arg\max_k\left\{e^T(t)\mathcal{P}_k BB^T \mathcal{P}_k e(t)\right\} \quad (4.22)$$

On the other hand, from the definition of the piecewise quadratic function, there always exist two positive constants $\delta_{\min}$ and $\delta_{\max}$ such that for any $t \ge t_0$,

$$\eta^-\left(\left\|e(t)\right\|\right) \le V(e,t) \le \eta^+\left(\left\|e(t)\right\|\right) \quad (4.23)$$

where $\eta^-\left(\left\|e(t)\right\|\right)$ and $\eta^+\left(\left\|e(t)\right\|\right)$ are given by

$$\eta^-\left(\left\|e(t)\right\|\right) \stackrel{\triangle}{=} \delta_{\min}\left\|e(t)\right\|^2$$
$$\eta^+\left(\left\|e(t)\right\|\right) \stackrel{\triangle}{=} \delta_{\max}\left\|e(t)\right\|^2 \quad (4.24)$$

It is obvious that any solution $e(t; t_0, e(t_0))$ of the error system is continuous. In addition, it follows from (4.22) and (4.23), that for any $t \geq t_0$, the following relation holds.

$$
\begin{aligned}
0 \leq \eta^- \left( \|e(t)\| \right) &\leq \mathcal{V}(e, t) = \mathcal{V}(e, t_0) + \int_{t_0}^t \frac{d}{dt} \mathcal{V}(e, \tau) d\tau \\
\mathcal{V}(e, t_0) + \int_{t_0}^t \frac{d}{dt} \mathcal{V}(e, \tau) d\tau &\leq \eta^+ \left( \|e(t_0)\| \right) - \int_{t_0}^t \eta^* \left( \|e(\tau)\| \right) d\tau + \int_{t_0}^t \sigma(\tau) d\tau
\end{aligned}
\tag{4.25}
$$

In (4.25), $\eta^* \left( \|e(t)\| \right)$ is defined as

$$
\eta^* \left( \|e(t)\| \right) \stackrel{\triangle}{=} \zeta_k \|e(t)\|^2
\tag{4.26}
$$

Therefore, from (4.25) we can obtain the following two results. Firstly, taking the limit as $t$ approaches infinity on both sides of the inequality (4.25), we have

$$
0 \leq \eta^+ \left( \|e(t_0)\| \right) - \lim_{t \to \infty} \int_{t_0}^t \eta^* \left( \|e(\tau)\| \right) d\tau + \lim_{t \to \infty} \int_{t_0}^t \sigma(\tau) d\tau
\tag{4.27}
$$

Thus one can see from (4.13) and (4.27) that

$$
\lim_{t \to \infty} \int_{t_0}^t \eta^* \left( \|e(\tau)\| \right) d\tau \leq \eta^+ \left( \|e(t_0)\| \right) + \sigma^*
\tag{4.28}
$$

On the other hand, from (4.25), we obtain

$$
0 \leq \eta^- \left( \|e(t)\| \right) \leq \eta^+ \left( \|e(t_0)\| \right) + \int_{t_0}^t \sigma(\tau) d\tau
\tag{4.29}
$$

It follows from (4.13) and (4.29) that

$$
0 \leq \eta^- \left( \|e(t)\| \right) \leq \eta^+ \left( \|e(t_0)\| \right) + \sigma^*
\tag{4.30}
$$

The relation (4.30) implies that $e(t)$ is uniformly bounded. Since $e(t)$ has been shown to be continuous, it follows that $e(t)$ is uniformly continuous. Therefore, one can see from the definition that $\eta^* \left( \|e(t)\| \right)$ is also uniformly continuous. Applying the **Lemma 3** ( Barbalat's lemma ) to (4.28) yields

$$
\lim_{t \to \infty} \eta^* \left( \|e(t)\| \right) = \lim_{t \to \infty} \zeta_k \|e(t)\| = 0
\tag{4.31}
$$

Namely, asymptotical stability of the uncertain error system (4.9) is ensured. Thus the uncertain linear system (4.1) is also stable.

Thus the proof of **Theorem 4** is completed.                                                                 □

**Remark 2.** *In this section, we consider the uncertain dynamical system (4.1) which has uncertainties in the state matrix only. The proposed robust controller can also be applied to the case that the uncertainties are included in both the system matrix and the input one. By introducing additional actuator dynamics and constituting an augmented system, uncertainties in the input matrix are embedded in the system matrix of the augmented system(36). Therefore the same design procedure can be applied.*

**Remark 3.** *In order to get the proposed controller, symmetric positive definite matrices* $S_k \in \mathbb{R}^{n \times n}$ $(k = 1, \cdots, N)$ *satisfying the assumption (4.3) are required. The condition (4.3) is reduced to the following rank condition.*

$$\text{rank}\left\{ \left( S_1 B \ S_2 B \ \cdots \ S_N B \right)^T \right\} = n \tag{4.32}$$

*However there is not a globally effective method to obtain matrices satisfying the conditions (4.32). In future work, we will examine the assumption (4.3) and the condition (4.32).*

**Remark 4.** *In this section, we introduce the compensation input (4.8). From (4.8) and (4.12), one can see that if* $e(t) = 0$, *then the relation* $\psi\left(x, e, \mathcal{L}, t\right) \equiv 0$ *is satisfied. Beside, we find that the variable gain matrix* $\mathcal{L}(x, e, t) \in \mathbb{R}^{m \times n}$ *can be calculated except for* $e(t) = 0$ *(see (24)).*

Now, we consider the condition (4.11) in **Theorem 4**. The condition (4.11) requires symmetric positive definite matrices $\mathcal{P}_k \in \mathbb{R}^{n \times n}$ and positive scalars $\gamma_j^{(k)} \in \mathbb{R}^1$ for stability. In this section, on the basis of the works of Oya et al.(23; 24), we consider the following inequalities instead of (4.11).

$$\left(\mathcal{P}_1 + \mathcal{P}_2 + \cdots + \mathcal{P}_N\right) A_{\mathcal{F}} + A_{\mathcal{F}}^T \left(\mathcal{P}_1 + \mathcal{P}_2 + \cdots + \mathcal{P}_N\right)$$

$$+ \sum_{j=1}^{N-1} \gamma_j^{(k)} \mathcal{P}_k B B^T \mathcal{P}_k + \mathcal{Q}_k < 0 \quad (k = 1, \cdots, N) \tag{4.33}$$

In addition, introducing complementary variables $\xi_j^{(k)} \triangleq \left(\gamma_j^{(k)}\right)^{-1}$ $(j = 1, \cdots, N-1, k = 1, \cdots, N)$ and using **Lemma 3** (Schur complement), we find that the condition (4.33) equivalent to the following LMIs.

$$\begin{pmatrix} \Psi\left(\mathcal{P}_1, \cdots, \mathcal{P}_N\right) + \mathcal{Q}_k & \mathcal{P}_k B & \mathcal{P}_k B & \cdots & \mathcal{P}_k B \\ B^T \mathcal{P}_k & -\xi_1^{(k)} I_m & 0 & \cdots & 0 \\ B^T \mathcal{P}_k & 0 & -\xi_2^{(k)} I_m & \cdots & 0 \\ \vdots & \vdots & \vdots & \ddots & \vdots \\ B^T \mathcal{P}_k & 0 & 0 & 0 & -\xi_{N-1}^{(k)} I_m \end{pmatrix} < 0, \tag{4.34}$$

$$\mathcal{P}_k > 0 \text{ and } \xi_j^{(k)} > 0 \quad (j = 1, \cdots, N-1, \ k = 1, \cdots, N)$$

where $\Psi\left(\mathcal{P}_1, \cdots, \mathcal{P}_N\right)$ in $(1,1)$-block of the LMIs (4.34) is given by

$$\Psi\left(\mathcal{P}_1, \cdots, \mathcal{P}_N\right) = \left(\mathcal{P}_1 + \mathcal{P}_2 + \cdots + \mathcal{P}_N\right) A_{\mathcal{F}} + A_{\mathcal{F}}^T \left(\mathcal{P}_1 + \mathcal{P}_2 + \cdots + \mathcal{P}_N\right) \tag{4.35}$$

Note that if there exist symmetric positive definite matrices $\mathcal{P}_k \in \mathbb{R}^{n \times n}$ and positive scalars $\gamma_j^{(k)} \in \mathbb{R}^1$ which satisfy the matrix inequalities (4.34), then the matrix inequality condition (4.11) is also satisfied (23; 24).

From the above discussion, one can see that in order to get the proposed robust controller, the positive scalars $\gamma_j^{(k)} \in \mathbb{R}^1$ and the symmetric positive definite matrices $\mathcal{P}_k \in \mathbb{R}^{n \times n}$ which satisfy the LMIs (4.34) and the assumption (4.3) are needed. Therefore firstly, we solve the LMIs (4.34) and next, we check the rank condition (4.32).

## 4.3 Illustrative examples

Consider the following uncertain linear system, i.e. $\mathcal{Z} = 2$.

$$\frac{d}{dt}x(t) = \begin{pmatrix} -4 & 1 \\ 0 & 2 \end{pmatrix} x(t) + \begin{pmatrix} 5 & -1 \\ 0 & 1 \end{pmatrix} \Delta(t) \begin{pmatrix} 1 & 1 \\ 0 & 1 \end{pmatrix} x(t) + \begin{pmatrix} 0 \\ 1 \end{pmatrix} u(t) \qquad (4.36)$$

By applying **Theorem 4**, we consider deriving the proposed robust controller. Now we select the weighting matrices $\mathcal{Q} \in \mathbb{R}^{2 \times 2}$ and $\mathcal{R} \in \mathbb{R}^{1 \times 1}$ such as $\mathcal{Q} = 1.0 I_2$ and $\mathcal{R} = 4.0$ for the quadratic cost function for the standard linear quadratic control problem for the nominal system, respectively. Then solving the algebraic Riccati equation (4.6), we obtain the optimal gain matrix

$$K = \begin{pmatrix} -5.15278 \times 10^{-3} & -4.06405 \end{pmatrix} \qquad (4.37)$$

In addition, setting the design parameters $\mathcal{Q}_{\mathcal{F}}$ and $\mathcal{R}_{\mathcal{F}}$ such as $\mathcal{Q}_{\mathcal{F}} = 10.0 \times 10^6 I_2$ and $\mathcal{R}_{\mathcal{F}} = 1.0$, respectively, we have the following fixed gain matrix.

$$\mathcal{F} = \begin{pmatrix} -1.23056 & -9.99806 \end{pmatrix} \times 10^3 \qquad (4.38)$$

Besides, selecting the matrices $\mathcal{Q}_k$ ($k = 1, 2$) in (4.34) as

$$\mathcal{Q}_1 = \begin{pmatrix} 20.0 & 1.0 \\ 1.0 & 1.0 \end{pmatrix}, \quad \mathcal{Q}_2 = \begin{pmatrix} 1.0 & 0.0 \\ 0.0 & 20.0 \end{pmatrix} \qquad (4.39)$$

and solving the LMI condition (4.34), we get

$$\begin{aligned} \mathcal{P}_1 &= \begin{pmatrix} 7.59401 \times 10^1 & 6.82676 \times 10^{-4} \\ 6.82676 \times 10^{-4} & 2.00057 \times 10^{-3} \end{pmatrix} \\ \mathcal{P}_2 &= \begin{pmatrix} 7.59401 \times 10^1 & 5.96286 \times 10^{-4} \\ 5.96286 \times 10^{-4} & 5.76862 \times 10^{-2} \end{pmatrix} \\ \gamma_1 &= 7.13182 \times 10^{-3}, \quad \gamma_2 = 7.13182 \times 10^{-3} \end{aligned} \qquad (4.40)$$

From (4.36) and (4.40), $\Omega_{\mathcal{S}_k}$ ($k = 1, 2$) can be written as

$$\begin{aligned} \Omega_{\mathcal{S}_1} &= \{ x \in \mathbb{R}^2 \mid 1.28240 x_1 + 7.80246 x_2 = 0 \} \\ \Omega_{\mathcal{S}_2} &= \{ x \in \mathbb{R}^2 \mid 1.28032 x_1 + 7.77319 x_2 = 0 \} \end{aligned} \qquad (4.41)$$

and thus the assumption (4.3) is satisfied.

On the other hand for the uncertain linear system (4.36), the quadratic stabilizing controller based on a fixed quadratic Lyapunov function cannot be obtained, because the solution of the LMI of (A.1) does not exist.

In this example, we consider the following two cases for the unknown parameter $\Delta(t)$.

- Case 1) : $\Delta(t) = \begin{pmatrix} -4.07360 & 8.06857 \\ 4.41379 & 3.81654 \end{pmatrix} \times 10^{-1}$

- Case 2) : $\Delta(t) = \begin{pmatrix} \cos(3.0\pi t) & 0 \\ 0 & -\sin(3.0\pi t) \end{pmatrix}$

Besides, for numerical simulations, the initial values for the uncertain linear system (4.36) and the nominal system are selected as $x(0) = \bar{x}(0) = (\,2.0\ -1.0\,)^T$ (i.c. $e(0) = (\,0.0\ 0.0\,)^T$), respectively, and we choose $\sigma(t) \in \mathbb{R}^+$ in (4.12) as $\sigma(t) = 5.0 \times 10^{12} \times \exp\left(-1.0 \times 10^{-3}t\right)$. The results of the simulation of this example are depicted in Figures 8–10. In these Figures, "Case 1)" and "Case 2)" represent the time-histories of the state variables $x_1(t)$ and $x_2(t)$ and the control input $u(t)$ for the proposed variable gain robust controller. "Desired" shows the desired time-response and the desired control input generated by the nominal system.

From Figures 8–10, we find that the proposed robust controller stabilizes the uncertain system (4.36) in spite of uncertainties. one can see from Figure 10 the proposed controller can avoid serious chattering. Therefore the effectiveness of the proposed controller is shown.

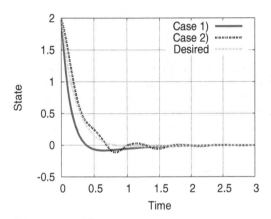

Fig. 8. Time histories of the state $x_1(t)$

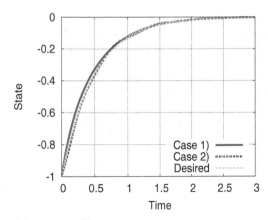

Fig. 9. Time histories of the state $x_2(t)$

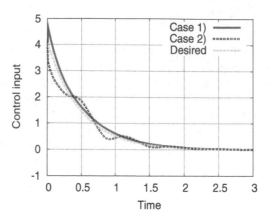

Fig. 10. Time histories of the control input $u(t)$

### 4.4 Summary
In this section, we have proposed a design method of a variable gain robust controller for a class of uncertain nonlinear systems. The uncertainties under consideration are composed of matched part and unmatched one, and by using the concept of piecewise Lyapunov functions, we have shown that the proposed robust controller can be obtained by solving LMIs (4.34) and cheking the rank condition (4.32). By numerical simulations, the effectiveness of the proposed controller has been presented.

## 5. Conclusions and future works

In this chapter, we have presented that the variable gain robust controller for a class of uncertain linear systems and through the numerical illustrations, the effectiveness of the proposed vaiable gain robust controllers has been shown. The advantage of the proposed controller synthesis is as follows; the proposed variable gain robust controller in which the real effect of the uncertainties can be reflected as on-line information is more flexible and adaptive than the conventional robust controller with a fixed gain which is derived by the worst-case design for the parameter variations. Additionally the proposed control systems are constructed by renewing the parameter which represents the perturbation region of unknown parameters, and there is no need to solve any other equation for the stability.

In Section 2 for linear systems with matched uncertainties, a design problem of variable gain robust state feedback controllers in order to achieve satisfactory transient behavior as closely as possible to desirable one generated by the nominal system is considered. Section 3 extends the result for the variable gain robust state feedback controller given in Section 2 to variable gain robust output feedback controllers. In this Section, some assumptions for the structure of the system parameters are introduced and by using these assumptions, an LMI-based the variable gain robust output feedback controller synthesis has been presented. In Section 4, the design method of variable gain robust state feedback controller via piecewise Lyapunov functions has been suggested. One can see that the crucial difference between the existing results and the proposed variable gain controller based on PLFs is that for uncertain linear systems which cannot be statilizable via the conventional quadratic stabilizing controllers, the proposed design procedure can stabilize it. Besides, it is obvious that the proposed variable robust control scheme is more effective for linear systems with larger uncertainties.

The future research subjects are an extension of the variable gain robust state feedback controller via PLFs to output feedback control systems. Besides, the problem for the extension to such a broad class of systems as uncertain large-scale systems, uncertain time-delay systems and so on should be tackled. Furthermore in future work, we will examine the condition (3.2) in section 3 and assumptions (4.3) and (4.32) in section 4.

On the other hand, the design of feedback controllers is often complicated by presence of physical constraints : saturating actuators, temperatures, pressures within safety margins and so on. If the constraints are violated, serious consequences may ensue, for example, physical components may be damaged, or saturation may cause a loss of closed-loop stability. In particular, input saturation is a common feature of control systems and the stabilization problems of linear systems with control input saturation have been studied (e.g. (17; 32)). Furthermore, some researchers have investigated analysis of constrained linear systems and reference managing for linear systems subject to input and state constraints (e.g. (10; 15)). Therefore, the future research subjects are to address the constrained robust control problems reducing the effect of unknown parameters.

## 6. Appendix

### 6.1 Quadratic stabilization

The following lemma provides a LMI-based design method of a robust controller via Lyapunov stability criterion.

**Lemma A.1.** *Consider the uncertain linear system (4.1) and the control law $u(t) = Hx(t)$. There exists the state feedback gain matrix $H \in \mathbb{R}^{m \times n}$ such that the control law $u(t) = Hx(t)$ is a quadratic stabilizing control, if there exist $\mathcal{X} > 0, \mathcal{Y}$ and $\delta > 0$ satisfying the LMI*

$$\begin{pmatrix} A\mathcal{X} + \mathcal{X}A^T + B\mathcal{Y} + \mathcal{Y}^T B^T + \delta \mathcal{D}\mathcal{D}^T & \mathcal{X}\mathcal{E}^T \\ \mathcal{E}\mathcal{X} & -\delta I_q \end{pmatrix} < 0 \tag{A.1}$$

*If the solution $\mathcal{X}, \mathcal{Y}$ and $\delta$ of the LMI (A.1) exists, then the gain matrix $H \in \mathbb{R}^{m \times n}$ is obtained as $H = \mathcal{Y}\mathcal{X}^{-1}$.*

*Proof.* Introducing the quadratic function $V(x,t) \triangleq ex^T(t)\mathcal{P}x(t)$ as a Lyapunov function candidate, we have

$$\frac{d}{dt}V(x,t) = x^T(t) \left\{ \mathcal{P}(A + BH) + (A + BH)^T \mathcal{P} \right\} x(t) + 2x^T(t)\mathcal{P}\mathcal{D}\Delta(t)\mathcal{E}x(t)$$

$$\leq x^T(t) \left\{ \mathcal{P}(A + BH) + (A + BH)^T \mathcal{P} \right\} x(t) + \delta x^T(t)\mathcal{P}\mathcal{D}\mathcal{D}^T\mathcal{P}x(t) + \frac{1}{\delta}x^T(t)\mathcal{E}^T\mathcal{E}x(t) \tag{A.2}$$

Here we have used the well-known relation (3.12). Thus the uncrtain linear system (4.1) is robustly stable provided that the following relation is satisfied.

$$\mathcal{P}(A + BH) + (A + BH)^T \mathcal{P} + \delta \mathcal{P}\mathcal{D}\mathcal{D}^T\mathcal{P} + \frac{1}{\delta}\mathcal{E}^T\mathcal{E} < 0 \tag{A.3}$$

We introduce the matrix $\mathcal{X} \triangleq \mathcal{P}^{-1}$ and consider the change of variable $\mathcal{Y} \triangleq H\mathcal{X}$. Then, by pre- and post-multiplying (A.3) by $\mathcal{X} = \mathcal{P}^{-1}$ , we have

$$A\mathcal{X} + \mathcal{X}A^T + B\mathcal{Y} + \mathcal{Y}^T B^T + \delta \mathcal{D}\mathcal{D}^T + \frac{1}{\delta}\mathcal{X}\mathcal{E}^T\mathcal{E}\mathcal{X} < 0 \tag{A.4}$$

One can see from **Lemma 2** (Schur complement) that the inequaity (A.4) is equivalent to the LMI (A.1). □

## 7. References

[1]  H. L. S. Almeida, A. Bhaya and D. M. Falcão, "A Team Algorithm for Robust Stability Analysis and Control Design of Uncertain Time-Varying Systems using Piecewise Quadratic Lyapunov Functions", Int. J. Robust and Nonlinear Contr., Vol.11, No.1, pp.357-371, 2001.

[2]  R. E. Benton, JR and D. Smith, "A Non-itarative LMI-based Algorithm for Robust Static-output-feedback Stabilization", Int. J. Contr., Vol.72, No.14, pp.1322-1330, 1999.

[3]  B. R. Bermish , M. Corless and G. Leitmann, "A New Class of Stabilizing Controllers for Uncertain Dynamical Systems", SIAM J. Contr. Optimiz. Vol.21, No.2, pp.246-255, 1983.

[4]  S. Boyd, L. El Ghaoui, E. Feron and V. Balakrishnan, Linear Matrix Inequalities in System and Control Theory, SIAM Studies in Applied Mathmatics, 1994.

[5]  Y. K. Choi, M. J. Chung and Z. Bien, "An Adaptive Control Scheme for Robot Manipulators", Int. J. Contr., Vol.44, No.4, pp.1185-1191, 1986.

[6]  J. C. Doyle, K. Glover, P. P. Khargonekar and B. A. Francis, "State-Space Solutions to Standarad $\mathcal{H}^2$ and $\mathcal{H}^\infty$ Control Problems", IEEE Trans. Automat. Contr., Vol.34, No.8, pp.831-847, 1989.

[7]  P. Gahinet, P. Apkarian and M. Chilali, "Affine Parameter Dependent Lyapunov Functions and Real Parameter Uncertainty", IEEE Trans. Automat. Contr., Vol.41, No.3, pp.436-442, 1996.

[8]  F. R. Gantmacher, "The Theory of Matrices", Vol.1, Chelsea Publishing Company, New York, 1960.

[9]  J. C. Geromel, C. C. De Souza and R. E. Skelton, "LMI Numerical Solution for Output Feedbadck Stabilization", Proc. of the 1994 American Contr. Conf., Baltimore, MD, USA, pp.40-44, 1994.

[10] E. G. Gilbert and I. Kolmanovsky, "Nonlinear Tracking Controlin the Presence of State and Control Constraints : A Generalized Reference Govonor", Automatica, Vol.38, No.12, pp.2071-2077, 2002.

[11] T. Iwasaki, R. E. Skelton and J. C. Geromel, "Linear Quadratic Suboptimal Control with Static Output Feedback", Syst. & Contr. Lett., Vol.23, No.6, pp.421-430, 1994.

[12] F. Jabbari and W. E. Schmitendolf, "Effect of Using Observers on Stabilization of Uncertain Linear Systems", IEEE Trans. Automat. Contr., Vol.38, No.2, pp.266-271, 1993.

[13] H. K. Khalil, "Nonlinear Systems, Third Edition", Prentice Hall, 2002.

[14] P. P. Khargonekar and M. A. Rotea, "Mixed $\mathcal{H}_2/\mathcal{H}_\infty$ Control , A Convex Optimization Approach", IEEE Trans. Automat. Contr., Vol.36, No.7, pp.824-837, 1991.

[15] K. Kogiso and K. Hirata, "Reference Governor for Contrained Systems with Time-Varying References", J. Robotics and Autonomous Syst., Vol.57, Issue 3, pp.289-295, 2009.

[16] V. Kučera and C. E. De Souza, "A Necessary and Sufficient Conditions for Output Feedback Stabilizability", Automatica , Vol.31, No.9, pp.1357-1359, 1995.

[17] Z. Lin, M. Pachter and S. Band, "Toward Improvement of Tracking Performance – Nonlinear Feedback for Linear Systems", Int. J. Contr., Vol.70, No.1, pp.1-11 (1998)

[18] M. Maki and K. Hagino, "Robust Control with Adaptation Mechanism for Improving Transient Behavior ", Int. J. Contr., Vol.72, No.13, pp.1218-1226, 1999.

[19] H. Oya and K. Hagino: "Robust Servo System with Adaptive Compensation Input for Linear Uncertain Systems", Proc. of the 4th Asian Contr. Conf., pp.972-977, SINGAPORE, 2002.

[20] H. Oya and K. Hagino : "Observer-based Robust Control Giving Consideration to Transient Behavior for Linear Systems with Structured Uncertainties", Int. J. Contr., Vol.75, No.15, pp.1231-1240, 2002.

[21] H. Oya and K. Hagino, "Robust Control with Adaptive Compensation Input for Linear Uncertain Systems", IEICE Trans. Fundamentals of Electronics, Communications and Computer Sciences, Vol.E86-A, No.6, pp.1517-1524, 2003.

[22] H. Oya and K. Hagino, "Adaptive Robust Control Scheme for Linear Systems with Structured Uncertainties", IEICE Trans. Fundamentals of Electronics, Communications and Computer Sciences, Vol.E87-A, No.8, pp.2168-2173, 2004.

[23] H. Oya, K. Hagino, S. Kayo and M. Matsuoka, "Adaptive Robust Stabilization for a Class of Uncertain Linear Systems via Variable Gain Controllers", Proc. of the 45th IEEE Conf. on Decision and Contr., pp.1183–1188, San Diego, USA, 2006.

[24] H. Oya, K. Hagino and S. Kayo, "Adaptive Robust Control Based on Piecewise Lyapunov Functions for a Class of Uncertain Linear Systems", Proc. of the European Contr. Conf. 2007 (ECC2007), pp.810–815, Kos, GREECE, 2007.

[25] H. Oya, K. Hagino and S. Kayo, "Synthesis of Adaptive Robust Output Feedback Controllers for a Class of Uncertain Linear Systems", Proc. of the 47th IEEE Conf.on Decision and Contr., pp.995-1000, Cancun, MEXICO, 2008.

[26] H. Oya and K. Hagino, "A New Adaptive Robust Controller Avoiding Chattering Phenomenon for a Class of Uncertain Linear Systems", Proc. of the 28th IASTED Int. Conf. on Modeling, Identification and Contr., pp.236–241, Innsbruck, 2009.

[27] I. R. Petersen, "A Riccati Equation Approach to the Design of Stabilizing Controllers and Observers for a Class of Uncertain Linear Systems", IEEE Trans. Automat. Contr., Vol.30, No.9, pp.904-907, 1985.

[28] I. R. Petersen and D. C. McFarlane, "Optimal Guaranteed Cost Control and Filtering for Uncertain Linear Systems", IEEE Trans. Automat. Contr., Vol.39, No.9, pp.1971-1977, 1994.

[29] I. R. Petersen and C. C. Hollot, "A Riccati Equation Approach to the Stabilization of Uncertain Linear Systems", Automatica, Vol.22, No.4, pp.397-411, 1986.

[30] E. S. Pyatnitskii, V. I. Skrodinskii, "Numerical Methods of Lyapunov Function Contruction and Their Application to the Absolute Stability Problem", Syst. & Contr. Lett., Vol.2, No.1, 1986.

[31] S. O. Reza Moheimani and I. R. Petersen : "Optimal Guaranteed Cost Control of Uncertain Systems via Static and Dynamic Output Feedback", Automatica, Vol.32, No.4, pp.575-579, 1996.

[32] M. C. Turner, I. Postlethwaite and D. J. Walker, "Non-linear Tracking Control for Multivariable Constrained Input Linear Systems", Int. J. Contr., Vol.73, No.12, pp.1160-1172, 2000.

[33] S. Ushida, S. Yamamoto and H. Kimura, "Quadratic Stabilization by $\mathcal{H}^\infty$ state feedback controllers with Adjustable Parameters", Proc. of the 35th IEEE Conf. Decision and Contr., pp.1003-1008, Kobe, JAPAN, 1996.

[34] V. Veselý, "Design of Robust Output Affine Quadratic Controller", Proc. of 2002 IFAC World Congress, pp.1-6, Barcelona, SPAIN, 2002.

[35]  L. Xie, S. Shishkin and M. Fu, "Piecewise Lyapunov Functions for Robust Stability of Linear Time-Varying Systems", Syst. & Contr. Letters, Vol.31, No.3, 1997.

[36]  K. Zhou and P. P. Khargonekar, "Robust Stabilization on Linear Systems with Norm Bounded Time-Varying Uncertainty", Syst. & Contr. Lett., Vol.10, No.1, pp.17-20, 1988.

[37]  K. Zhou, "Essentials of Robust Control", Prentice Hall Inc., New Jersey, USA, 1998.

# 6

# A Model-Free Design of the Youla Parameter on the Generalized Internal Model Control Structure with Stability Constraint

Kazuhiro Yubai, Akitaka Mizutani and Junji Hirai
*Mie University*
*Japan*

## 1. Introduction

In the design of the control system, the plant perturbations and the plant uncertainties could cause the performance degradation and/or destabilization of the control system. The $H_\infty$ control synthesis and the $\mu$ synthesis are well known as the suitable controller syntheses for the plant with the large plant perturbations and/or the plant uncertainties (Zhou & Doyle, 1998), and many successful applications are also reported in various fields. However, these controller syntheses provide the controller robustly stabilizing the closed-loop system for the worst-case and overestimated disturbances and uncertainties at the expense of the nominal control performance. It means that there exists a trade-off between the nominal control performance and the robustness in the design of the control system.

Meanwhile from the view point of the control architecture, the Generalized Internal Model Control (GIMC) structure is proposed by Zhou using Youla parameterization (Vidyasagar, 1985) to resolve the above-mentioned trade-off (Campos-Delgado & Zhou, 2003; Zhou & Ren, 2001). The GIMC structure is interpreted as an extension of the Internal Model Control (IMC) (Morari & Zafiriou, 1997), which is only applicable to stable plants, to unstable plants by introducing coprime factorization. The GIMC structure consists of a conditional feedback structure and an outer-loop controller. The conditional feedback structure can detect model uncertainties and any disturbances, and they are compensated through the Youla parameter. It means that the robustness of the control system in the GIMC structure is specified by the Youla parameter. On the other hand, in case where there exist no plant uncertainties and no disturbances, the conditional feedback structure would detect nothing, and the feedback control system would be governed only by the outer-loop controller. Since the nominal control performance is independent of the Youla parameter, the outer-loop controller can be designed according to various controller design techniques, and the trade-off between the nominal control performance and the robustness is resolved.

For the design of the Youla parameter, we proposed the design method using the dual Youla parameter which represents the plant perturbation and/or the plant uncertainties (Matsumoto et al., 1993; Yubai et al., 2007). The design procedure is as follows: The dual Youla parameter is identified by the Hansen scheme (Hansen et al., 1989) using appropriate identification techniques, and the Youla parameter is designed based on the robust controller synthesis. However, since it is difficult to give a physical interpretation to the dual Youla parameter in general, we must select the weighting function for identification and the order of the identified model by trial and error. For implementation aspect, a low-order controller is much preferable, which means that a low-order model of the dual Youla parameter should be identified. However, it is difficult to identify the low-order model of the dual Youla parameter which contains enough information on the actual dual Youla parameter to design the appropriate Youla parameter. Moreover, there may be the cases where an accurate and reasonably low-order model of the dual Youla parameter can not be obtained easily.

To avoid these difficulties in system identification of the dual Youla parameter, this article addresses the design method of the Youla parameter by model-free controller synthesis. Model-free controller syntheses have the advantages that the controller is directly synthesized or tuned only from the input/output data collected from the plant, and no plant mathematical model is required for the controller design, which avoids the troublesome model identification of the dual Youla parameter. Moreover, since the order and the controller structure are specified by the designer, we can easily design a low-order Youla parameter by model-free controller syntheses.

A number of model-free controller syntheses have been proposed, e.g., the Iterative Feedback Tuning (IFT) (Hjalmarsson, 1998), the Virtual Reference Feedback Tuning (VRFT) (Campi et al., 2002), and the Correlation-based Tuning (CbT) (Miskovic et al., 2007) and so on. These model-free controller syntheses address the model matching problem as a typical control objective. Since the IFT and the CbT basically deal with nonlinear optimization problems, they require the iterative experiments to update the gradient of the cost function and the Hessian for the Gauss-Newton method at each iterative parameter update. On the other hand, the VRFT brings controllers using only a single set of input/output data collected from the plant if the controllers are linearly parameterized with respect to the parameter vector to be tuned. This article adopts the VRFT to design the Youla parameter to exploit the above-mentioned feature. However, the model-free controller syntheses have a common disadvantage that the stability of the closed-loop system can not be evaluated in advance of controller implementation because we have no mathematical plant model to evaluate the stability and/or the control performance. From the view point of safety, destabilization of the control system is not acceptable. Recently, the data-driven test on the closed-loop stability before controller implementation (Karimi et al., 2007; Yubai et al., 2011) and the data-driven controller synthesis at least guaranteeing the closed-loop stability (Heusden et al., 2010) are developed for the standard unity feedback control structure.

This article derives the robust stability condition for the design of the Youla parameter, and its sufficient condition is described as the $H_\infty$ norm of the product of the Youla and the dual Youla parameters. Moreover, the $H_\infty$ norm is estimated using the input/output data collected from the plant in the closed-loop manner. This sufficient condition of the robust stability is imposed as the stability constraint to the design problem of the Youla parameter based on the VRFT previously proposed by the authors (Sakuishi et al., 2008). Finally, the Youla parameter guaranteeing the closed-loop stability is obtained by solving the convex optimization.

The discussion is limited to SISO systems in this article.

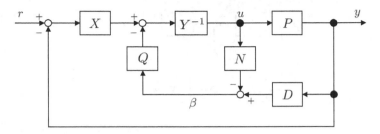

Fig. 1. GIMC structure.

## 2. Robust control by the GIMC structure

This section gives a brief review of the GIMC (Generalized Internal Model Control) structure and it is a control architecture solving the trade-off between the control performance and the robustness.

### 2.1 GIMC structure

A linear time-invariant plant $P_0$ is assumed to have a coprime factorization (Vidyasagar, 1985) on $\mathcal{RH}_\infty$ as

$$P_0 = ND^{-1}, \quad N, D \in \mathcal{RH}_\infty, \tag{1}$$

where $\mathcal{RH}_\infty$ denotes the set of all real rational proper stable transfer functions. A nominal controller $C_0$ stabilizing $P_0$ is also assumed to have a coprime factorization on $\mathcal{RH}_\infty$ as

$$C_0 = XY^{-1}, \quad X, Y \in \mathcal{RH}_\infty, \tag{2}$$

where $X$ and $Y$ satisfy the Bezout identity $XN + YD = 1$. Then a class of all stabilizing controllers $C$ is parameterized as (3), which is called as Youla parameterization, by introducing the Youla parameter $Q \in \mathcal{RH}_\infty$ (Vidyasagar, 1985):

$$C = (Y - QN)^{-1}(X + QD), \tag{3}$$

where $Q$ is a free parameter and is determined arbitrarily as long as

$$\det(Y(\infty) - Q(\infty)N(\infty)) \neq 0.$$

Then, the GIMC structure is constructed as Fig. 1 by using (1) and (3), where $r$, $u$, $y$ and $\beta$ represent reference inputs, control inputs, observation outputs and residual signals, respectively. The only difference between the GIMC structure and a standard unity feedback control structure shown in Fig. 2 is that the input of $D$ is $y$ in the GIMC structure instead of $e$. Since the GIMC structure has a conditional feedback structure, the Youla parameter $Q$ is only activated in the case where disturbances are injected and/or there exist plant uncertainties. If there is no disturbance and no plant uncertainty ($\beta = 0$), $Q$ in the GIMC structure does not generate any compensation signals and the control system is governed by only a nominal controller $C_0$. It means that the nominal control performance is specified by only the nominal controller $C_0$. On the other hand, if there exist disturbances and/or plant uncertainties ($\beta \neq 0$),

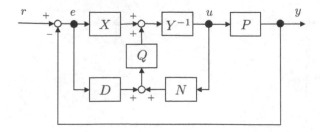

Fig. 2. A unity feedback control structure.

the inner loop controller $Q$ generates the compensation signal to suppress the effect of plant uncertainties and disturbances in addition to the nominal controller $C_0$.

In this way, the role of $C_0$ and that of $Q$ are clearly separated: $C_0$ could be designed to achieve the higher nominal control performance, while $Q$ could be designed to attain the higher robustness for plant uncertainties and disturbances. This is the reason why the GIMC structure is one of promising control architectures which solve the trade-off between the nominal control performance and the robustness in the design of the feedback control system. In this article, we address the design problem of the Youla parameter $Q$ using the input/output data set to generate an appropriate compensation signal to reduce the effect of plant uncertainties and/or disturbances on the assumption that the nominal controller $C_0$ which meets the given nominal control performance requirements has been already available.

### 2.2 Dual Youla parameterization and robust stability condition

For appropriate compensation of plant uncertainties, information on plant uncertainties is essential. In the design of the Youla parameter $Q$, the following parameterization plays an important role. On the assumption that the nominal plant $P_0$ factorized as (1) and its deviated version, $P$, are stabilized by the nominal controller $C_0$, then $P$ is parameterized by introducing a dual Youla parameter $R \in \mathcal{RH}_\infty$ as follows:

$$P = (N + YR)(D - XR)^{-1}. \tag{4}$$

This parameterization is called as the dual Youla parameterization, which is a dual version of the Youla parameterization mentioned in the previous subsection. It says that the actual plant $P$, which is deviated from the nominal plant $P_0$, can be represented by the dual Youla parameter $R$. By substituting (4) to the block-diagram shown by Fig. 1, we obtain the equivalent block-diagram shown by Fig. 3. From this block-diagram, the robust stability condition when the controlled plant deviates from $P_0$ to $P$ is derived as

$$(1 + RQ)^{-1} \in \mathcal{RH}_\infty. \tag{5}$$

We must design $Q$ so as to meet this stability condition.

### 3. Direct design of the Youla parameter from experimental data

As stated in the previous subsection, the role of $Q$ is to suppress plant variations and disturbances. This article addresses the design problem of $Q$ to approach the closed-loop performance from $r$ to $y$, denoted by $G_{ry}$, to the its nominal control performance as an

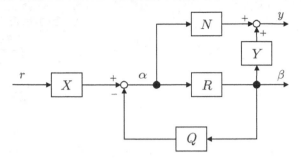

Fig. 3. Equivalent block-diagram of GIMC.

example. This design problem is formulated in frequency domain as a model matching problem;

$$Q = \arg \min_{\tilde{Q}} J_{MR}(\tilde{Q}), \tag{6}$$

where

$$J_{MR}(Q) = \left\| W_M \left( M - \frac{(N + RY)X}{1 + RQ} \right) \right\|_2^2. \tag{7}$$

$M$ is a reference model for $G_{ry}$ given by the designer and it corresponds to the nominal control performance. $W_M$ is a frequency weighting function.

According to the model-based controller design techniques, the following typical controller design procedure is taken place: Firstly, we identify the dual Youla parameter $R$ using the input/output data set. Secondly, the Youla parameter $Q$ is designed based on the identified model of $R$. However, since the dual Youla parameter $R$ is described as

$$R = D(P - P_0)\{Y(1 + PC_0)\}^{-1}, \tag{8}$$

it depends on the coprime factors, $N$, $D$, $X$ and $Y$, which makes it difficult to give a physical interpretation for $R$. As a result, the identification of $R$ requires trial-and-error for the selection of the structure and/or the order of $R$. As is clear from (8), $R$ should be modeled as a high order model, the designed $Q$ tends to be a high order controller, which is a serious problem for implementation.

In this article, we address the direct design problem of the fixed-order and fixed-structural $Q$ from the input/output data set minimizing the evaluation function (7) without any model identification of $R$.

### 3.1 Review of the Virtual Reference Feedback Tuning (VRFT)

The Virtual Reference Feedback Tuning (VRFT) is one of model-free controller design methods to achieve the model matching. The VRFT provides the controller parameters using only the input/output data set so that the actual closed-loop property approaches to its reference model given by the designer. In this subsection, the basic concept and its algorithm are reviewed.

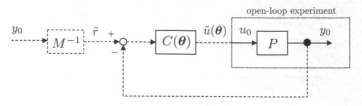

Fig. 4. Basic concept of the VRFT.

The basic concept of the VRFT is depicted in Fig. 4. For a stable plant, assume that the input/output data set $\{u_0(t), y_0(t)\}$ of length $N$ has been already collected in open-loop manner. Introduce the virtual reference $\tilde{r}(t)$ such that

$$y_0(t) = M\tilde{r}(t),$$

where $M$ is a reference model to be achieved. Now, assume that the output of the feedback system consisting of $P$ and $C(\theta)$ parameterized by the parameter vector $\theta$ coincides with $y_0(t)$ when the virtual reference signal $\tilde{r}(t)$ is given as a reference signal. Then, the output of $C(\theta)$, denoted by $\tilde{u}(t, \theta)$ is represented as

$$\tilde{u}(t, \theta) = C(\theta)(\tilde{r}(t) - y_0(t))$$
$$= C(\theta)(M^{-1} - 1)y_0(t).$$

If $\tilde{u}(t, \theta) = u_0(t)$, then the model matching is achieved, i.e.,

$$M = \frac{PC(\theta)}{1 + PC(\theta)}.$$

Since the exact model matching is difficult in practice due to the restricted structural controller, the measurement noise injected to the output etc., we consider the alternative optimization problem:

$$\hat{\theta} = \arg \min_{\theta} J_{VR}^N(\theta),$$

where

$$J_{VR}^N(\theta) = \frac{1}{N} \sum_{t=1}^{N} [L(u_0(t) - \tilde{u}(t, \theta))]^2$$
$$= \frac{1}{N} \sum_{t=1}^{N} [Lu_0(t) - C(\theta)L(\tilde{r}(t) - y_0(t))]^2$$

$L$ is a prefilter given by the designer. By selection of $L = W_M M(1 - M)$, $\hat{\theta}$ would be a good approximation of the exact solution of the model matching problem $\bar{\theta}$ even if $\tilde{u}(t, \theta) \neq u_0(t)$ (Campi et al., 2002). Especially, in case where the controller $C(\theta)$ is linearly parameterized with respect to $\theta$ using an appropriate transfer matrix $\sigma$, i.e., $C(\theta) = \sigma^T \theta$, the optimal solution

$\hat{\theta}$ is calculated by the least-squares method as

$$\hat{\theta} = \left[ \sum_{t=1}^{N} \varphi(t)\varphi^{T}(t) \right]^{-1} \sum_{t=1}^{N} \varphi(t)u_{L}(t),$$

where $\varphi(t) = L\sigma(\tilde{r}(t) - y_0(t))$, $u_L(t) = Lu_0(t)$.

### 3.2 Direct tuning of $Q$ from experimental data by the VRFT

This subsection describes the application of the VRFT to the design of the Youla parameter $Q$ without any model identification of the dual Youla parameter $R$. The experimental data set used in the controller design, $\{r_0(t), u_0(t), y_0(t)\}$, is collected from the closed-loop system composed of the perturbed plant $P$ and the nominal controller $C_0$. Define the Youla parameter $Q(z, \theta)$ linearly parameterized with respect to $\theta$ as

$$Q(z, \theta) = \sigma(z)^{T}\theta, \tag{9}$$

where $\sigma(z)$ is a discrete-time transfer function vector defined as

$$\sigma(z) = [\sigma_1(z), \sigma_2(z), \cdots, \sigma_n(z)]^{T}, \tag{10}$$

and $\theta$ is a parameter vector of length $n$ defined as

$$\theta = [\theta_1, \theta_2, \cdots, \theta_n]^{T}. \tag{11}$$

Then the model matching problem formulated as (6) can be rewritten with respect to $\theta$ as

$$\bar{\theta} = \arg \min_{\theta} J_{MR}(\theta), \tag{12}$$

where

$$J_{MR}(\theta) = \left\| W_M \left( M - \frac{(N + RY)X}{1 + RQ(\theta)} \right) \right\|_2^2. \tag{13}$$

Under the condition that the dual Youla parameter $R$ is unknown, we will obtain the minimizer $\bar{\theta}$ of $J_{MR}(\theta)$ using the closed-loop experimental data set $\{r_0(t), u_0(t), y_0(t)\}$.
Firstly, we obtain the input and the output data of $R$ denoted by $\alpha(t)$, and $\beta(t)$, respectively. In Fig. 1, we treat the actual plant $P$ as the perturbed plant described by (4) and set $Q = 0$ since $Q$ is a parameter to be designed. Then, we calculate $\alpha(t)$ and $\beta(t)$ using the input/output data, $\{u_0(t), y_0(t)\}$ collected from the plant when the appropriate reference signal $r_0(t)$ is applied to the standard unity feedback control structure as shown in Fig. 5. The signals $\alpha(t)$ and $\beta(t)$ are calculated as follows:

$$\alpha(t) = Xy_0(t) + Yu_0(t)$$
$$= Xr_0(t), \tag{14}$$
$$\beta(t) = Dy_0(t) - Nu_0(t). \tag{15}$$

Although $\alpha(t)$ is an internal signal of the feedback control system, $\alpha(t)$ is an function of the external signal $r_0(t)$ given by the designer as is clear from (14). This means that the loop-gain from $\beta$ to $\alpha$ is equivalent to 0, and that the input-output characteristic from $\beta$ to $\alpha$ is an open-loop system, which is also understood by Fig. 3 with $Q = 0$. Moreover, since $R$ belongs to $\mathcal{RH}_\infty$ according to the dual Youla parameterization, the input/output data set of $R$ is always available by an open-loop experiment. As a result, the basic requirement for the VRFT is always satisfied in this parameterization.

Secondly, we regard $y_0(t)$ as the output of the reference model $M$, and obtain the virtual reference $\tilde{r}(t)$ such that

$$y_0(t) = M\tilde{r}(t). \tag{16}$$

If there exists the parameter $\theta$ such that $\alpha(t) = X\tilde{r}(t) - Q(\theta)\beta(t)$, the exact model matching is achieved ($G_{ry} = M$). According to the concept of the VRFT, the approximated solution of the model matching problem, $\hat{\theta}$, is obtained by solving the following optimization problem:

$$\hat{\theta} = \arg \min_{\theta} J_{\text{VR}}^N(\theta), \tag{17}$$

where

$$J_{\text{VR}}^N(\theta) = \frac{1}{N} \sum_{t=1}^{N} [L_M(\alpha(t) - X\tilde{r}(t) + Q(\theta)\beta(t))]^2.$$

Since $Q(\theta)$ is linear with respect to the parameter vector $\theta$ as defined in (9), $J_{\text{VR}}^N(\theta)$ is rewritten as

$$J_{\text{VR}}^N(\theta) = \frac{1}{N} \sum_{t=1}^{N} [y_L(t) - \varphi(t)^{\text{T}}\theta]^2, \tag{18}$$

where

$$\varphi(t) = -L_M \sigma \beta(t),$$
$$y_L(t) = L_M(\alpha(t) - X\tilde{r}(t)).$$

The minimizer of $J_{\text{VR}}^N(\theta)$ is then calculated using the least-squares method as

$$\hat{\theta} = \left[ \sum_{t=1}^{N} \varphi(t)\varphi^{\text{T}}(t) \right]^{-1} \sum_{t=1}^{N} \varphi(t)y_L(t). \tag{19}$$

The filter $L_M$ is specified by the designer. By selecting $L_M = W_M M Y \Phi_\alpha(\omega)^{-1}$, $\hat{\theta}$ could be a good approximation of $\bar{\theta}$ in case $N \to \infty$, where $\Phi_\alpha(\omega)$ is a spectral density function of $\alpha(t)$. Moreover, this design approach needs an inverse system of the reference model, $M^{-1}$, when $\tilde{r}(t)$ is generated. However, by introducing $L_M$, we can avoid overemphasis by derivation in $M^{-1}$ in the case where the noise corrupted data $y_0(t)$ is used.

### 3.3 Stability constraint on the design of $Q$ by the VRFT

The design method of $Q$ based on the VRFT stated in the previous subsection does not explicitly address the stability issue of the resulting closed-loop system. Therefore, we can not evaluate whether the resulting Youla parameter $Q(\theta)$ actually stabilizes the closed-loop

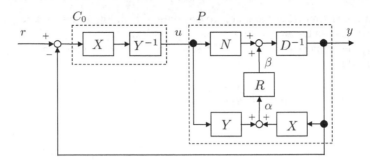

Fig. 5. Data acquisition of $\alpha(t)$ and $\beta(t)$.

system or not in advance of its implementation. To avoid the instability, the data-based stability constraint should be introduced in the optimization problem (17).

As stated in the subsection 2.2, the robust stability condition when the plant perturbs from $P_0$ to $P$ is described using $R$ and $Q$ as (5). However, (5) is non-convex with respect to the parameter $\theta$, and it is difficult to incorporate this stability condition into the least-squares based VRFT as the constraint. Using the small-gain theorem, the sufficient condition of the robust stability is derived as

$$\delta = \|RQ(\theta)\|_\infty < 1. \tag{20}$$

The alternative constraint (20) is imposed instead of (5), and the original constrained optimization problem is reduced to the tractable one (Matsumoto et al., 1993). Since model information on the plant can not be available in the model-free controller syntheses such as the VRFT, we must evaluate (20) using only the input/output data set $\{u_0(t), y_0(t)\}$ obtained from the closed-loop system. As is clear from Fig. 3, since the input and the output data of $R$ are $\alpha(t)$ and $\beta(t)$, respectively, the open-loop transfer function from $\alpha$ to $\xi(\theta)$ corresponds to $RQ(\theta)$ by introducing the virtual signal $\xi(t, \theta) = Q(\theta)\beta(t)$. Assuming that $\alpha(t)$ is a $p$ times repeating signal of a periodic signal with a period $T$, i.e., $\alpha(t)$ is of length $N = pT$, the $H_\infty$ norm of $RQ(\theta)$ denoted by $\delta(\theta)$ can be estimated via the spectral analysis method as the ratio between the power spectral density function of $\alpha(t)$, denoted by $\Phi_\alpha(\omega_k)$, and the power cross spectral density function between $\alpha(t)$ and $\xi(t, \theta)$, denoted by $\Phi_{\alpha\xi}(\omega_k)$ (Ljung, 1999).

From the Wiener-Khinchin Theorem, $\Phi_\alpha(\omega_k)$ is represented as a discrete Fourier transform (DFT) of an auto-correlation of $\alpha(t)$, denoted by $R_\alpha(\tau)$:

$$\Phi_\alpha(\omega_k) = \frac{1}{T} \sum_{\tau=0}^{T-1} R_\alpha(\tau) e^{-i\tau\omega_k}, \tag{21}$$

where

$$R_\alpha(\tau) = \frac{1}{T} \sum_{\tau=1}^{T-1} \alpha(t - \tau)\alpha(t),$$

$\omega_k = 2\pi k/(TT_s)$ $(T = 0, \cdots, (T-1)/2)$, and $T_s$ is a sampling time. The frequency points $\omega_k$ must be defined as a sequence with a much narrow interval for a good estimate of $\delta(\theta)$.

A shorter sampling time $T_s$ is preferable to estimate $\delta(\theta)$ in higher frequencies, and a longer period $T$ improves the frequency resolution.

Similarly, $\Phi_{\alpha\xi}(\omega_k, \theta)$ is estimated as a DFT of the cross-correlation between $\alpha(t)$ and $\xi(t, \theta)$, denoted by $\hat{R}_{\alpha\xi}(\tau)$:

$$\hat{\Phi}_{\alpha\xi}(\omega_k, \theta) = \frac{1}{T} \sum_{\tau=0}^{T-1} \hat{R}_{\alpha\xi}(\tau, \theta) e^{-i\tau\omega_k}, \tag{22}$$

where

$$\hat{R}_{\alpha\xi}(\tau, \theta) = \frac{1}{N} \sum_{\tau=1}^{N} \alpha(t - \tau)\xi(t, \theta).$$

Using the $p$-periods cyclic signal $\alpha(t)$ in the estimate of $\hat{R}_{\alpha\xi}(\tau, \theta)$, the effect of the measurement noise involved in $\xi(t, \theta)$ is averaged and the estimate error in $\Phi_{\alpha\xi}(\omega_k, \theta)$ is then reduced. Especially, the measurement noise is normalized, the effect on the estimate of $\Phi_{\alpha\xi}(\omega_k, \theta)$ by the measurement noise is asymptotically reduced to 0.

Since $Q(\theta)$ is linearly defined with respect to $\theta$, $\hat{R}_{\alpha\xi}(\tau, \theta)$ and $\hat{\Phi}_{\alpha\xi}(\omega_k, \theta)$ are also linear with respect to $\theta$. As a result, the stability constraint of (20) is evaluated using only the input/output data as

$$\hat{\delta}(\theta) = \max_{\{\omega_k|\Phi_\alpha(\omega_k)\neq 0\}} \left| \frac{\hat{\Phi}_{\alpha\xi}(\omega_k, \theta)}{\Phi_\alpha(\omega_k)} \right| < 1. \tag{23}$$

Since this constraint is convex with respect to $\theta$ at each frequency point $\omega_k$, we can integrate this $H_\infty$ norm constraint into the optimization problem (17) and solve it as a convex optimization problem.

### 3.4 Design algorithm

This subsection describes the design algorithm of $Q(\theta)$ imposing the stability constraint.

[step 1]  Collect the input/output data set $\{u_0(t), y_0(t)\}$ of length $N$ in the closed-loop manner in the unity feedback control structure shown in Fig. 5 when the appropriate reference signal $r_0(t)$ is applied.

[step 2]  Calculate $\alpha(t)$ and $\beta(t)$ using the data set $\{r_0(t), u_0(t), y_0(t)\}$ as

$$\alpha(t) = Xr_0(t),$$
$$\beta(t) = Dy_0(t) - Nu_0(t).$$

[step 3]  Generate the virtual reference $\tilde{r}(t)$ such that

$$y_0(t) = M\tilde{r}(t).$$

[step 4]  Solve the following convex optimization problem;

$$\hat{\theta} = \arg \min_{\theta} J_{\mathrm{VR}}^N(\theta),$$

Fig. 6. Experimental set-up of a belt-driven two-mass system.

subject to

$$\left| \frac{1}{T} \sum_{\tau=0}^{T-1} \hat{R}_{\alpha\zeta}(\tau,\theta)e^{-i\tau\omega_k} \right| < \left| \frac{1}{T} \sum_{\tau=0}^{T-1} R_\alpha(\tau)e^{-i\tau\omega_k} \right|,$$

$$\omega_k = 2\pi k/T, \quad k = 0,\ldots,(T-1)/2.$$

## 4. Design example

To verify the effectiveness of the proposed design method, we address a velocity control problem of a belt-driven two-mass system frequently encountered in many industrial processes.

### 4.1 Controlled plant

The plant to be controlled is depicted as Fig. 6. The velocity of the drive disk is controlled by the drive motor connected to the drive disk. The pulley is connected to the load disk through the flexible belt, the restoring force of the flexible belt affects the velocity of the drive disk, which causes the resonant vibration of the drive disk. The resonant frequency highly depends on the position and the number of the weights mounted on the drive disk and the load disk. We treat this two-mass resonant system as the controlled plant $P$. Since the position and the number of the weights mainly changes the resonant frequency, a rigid model is treated as the nominal plant $P_0$ identified easily, which changes little in response to load change. The nominal plant $P_0$ is identified by the simple frequency response test as

$$P_0 = \frac{4964}{s^2 + 136.1s + 8.16}. \tag{24}$$

Moreover, the delay time of 14 ms is emulated by the software as the plant perturbation in $P$, but it is not reflected in $P_0$. Due to the delay time, the closed-loop system tends to be destabilized when the gain of the feedback controller is high. This means that if the reference model with the high cut-off frequency is given, the closed-loop system readily destabilized.

## 4.2 Experimental condition

For the simplicity, the design problem is restricted to the model matching of $G_{ry}$ approaching to its reference model $M$ in the previous section. However, the proposed method readily address the model matching of multiple characteristics. In the practical situations, we must solve the trade-off between several closed-loop properties. In this experimental set-up, we show the design result of the simultaneous optimization problem approaching the tracking performance, $G_{ry}$, and the noise attenuation performance, $G_{ny}$ to their reference models, $M$ and $T$, respectively. The evaluation function is defined as

$$J_{MR}(\theta) = \left\| W_M \left( M - \frac{(N+RY)X}{1+RQ(\theta)} \right) \right\|_2^2 + \left\| W_T \left( T - \frac{(N+RY)(X+Q(\theta)D)}{1+RQ(\theta)} \right) \right\|_2^2. \tag{25}$$

To deal with the above multiobjective optimization problem, we redefine $\varphi(t)$ and $y_L(t)$ in (18) as

$$\varphi(t) = [-L_M \sigma \beta(t), \; -L_T \sigma(\beta(t) - D\tilde{n}(t))],$$

$$y_L(t) = [L_M(\alpha(t) - X\tilde{r}(t)), \; L_T(\alpha(t) - X\tilde{n}(t))]^T,$$

where $\tilde{n}(t)$ is a virtual reference such that $y_0(t) = T\tilde{n}(t)$, $L_T$ is a filter selected as $L_T = W_T T \Phi_\alpha(\omega)^{-1}$. The reference models for $G_{ry}$ and $G_{ny}$ are given by discretization of

$$M = \frac{50^2}{(s+50)^2}, \text{ and}$$

$$T = \frac{50^2}{(s+50)^2}$$

with the sampling time $T_s = 1$ [ms].

The nominal controller stabilizing $P_0$ is evaluated from the relation

$$M = \frac{P_0 C_0}{1 + P_0 C_0}$$

as

$$C_0 = \frac{M}{(1-M)P_0}$$

$$= \frac{0.5036s^2 + 68.52s + 4.110}{s(s+100)}.$$

The weighting functions $W_M$ and $W_T$ are given to improve the tracking performance in low frequencies and the noise attenuation performance in high frequencies as

$$W_M = \frac{200^2}{(s+200)^2}, \text{ and}$$

$$W_T = \frac{s^2}{(s+200)^2}.$$

The Youla parameter $Q(s, \boldsymbol{\theta})$ is defined in the continuous-time so that the properness of $Q(s, \boldsymbol{\theta})$ and the relation, $Q \in \mathcal{RH}_\infty$, are satisfied as

$$Q(s, \boldsymbol{\theta}) = \frac{\theta_1 s + \theta_2 s^2 + \theta_3 s^3 + \theta_4 s^4 + \theta_5 s^5}{(0.06s + 1)^5}$$

$$= \frac{1}{(0.06s + 1)^4} \begin{bmatrix} s & s^2 & s^3 & s^4 & s^5 \end{bmatrix} \begin{bmatrix} \theta_1 \\ \theta_2 \\ \theta_3 \\ \theta_4 \\ \theta_5 \end{bmatrix}$$

$$= \sigma(s)^\mathsf{T} \boldsymbol{\theta}.$$

The discrete-time Youla parameter $Q(z, \boldsymbol{\theta})$ is defined by discretization of $Q(s, \boldsymbol{\theta})$, i.e., $\sigma(s)$, with the sampling time $T_s = 1$ [ms]. In order to construct the type-I servo system even if the plant perturbs, the constant term of the numerator of $Q(s, \boldsymbol{\theta})$ is set to 0 such that $Q(s, \boldsymbol{\theta})|_{s=0} = 0$ in the continuous-time (Sakuishi et al., 2008).

### 4.3 Experimental result
The VRFT can be regarded as the open-loop identification problem of the controller parameter by the least-squares method. We select the pseudo random binary signal (PRBS) as the input for identification of the controller parameter as same as in the general open-loop identification problem, since the identification input should have certain power spectrum in all frequencies. The PRBS is generated through a 12-bit shift register (i.e., $T = 2^{12} - 1 = 4095$ samples), the reference signal $r_0$ is constructed by repeating this PRBS 10 times (i.e., $p = 10$, $N = 40950$). Firstly, we obtain the parameter $\hat{\boldsymbol{\theta}}_{w/o}$ as (26) when the stability constraint is not imposed.

$$\hat{\boldsymbol{\theta}}_{w/o} = \begin{bmatrix} -2.878 \times 10^{-2} \\ 1.429 \times 10^{-2} \\ -1.594 \times 10^{-3} \\ 1.184 \times 10^{-5} \\ 1.339 \times 10^{-6} \end{bmatrix} \tag{26}$$

Secondly, we obtain the parameter $\hat{\boldsymbol{\theta}}_{w/}$ as (27) when the stability constraint is imposed.

$$\hat{\boldsymbol{\theta}}_{w/} = \begin{bmatrix} 1.263 \times 10^{-1} \\ 1.261 \times 10^{-2} \\ 7.425 \times 10^{-4} \\ 4.441 \times 10^{-6} \\ 4.286 \times 10^{-7} \end{bmatrix} \tag{27}$$

The estimates of $\delta(\boldsymbol{\theta})$ for $Q(z, \hat{\boldsymbol{\theta}}_{w/o})$ and $Q(z, \hat{\boldsymbol{\theta}}_{w/})$ are shown in Fig. 7. For $Q(z, \hat{\boldsymbol{\theta}}_{w/o})$, the stability constraint is not satisfied around 60 rad/s, and $\hat{\delta}(\hat{\boldsymbol{\theta}}_{w/o}) = 7.424$. Since the sufficient condition for the robust stability is not satisfied, we can predict in advance of implementation that the closed-loop system might be destabilized if the Youla parameter $Q(z, \hat{\boldsymbol{\theta}}_{w/o})$ was implemented. On the other hand, $\hat{\delta}(\hat{\boldsymbol{\theta}}_{w/}) = 0.9999$ for $Q(z, \hat{\boldsymbol{\theta}}_{w/})$, which satisfies the stability

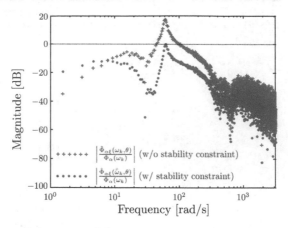

Fig. 7. Estimate of $\delta(\boldsymbol{\theta})$, $\hat{\delta}(\hat{\boldsymbol{\theta}}_{\mathrm{w/o}})$ and $\hat{\delta}(\hat{\boldsymbol{\theta}}_{\mathrm{w/}})$.

constraint. Therefore, we can predict in advance of implementation that the closed-loop system could be stabilized if the Youla parameter $Q(z, \hat{\boldsymbol{\theta}}_{\mathrm{w/}})$ was implemented.

Figure 8 shows the step responses of the GIMC structure with implementing $Q(z, \hat{\boldsymbol{\theta}}_{\mathrm{w/o}})$ and $Q(z, \hat{\boldsymbol{\theta}}_{\mathrm{w/}})$. In the case of $Q(z, \hat{\boldsymbol{\theta}}_{\mathrm{w/o}})$, its response vibrates persistently, the tracking performance, $G_{ry}$, degrades compared with the case that the control system is governed by only the nominal controller $C_0$, i.e., $Q = 0$. On the other hand, in the case of $Q(z, \hat{\boldsymbol{\theta}}_{\mathrm{w/}})$, its response does not coincides with the output of the reference model due to the long delay time, but Fig. 8 shows that the control system is at least stabilized. Moreover, we can confirm that the vibration is suppressed compared with the case of $Q = 0$ and the proposed method provides the Youla parameter reflecting the objective function without destabilizing the closed-loop system. Although $J_{\mathrm{VR}}^N(\hat{\boldsymbol{\theta}}_{\mathrm{w/o}}) < J_{\mathrm{VR}}^N(\hat{\boldsymbol{\theta}}_{\mathrm{w/}})$, the response for $Q(z, \hat{\boldsymbol{\theta}}_{\mathrm{w/}})$ is much closer to the output of the reference model than that for $Q(z, \hat{\boldsymbol{\theta}}_{\mathrm{w/o}})$. This observation implies

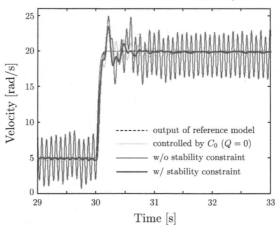

Fig. 8. Step responses for a belt-driven two-mass system with and without stability constraint.

that only minimization of the 2-norm based cost function may not provide the appropriate stabilizing controller in model-free controller syntheses.

## 5. Conclusion

In this article, the design method of the Youla parameter in the GIMC structure by the typical model-free controller design method, VRFT, is proposed. By the model-free controller design method, we can significantly reduce the effort for identification of $R$ and the design of $Q$ compared with the model-based control design method. We can also specify the order and the structure of $Q$, which enable us to design a low-order controller readily. Moreover, the stability constraint derived from the small-gain theorem is integrated into the 2-norm based standard optimization problem. As a result, we can guarantee the closed-loop stability by the designed $Q$ in advance of the controller implementation. The effectiveness of the proposed controller design method is confirmed by the experiment on the two-mass system.

As a future work, we must tackle the robustness issue. The proposed method guarantees the closed-loop stability only at the specific condition where the input/output data is collected. If the load condition changes, the closed-loop stability is no longer guaranteed in the proposed method. We must improve the proposed method to enhance the robustness for the plant perturbation and/or the plant uncertainties. Morevover, though the controller structure is now restricted to the linearly parameterized one in the proposed method, the fully parameterized controller should be tuned for the higher control performance.

## 6. References

M. C. Campi, A. Lecchini and S. M. Savaresi: "Virtual Reference Feedback Tuning: a Direct Method for the Design of Feedback Controllers", *Automatica*, Vol. 38, No. 8, pp. 1337–1346 (2002)

D. U. Campos-Delgado and K. Zhou: "Reconfigurable Fault Tolerant Control Using GIMC Structure", *IEEE Transactions on Automatic Control*, Vol. 48, No. 5, pp. 832–838 (2003)

F. Hansen, G. Franklin and R. Kosut: "Closed-Loop Identification via the Fractional Representation: Experiment Design", *Proc. of American Control Conference 1989*, pp. 1422–1427 (1989)

K. van Heusden, A. Karimi and D. Bonvin: "Non-iterative Data-driven Controller Tuning with Guaranteed Stability: Application to Direct-drive Pick-and-place Robot", *Proc. of 2010 IEEE Multi-Conference on Systems and Control*, pp. 1005–1010 (2010)

K. van Heusden, A. Karimi and D. Bonvin: "Data-driven Controller Tuning with Integrated Stability Constraint", *Proceedings of 47th IEEE Conference on Decision and Control*, pp. 2612–2617 (2008)

H. Hjalmarsson, M. Gevers, S. Gunnarsson and O. Lequin: "Iterative Feedback Tuning: Theory and Applications", *IEEE Control Systems Magazine*, Vol. 18, No. 4, pp. 26–41 (1998)

A. Karimi, K. van Heusden and D. Bonvin: "Noniterative Data-driven Controller Tuning Using the Correlation Approach", *Proc. of European Control Conference 2007*, pp. 5189–5195 (2007)

L. Ljung: System Identification Theory for the User (second edition), Prentice Hall (1999)

K. Matsumoto, T. Suzuki, S. Sangwongwanich and S. Okuma: "Internal Structure of Two-Degree-of-Freedom controller and a Design Method for Free Parameter of Compensator", *IEEJ Transactions on Industry Applications*, Vol. 113-D, No. 6, pp. 768–777 (1993) (in Japanese)

L. Mišković, A. Karimi, D. Bonvin and M. Gevers: "Correlation-Based Tuning of Linear Multivariable Decoupling Controllers", *Automatica*, Vol. 43, No. 9, pp. 1481–1494 (2007)

M. Morari and E. Zafiriou: Robust Process Control, Prentice Hall (1997)

T. Sakuishi, K. Yubai and J. Hirai: "A Direct Design from Input/Output Data of Fault-Tolerant Control System Based on GIMC Structure", *IEEJ Transactions on Industry Applications*, Vol. 128, No. 6, pp. 758–766 (2008) (in Japanese)

M. Vidyasagar: Control System Synthesis: A Factorization Approach, The MIT Press (1985)

K. Yubai, S. Terada and J. Hirai: "Stability Test for Multivariable NCbT Using Input/Output Data", *IEEJ Transactions on Electronics, Information and Systems*, Vol. 130, No. 4 (2011)

K. Yubai, T. Sakuishi and J. Hirai: "Compensation of Performance Degradation Caused by Fault Based on GIMC Structure", *IEEJ Transactions on Industry Applications*, Vol. 127, No. 8, pp. 451–455 (2007) (in Japanese)

K. Zhou and Z. Ren: "A New Controller Architecture for High Performance, Robust, and Fault-Tolerant Control", *IEEE Transactions on Automatic Control*, Vol. 46, No. 10, pp. 1613–1618 (2001)

K. Zhou and J. C. Doyle: Essentials of Robust Control, Prentice Hall (1998)

# 7

# Model Based $\mu$-Synthesis Controller Design for Time-Varying Delay System

Yutaka Uchimura
*Shibaura Institute of Technology*
*Japan*

## 1. Introduction

Time delay often exists in engineering systems such as chemical plants, steel making processes, etc. and studies on time-delay system have long historical background. Therefore the system with time-delay has attracted many researchers' interest and various studies have been conducted. It had been a classic problem; however evolution of the network technology and spread of the Internet brought it back to the main stage. Rapid growth of computer network technology and wide spread of the Internet have been brought remarkable innovation to the world. They enabled not only the speed-of-light information exchange but also offering various services via Internet. Even the daily lives of people have been changed by network based services such as emails, web browsing, twitter and social networks.

In the field of motion control engineering, computer networks are utilized for connecting sensors, machines and controllers. Network applications in the machine industry are replacing bunch of traditional wiring, which is complex, heavy and requires high installation costs (Farsi et al., 1999). Especially, the weight of the signal wires increases the gas consumption of automobiles, which is nowadays not only an issue on the driving performance but also on the environmental issue.

Much research and development is also being conducted in application level, such as tele-surgery (Ghodoussi et al., 2002), tele-operated rescue robots (Yeh et al., 2008), and bilateral control with force feedback via a network (Uchimura & Yakoh, 2004). These applications commonly include sensors, actuators and controllers that are mutually connected and exchange information via a network.

When transmitting data on a network, transmission delays are accumulated due to one or more of the following factors: signal propagation delay, non-deterministic manner of network media access, waiting time in queuing, and so on. The delays sometimes become substantial and affect the performance of the system. Especially, delays in feedback not only weaken system performance, but also cause system unstable in the worst case. Various studies have investigated ways to deal the system with transmission delay. Time-delay systems belong to the class of functional differential equations which are infinite dimensional. It means that there exists infinite number of eigenvalues and conventional control methods developed for the linear time-invariant system do not always reach the most optimized solution.

Therefore many methods for the time-delay systems were proposed. A classic but prominent method is the Smith compensator (Smith, 1957). The Smith compensator essentially assumes that a time delay is constant. If the delay varies, the system may become unstable (Palmor, 1980). Vatanski et.al. (Vatanski et al., 2009) proposed a modified Smith predictor method by measuring time varying delays on the network, which eliminates the sensor time delay (the delay from a plant to a controller). The gain (P gain) of the controller is adjusted based on the amount of time delay to maintain stability of the system. Passivity based control using scattering transformation does not requires an upper bound of delay (Anderson & Spong, 1989); however, as noted in previous research (Yokokohji et al., 1999), the method tends to be conservative and to consequently deteriorate overall performance.

One of the typical approaches is a method base on robust control theory. Leung proposed to deal with time delay as a perturbation and a stabilizing controller was obtained in the frame work of $\mu$-synthesis (Leung et al., 1997). Chen showed a robust asymptotic stability condition by a structured singular value (Chen & Latchman, 1994). The paper also discussed on systems whose state variables include multiple delays.

Another typical approach is to derive a sufficient condition of stability using Lyapunov-Krasovskii type function (Kharitonov et al, 2003). The conditions are mostly shown in the form of LMI (Linear Matrix Inequality)(Mahmoud & AI-bluthairi, 1994)(Skelton et al., 1998). Furthermore, a stabilizing controller for a time invariant uncertain plant is also shown in the form of LMI (Huang & Nguang, 2007). However, Lyapunov-Krasovskii based approaches commonly face against conservative issues. For example, if the Lyapunov function is time independent (Verriest et al., 1993), the system tends to be very conservative. Thus, many different Lyapunov-Krasovskii functions are proposed to reduce the conservativeness of the controller (Yue et al., 2004)(Richard, 2003). Lyapunov-Krasovskii based methods deal with systems in the time domain, whereas robust control theory is usually described in the frequency domain.

Even though those two methods deal with the same object, their approaches seem to be very different. Zhang (Zhang et al., 2001) showed an interconnection between those two approaches by introducing the scaled small gain theory and a system named comparison system. The paper also examined on conservativeness of several stability conditions formulated in LMI and $\mu$-synthesis based design, which concluded that $\mu$-synthesis based controller was less conservative than other LMI based controllers. Detail of this examination is shown in the next section.

In fact, conservativeness really depends how much information of the plant is known. It is obvious that delay-independent condition is more conservative than delay-dependent condition. Generally, the more you know the plant, you possibly gain the chance to improve. For example, time delay on a network is not completely uncertain, in other words it is measurable. If the value of delay is known and explicitly used for control, performance would be improved. Meanwhile, in the model based control, the modeling error between the plant model and the real plant can affect the performance and stability of the system. However, perfect modeling of the plant is very difficult, because the properties of the real plant may vary due to the variation of loads or deterioration by aging. Thus modeling error is inevitable. The modeling error is considered to be a loop gain variation (multiplicative uncertainty) . The error seriously affects the stability of the feedback system. In order to consider the adverse effect of the modeling error together with time delay, we exploited a $\mu$-synthesis to avoid the instability due to uncertainty.

This chapter proposes a model based controller design with $\mu$-synthesis for a network based system with time varying delay and the plant model uncertainty. For the time delay, the explicit modeling is introduced, while uncertainty of the plant model is considered as a perturbation based on the robust control theory.

The notations in this chapter are as follows: $\mathbf{R}$ is the set of real numbers, $\mathbf{C}$ is the set of complex numbers, $\mathbf{R}^{n \times m}$ is the set of all real $n \times m$ matrices, $I_n$ is $n \times n$ identity matrix, $W^T$ is the transpose of matrix $W$, $P > 0$ indicates that $P$ is a symmetric and positive definite matrix,

$\|\cdot\|_\infty$ indicates $H_\infty$ norm defined by $\|G\|_\infty := \sup_{\omega \in \mathbf{R}} \bar{\sigma}[G(j\omega)]$ where $\bar{\sigma}(M)$ is the maximum singular value of complex matrix $M$. Let $(A, B, C, D)$ be a minimal realization of $G(s)$ with

$$G(s) = \left[\begin{array}{c|c} A & B \\ \hline C & D \end{array}\right].$$

(1)

## 2. Related works and comparison on conservativeness

### 2.1 Stability analysis approaches, eigen values, small gain and LMI

Time-delay system attracts much interest of researchers and many studies have been conducted. In the manner of classic frequency domain control theory, the system seems to have infinite order, i.e. it has infinite poles, which makes it intractable problem. Since time delay is a source of instability of the system, stability analysis has been one of the main concerns. These studies roughly categorized into frequency domain based methods and time domain based methods. Frequency domain based methods include Nyquist criterion, Pade approximation and robust control theory such as $H_\infty$ control based approaches.

Meanwhile time domain based methods are mostly offered with conditions which are associated with Lyapunov-Krasovskii functional. The condition is formulated in terms of LMI, hence can be solved efficiently.

Consider a time-delay system in (2),

$$\dot{x}(t) = Ax(t) + A_d x(t - \delta(t))$$

(2)

where $x(t) \in \mathbf{R}^n$ which is a state variable, $A \in \mathbf{R}^{n \times n}, A_d \in \mathbf{R}^{n \times n}$ are parameters of state space model of a plant and $\delta(t)$ corresponds to the delay on transmission such as network communication delay.

Much interest in the past literature has focused on searching less conservate conditions. Conservativeness is often measured by the amount of $\delta(t)$, that is, the larger $\delta(t)$ is the better. In fact, constraints on $\delta(t)$ plays an important role on conservativeness measure. Conservativeness strongly depends on the following constraints:

1. Delay dependent or independent. Whether or not there exists the upper bound of delay $\bar{\delta}$, where $\delta(t) < \bar{\delta}$.

2. $\delta(t)$ is time variant or time invariant (variable delay or constant delay).

3. The value of upper bound of $\dot{\delta}(t)$, $\nu$, where $\dot{\delta}(t) < \nu$.

As for the first constraint, stability condition is often referred as delay-dependent/independent. If the stability condition is delay-independent, it allows amount of time-delay to be infinity.

### 2.2 Delay independent stability analysis in time domain

Verriest (Verriest et al., 1993) showed that the system in (2) is uniformly asymptotically stable, if there exist symmetric positive definite matrix $P$ and $Q$ such that

$$\begin{bmatrix} PA + A^T P + Q & PA_d \\ A_d^T P & -Q \end{bmatrix} < 0.$$

(3)

The condition (3) is a sufficient condition for delay-independent case. One may notice that the matrix form is similar to that of the bounded real lemma.

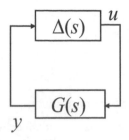

Fig. 1. Interconnection of a plant and time delay

**Lemma 1** *(Bounded real lemma)*: Assume $G(s)$ which is the transfer function of a system, i.e. $G(s) := C(sI - A)^{-1}B$. $\|G(s)\|_\infty < \gamma$, if and only if there exists a matrix $P > 0$,

$$\begin{bmatrix} PA + A^T P + \frac{C^T C}{\gamma} & PA_d \\ A_d^T P & -\gamma I_n \end{bmatrix} < 0. \tag{4}$$

Suppose $(A, B, C, D)$ of system (2) is $(A, A_d, I_n, 0)$ and let $G(s) = (sI_n - A)^{-1}A_d$ be a transfer function of the system and $\gamma = 1$ in (4), (3) and (4) are identical. This fact implies that a system with time delay is stable regardless the value of time delay, if $\|G(s)\|_\infty < 1$. This condition corresponds to the small gain theorem.

Fig.1 shows an interconnection of system $G(s)$ and delay block $\Delta(s)$, where $u(t) = y(t - \delta(t))$. In the figure, $\Delta(s)$ is a block of time delay whose $H_\infty$ norm $\|\Delta(s)\|_\infty$ is induced by (5) .

$$\|\Delta(s)\|_\infty = \sup_{y \in L_2} \frac{\sqrt{\int_0^\infty u^T(t)u(t)dt}}{\sqrt{\int_0^\infty y^T(t)y(t)dt}} = \sup_{y \in L_2} \frac{\|u\|_2}{\|y\|_2} \tag{5}$$

Because the input energy to the delay block is same as the output energy, $H_\infty$ norm of $\Delta(s)$ is equal to 1, i.e. $\|\Delta(s)\|_\infty = 1$. Hence, the interconnected system is stable because $\|G(s)\Delta(s)\|_\infty < 1$. This implies that if $\|G(s)\Delta(s)\|_\infty > 1$, the system becomes unstable when the delay exceeds the limitation. If the delay $\delta(t)$ is bounded by the maximum value $\bar{\delta}$, system in (2) is stable even if $\|G(s)\Delta(s)\|_\infty > 1$. Evaluation of conservativeness is often measured by the upper bound $\bar{\delta}$ for the given system. A condition which gives larger $\bar{\delta}$ is regarded as less conservative.

### 2.3 Delay dependent stability analysis with Lyapnouv-Krasovskii functional

Delay independent stability condition is generally very conservative, because it allows infinite time delay and requires the system $G(s)$ to be small in terms of the system gain. However, the given system is not always $\|G(s)\|_\infty < 1$. For the system whose $H_\infty$ norm is more than one, there exist an upper bound of delay. Generally, an upper bound of delay is given and stability conditions of the system with the upper bound are shown. There have been many studies on Lyapnouv-Krasovskii based analysis for time varying delay system. These have been refining forms of Lyapnouv-Krasovskii functional to reduce conservativeness. Following theorems are LMI based stability conditions for a system with time-varying delay.

**Theorem 1** *(Li & de Souza, 1996)*:

The system given in (6) with time-varying delay is asymptotically stable for any delay $\delta(t)$ satisfying condition (7) if there exist matrix $X > 0$ and constants $\beta_1 > 0$ and $\beta_2 > 0$ satisfying

(8)

$$\dot{x}(t) = Ax(t) + A_d x(t - \delta(t)) \tag{6}$$

$$0 \le \delta(t) < \bar{\delta} \tag{7}$$

$$\begin{bmatrix} \Omega_1 & XA_dA & XA_dA_d \\ * & \beta_1^{-1}X & 0 \\ * & * & \beta_2^{-1}X \end{bmatrix} > 0 \tag{8}$$

where

$$\Omega_1 = -\bar{\delta}^{-1}\left[(A + A_d)^T X + X(A + A_d)\right] - (\beta_1^{-1} + \beta_2^{-1})X. \tag{9}$$

**Theorem 2** (Park, 1999):
The system given in (6) with time-varying delay is asymptotically stable for any delay $\delta(t)$ satisfying condition (7) if there exist matrix $P > 0, Q > 0, V > 0$, and $W$ such that

$$\begin{bmatrix} \Omega_2 & -W^T A_d & A^T A_d^T V & \Theta \\ * & -Q & A_d^T A_d^T B & 0 \\ * & * & -V & 0 \\ * & * & * & -V \end{bmatrix} > 0 \tag{10}$$

where

$$\Omega_2 = (A + A_d)^T P + P(A + B) + W^T B + B^T W + Q \tag{11}$$

$$\Theta = \bar{\delta}(W^T + P). \tag{12}$$

**Theorem 3** *(Tang & Liu, 2008)*:
The system given in (6) with time-varying delay which satisfies (7) is asymptotically stable for any delay $\delta(t)$ which satisfies (13), if there exist matrices $P > 0, Q > 0, Z > 0, Y$ and $W$ such that the following linear matrix inequality (LMI) holds:

$$0 \le \delta(t) < \bar{\delta}, \ \dot{\delta}(t) \le \nu < 1 \tag{13}$$

$$\begin{bmatrix} \Omega_3 & -Y + PA_d + W^T & -Y & \bar{d}A^T Z \\ * & -W - W^T - (1-\nu)Q & -W & dA_d^T Z \\ * & * & -Z & 0 \\ * & * & * & -Z \end{bmatrix} < 0 \tag{14}$$

where

$$\Omega_3 = PA + A^T P + Y + Y^T + Q. \tag{15}$$

In packet based networked system, the condition $\dot{\delta}(t) < 1$ implies that the preceding packet is not caught up by the successive packet.

## 2.4 Delay dependent stability analysis in frequency domain

In frequency domain based, Nyquist criterion gives necessary and sufficient condition and the eigen value based analysis described below is another option of the analysis.

**Lemma 2** The system (2) is asymptotically stable for all $\delta \in [0, \bar{\delta}]$, if and only if $\psi(j\omega, \delta) \neq 0, \forall \omega > 0$ where $\psi(s, \delta) := (sI_n - A - A_d e^{-s\delta})$.

**Corollary 1** The system (2) is asymptotically stable for all $\delta \in [0, \bar{\delta}]$, if and only if

$$det[I_n - G(j\omega)\Phi(j\delta\omega)] \neq 0, \forall \omega \ge 0, \tag{16}$$

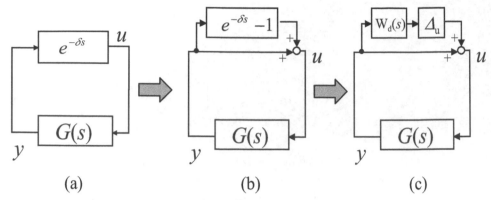

Fig. 2. Robust control based method

where $G(s) = F(sI_n - \bar{A})^{-1}H$, $A_d = HF$, $\bar{A} := A + A_d$ and $\Phi(\delta s) = \phi(\delta s)I_q$, $\phi(\delta s) = e^{-\delta s} - 1$.
Lemma 2 and Corollary 1 requires solving a transcendental equation. Thus, another set $\Delta(j\omega)$
which covers $\Phi(\delta s)$ is chosen. This selection of set $\Delta(j\omega)$ seriously effects on conservativeness.
Zhang proposed very less conservative method using modified Pade approximation. It gives
very less conservative $\bar{\delta}$ which is very close to the Nyquist criterion.
The eigen value analysis including Pade based method can be only applicable for time
invariant delay. For time variant delay, stability analysis with robust control based methods
has been proposed.
The robust control based method regards a set $\Delta(j\omega)$ as the frequency dependent worst case
gain (Leung et al., 1997). In the method, a weighting function is chosen to cover the gain of
$\Phi(\delta s)$. Fig. 2 illustrates the block diagram of robust control method. Fig. 2 (a) shows a system
with a single delay and it can be converted to Fig. 2 (b), i.e. $\Phi(\delta s) = \phi(\delta s) = e^{-\delta s} - 1$. Fig. 2
(c) represents multiplicable uncertainty with associated weighting function $W_d(s)$ and $\Delta_u$ is a
unit disk ($\|\Delta_u\|_\infty = 1$).
$W_d(s)$ is chosen such that $H_\infty$ gain of $W_d(s)$ is more than $\phi(\delta s) - 1$, i.e. $\|\phi(\delta s) - 1\|_\infty < \|W_d(s)\|_\infty$.
Fig. 3 shows the bode plot of $\phi(\delta s) = e^{-\delta s} - 1$, where (a) shows the plot of $\delta = 0.1$, (b) shows
the plot of $\delta = 1$ and (c) shows the case of $\delta = 10$. As shown in the figures, the bode plot
shifts along frequency axis by changing value of $\delta$. It shifts towards the low frequency when
$\delta$ becomes large.
The robust control method gives a sufficient condition based on the small gain theory by
choosing a unit disk with a weighting function $W_d(s)$ for a set $\Delta(j\omega)$.

### 2.5 Conservation examination on LMI based method and robust control method
We examined conservativeness of LMI based conditions including Theorem 1, 2, 3 and
previously introduced robust control based method.

### 2.5.1 Numerical example
Suppose a second order LTI system whose parameters are

$$A = \begin{bmatrix} 0 & 1 \\ -1 & -2\zeta \end{bmatrix}, \qquad A_d = \begin{bmatrix} 0 & 0 \\ -1.1 & 0 \end{bmatrix} \qquad (17)$$

where $\zeta$ corresponds to a damping factor.

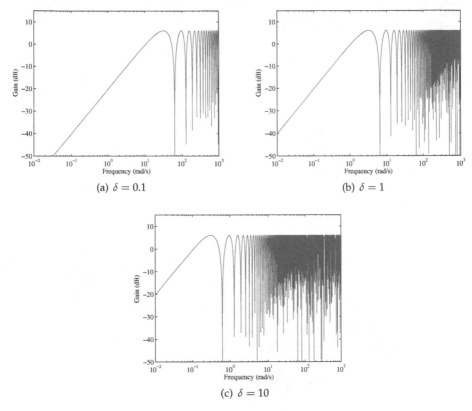

(a) $\delta = 0.1$        (b) $\delta = 1$

(c) $\delta = 10$

Fig. 3. Bode plot of $e^{-\delta s} - 1$

| $\zeta$ \ | Nyquist | Li'96 | Park'99 | Tang0 | Tang1 | Robust |
|---|---|---|---|---|---|---|
| 0.1 | 0.1838 | 0.1818 | 0.1834 | 0.1834 | 0.1818 | 0.1809 |
| 0.3 | 0.6096 | 0.5455 | 0.5933 | 0.5933 | 0.5455 | 0.5289 |
| 0.5 | 1.2965 | 0.9091 | 1.1927 | 1.1927 | 0.9091 | 0.8690 |
| 0.7 | 2.9816 | 1.2727 | 2.4815 | 2.4815 | 1.2727 | 1.4210 |
| 1.0 | 7.9927 | 1.8182 | 6.0302 | 6.0302 | 1.8182 | 3.2000 |
| 10.0 | 117.0356 | 18.1818 | 85.0562 | 85.0562 | 18.1818 | 23.0000 |

Table 1. Upper bound of $\delta$ ($\bar{\delta}$)

By using YALMIP (Lofberg, 2005) with Matlab for the problem modeling and CSDP (CSDP, 1999) for the LMI solver, we calculated the maximum value of $\delta$ by solving LMI feasibility problem with iteration operations.
Table 1 shows the maximum value $\bar{\delta}$ which measures conservativeness of the conditions. In the table, Li'96 and Park'99 are obtained by the Theorem 1 and 2 respectively. Tang0 is the result when $\nu = 0$ and Tang1 is that of $\nu = 1$, where $\nu$ is in (13).

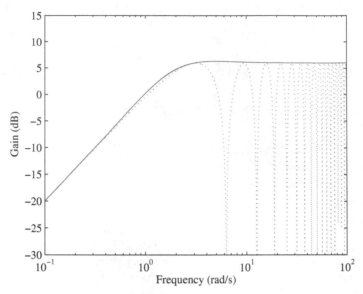

Fig. 4. Bode plots of $W_d(s)$ (blue line) and $e^{-Ts} - 1$ (red dotted line)

Robust in Table 1 shows the results of the robust control method which regards the varying delay as a perturbation, where the following weighting function was used.

$$W_d(s) = \frac{2s(T^2 s^2/4 + (T + T/4)s + 1)}{(s + 2/T)(T^2 s^2/4 + Ts + 1)} \tag{18}$$

Fig. 4 shows the bode plots of $W_d(s)$ and $e^{-Ts} - 1$ where $T = 1$.
Notice that the results of Li'96 are exactly same as Tang1 and Park'99 are the same as Tang1. This implies these two pairs are equivalent conditions. In fact, $\nu = 0$ corresponds that time delay is constant because $\nu = \dot{\delta}(t)$. Robust control results lie between Tang0 and Tang1, i.e. between $\nu = 0$ and $\nu = 1$. In fact, the perturbation assumed by robust control shall include the case $\nu = 1$, thus these results imply that the robust control approach seems to be less conservative.
So far, Lyapunov-Krasovskii controllers are mostly designed with (memory less) static feedback of the plant state (Jiang & Han, 2005). From the performance point of view, the static state feedback performs often worse than the dynamic controller such as $H_\infty$ based controllers.

### 2.5.2 Examination on LMI based method and $\mu$-synthesis
Zhang also examined conservativeness on stability conditions formulated in LMI form and robust control (Zhang et al., 2001), both delay independent and dependent condition were also discussed. In the examination, a system in (2) with parameters in (19) and (20) was used, which was motivated by the dynamics of machining chatter (Tlusty, 1985).

$$A = \begin{bmatrix} 0 & 0 & 1 & 0 \\ 0 & 0 & 0 & 1 \\ -(10.0 + K) & 10.0 & 1 & 0 \\ 5.0 & -15.0 & 0 & -0.25 \end{bmatrix} \tag{19}$$

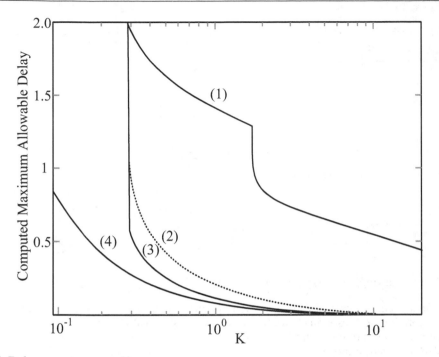

Fig. 5. Delay margin versus K.

$$A_d = \begin{bmatrix} 0 & 0 & 0 & 0 \\ 0 & 0 & 0 & 0 \\ K & 0 & 0 & 0 \\ 0 & 0 & 0 & 0 \end{bmatrix} \tag{20}$$

The paper examined conservativeness with μ-synthesis based method which is a representative method of the robust control. Specifically, it calculates the structured singular value $\mu_{\Delta_r}(G(jw))$ defined in (21) with respect to a block structure $\Delta_r$ in (22).

$$\mu_{\Delta_r}(G(jw)) = [\min\{\bar{\sigma}(\Delta) : \det(I - G\Delta) = 0, \Delta \in \Delta_r\}]^{-1} \tag{21}$$

$$\Delta_r := \{\mathrm{diag}[\lambda_1 I_{n_1}, \lambda_2 I_{n_2}] : \lambda_i \in \mathbf{C}\}. \tag{22}$$

Because calculating of μ is NP-hard (non-deterministic polynomial-time hard), its upper bound with $D$ scales defined in (23) and (24) was used.

$$\sup_{w \in \mathbf{R}} \inf_{D \in \mathbf{D_r}} \bar{\sigma}\left(DG(jw)D^{-1}\right) < 1 \tag{23}$$

$$\mathbf{D_r} := \{\mathrm{diag}[D_1, D_2] \,|\, D_i \in \mathbf{C}^{n \times n}, D_i = D_i^* > 0\} \tag{24}$$

The analytical results are shown in Fig. 5 (Zhang et al., 2001). In the figure, the plot (1) shows the case of Nyquist Criterion, (2) shows μ upper bound with frequency-dependent D scaling, (3) shows the upper bound by Theorem 2 and (3) shows the upper bound by Theorem 1. The results show that the LMI based conditions are more conservative than $D$-scaled μ based method. The reason of this is stated that the scale matrix $D$ in μ method is frequency

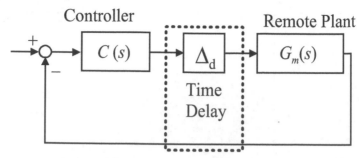

Fig. 6. Basic structure of network based system

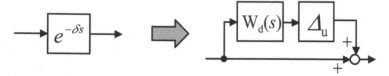

Fig. 7. Time varying delay as a perturbation

dependent function which is obtained by frequency sweeping of $G(j\omega)$. On contrary, LMI formed condition corresponds to fix $D$ scale a real constant value. Constant $D$ scaling is well known to provide a more conservative result than frequency-dependent $D$ scaling. This result revealed that Lyapunov-Krasovskii based conditions formulated in LMI may be caught into conservative issue and their robust margin possibly becomes smaller than $\mu$ based controller. Through the investigations stated above, we determined to exploit a $\mu$-synthesis based controller design. Because $\mu$-synthesis based controller is designed based on the robust control theory. In the next section, we describe a model based $\mu$ controller design for a system with time delay and model uncertainty.

## 3. Model based $\mu$-synthesis controller

Fig. 6 shows basic structure of a network based system where $C(s)$ is a controller and $G_m(s)$ is a remote plant. The block $\Delta_d$ is a delay factor which represents transmission delay on a network. It represents round trip delay, which accumulates forward and backward delays. The time varying delay $\delta(t)$ is bounded with $0 \leq \delta(t) \leq \bar{\delta}$. If the time delay $\delta(t)$ is a constant value $\delta_c$, the block can be written as $\Delta_d = e^{-\delta_c s}$ in frequency domain, however $e^{-\delta s}$ is not accurate expression for time varying delay $\delta$. As described in the previous section, Leung proposed to regard time varying delay as an uncertainty and the delay is represented as a perturbation associated with a weighting function (Leung et al., 1997) . In particular, time delay factor can be denoted as shown in Fig. 7, where $\Delta_u$ is unknown but assure to be stable with $\|\Delta_u(s)\|_\infty \leq 1$ and $W_d(s)$ is a weighting function which holds $|e^{-\bar{\delta}s} - 1| < |W_d(j\omega)|, \forall \omega \in \mathbf{R}$, i.e. $W_d(s)$ covers the upper bound of gain $e^{-\bar{\delta}s} - 1$ . Applying the small gain theory considering $\|W_d(s)\Delta_u(s)\|_\infty \leq \|W_d(s)\|_\infty$, the system is stable if the condition (25) holds.

$$\|C(s)G_m(s)(1 + W_d(s))\|_\infty < 1 \tag{25}$$

(25) is rewritten in (26)

$$\|C(s)\|_\infty < \frac{1}{\|G_m(s)(1 + W_d(s))\|_\infty}. \tag{26}$$

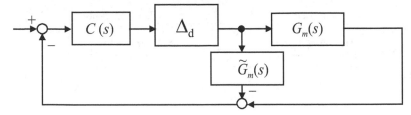

Fig. 8. Model based control structure

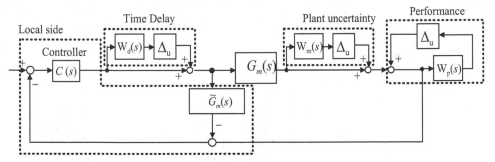

Fig. 9. Overall structure with perturbations

(26) implies the maximum gain of $C(s)$ is limited by the norm of $G_m(s)$ and $(1 + W_d(s))$. If the gain of $C(s)$ is small, even the norm sensitivity function without delay cannot become small as shown in (27).

$$\|S(s)\|_\infty = \left\| \frac{1}{1 + C(s)G_m(s)} \right\|_\infty \qquad (27)$$

In general, the norm of the sensitivity function directly represents the performance of the system such as servo response and disturbance attenuation. The restriction due to the bounded norm of the controller may degrade the performance of the system. In order to avoid it, we propose a unification of model based control with μ-synthesis robust control design.

Fig. 8 shows a proposed model based control structure which includes the model of time delay and the remote plant where $\tilde{G}_m(s)$ is a model of the plant. In the real implementation, a model of time delay is also employed, which exactly measures the value of time delay. The measurement of delay can be implemented by time-stamped packets and synchronization of the local and remote node (Uchimura et al., 2007). By introducing the plant model, the upper bound restriction of $C(s)$ is relaxed if the model $\tilde{G}_m(s)$ is close to $G_m(s)$, i.e. if $\|\tilde{G}_m(s) - G_m(s)\|_\infty$ is smaller than $\|G_m(s)\|_\infty$.

$$\|C(s)\|_\infty < \frac{1}{\|(G_m(s) - \tilde{G}_m(s))(1 + W_d(s))\|_\infty} \qquad (28)$$

In fact, perfect modeling of $G_m(s)$ is impossible and property of the remote model may vary in time due to various factors such as aging or variation of loads. Therefore we need to admit the difference between $\tilde{G}_m(s)$ and $G_m(s)$ and need to deal with it as a perturbation of the remote plant $G_m(s)$. Then another perturbation factor associated with a weighting function $W_m(s)$ is added. Additionally, another perturbation factor with $W_p(s)$ after the remote plant is also added to improve the performance of the system. $W_p^{-1}(s)$ works to restrict the upper bound

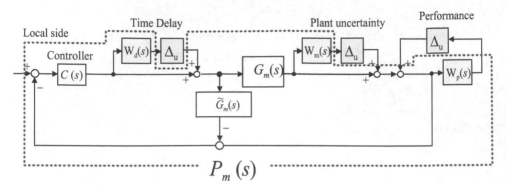

Fig. 10. Augmented plant $P_m$

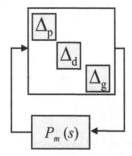

Fig. 11. Simplified block diagram of the augmented plant $P_m(s)$

of the norm of the sensitivity function $S(s)$. In the experiment described in later, the gain of $W_p(s)$ is large at low frequency range.

Fig. 9 shows the overall structure with perturbations of the proposed control system. There are three perturbations in the system and each perturbation has no correlation with others. Therefore we applied $\mu$-synthesis to design the controller $C(s)$. As previously mentioned, the value of $\mu$ is hard to calculate thus we also employed frequency dependent scale $D(j\omega)$ to calculate the upper bound of $\mu_{\mathbf{D_r}}$ as follows.

$$\mu_{\mathbf{D_r}} = \sup_{\omega \in \mathbf{R}} \inf_{D \in \mathbf{D_r}} \bar{\sigma} \left( D(j\omega) P_m(j\omega) D(j\omega)^{-1} \right) \tag{29}$$

Since there exist three perturbations in the proposed method, class of $\mathbf{D_r}$ is defined in (30).

$$\mathbf{D_r} := \{ \mathrm{diag}[d_1, d_2, d_3] \mid d_i \in \mathbf{C} \} \tag{30}$$

$P_m(s)$ in (29) is the transfer function matrix of the augmented plant with three inputs and three outputs. The plant $P_m(s)$ includes three weighting functions $W_d(s)$, $W_m(s)$, $W_p(s)$ and controller $C(s)$. Fig. 10 shows the augmented plant $P_m(s)$ where the area surrounded by dotted line corresponds to $P_m(s)$ and it can be simplified to the block diagram shown in Fig. 11.

Because finding $D(s)$ and $C(s)$ simultaneously is difficult, so called D-K iteration is used to find a adequate combination of $D(s)$ and $C(s)$.

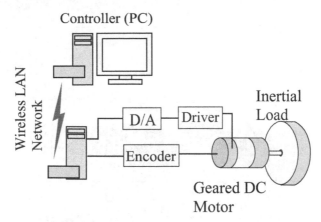

Fig. 12. Experimental setup and system configuration

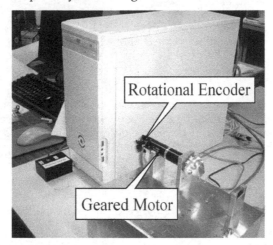

Fig. 13. Overview of the experimental device

## 4. Design of model based $\mu$ controller and experimental evaluation

### 4.1 Design procedure of a controller

In order to evaluate the performance of proposed controller, we set up an experiment. Fig. 12 shows the configuration of the experiment. As shown in the figure, we used wireless LAN to transmit data in between local controller and remote plant. Fig. 13 shows the overview of the experimental device of the remote plant (geared motor). In the experiment, we used a geared DC motor with an inertial load on the output axis. We assumed load variation, thus two different inertial loads are prepared. Through the examination of identification tests, the nominal plant $G_m(s)$ was identified as a first order transfer function in (31).

$$G_m(s) = \frac{260.36}{s + 154.28} \tag{31}$$

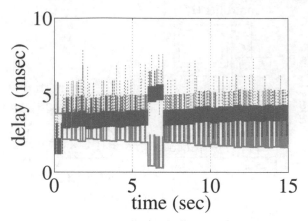

Fig. 14. Measurement results of time delay

We intentionally chose different transfer function for a plant model $\tilde{G}_m$ in (32). It aimed to evaluate robust performance against unexpected load variations.

$$\tilde{G}_m(s) = \frac{182.25}{s + 108.0} \tag{32}$$

Fig. 14 shows one of the measurement results of time delay, green plot shows transmission delay from local to remote and the blue plot shows ones from remote to local. Based on measurements under various circumstances, we chose the upper bound of time delay as 100 [msec] and the weighing function $W_d$ was chosen to be

$$W_d(s) = \frac{2.1s}{s + 10}. \tag{33}$$

The second weighting function $W_m(s)$ which is associated with model uncertainty was chosen to cover the difference of $G_m(s)$ and $\tilde{G}_m(s)$ as shown in (32).

$$W_m(s) = \frac{78s^2 + 12050s}{260s^2 + 92390s + 8056000} \tag{34}$$

The third weighting function $W_p(s)$ for performance is determined to maintain the value of the sensitivity function to be small. It also aimed to attenuate the disturbance at low frequency.

$$W_p(s) = \frac{0.421s + 4.21}{s + 0.01} \tag{35}$$

We used Robust Toolbox of Matlab for numerical computation including $D$-$K$ iteration and obtained a solution of $C(s)$ which satisfied the condition $\mu_{D_r} < 1$. After 8 times $D$-$K$ iterations, peak $\mu$ value was converged to $\mu = 0.991$ and a controller with 17th order was obtained. The Bode plot of the obtained controller $C(s)$ is shown in Fig.15.

### 4.2 Experimental result

We implemented obtained controller on PC hardware by transferring it into the discrete-time controller with 1 [msec] sampling time. The controller tasks with motor control tasks

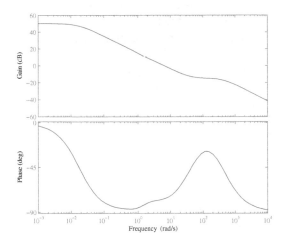

Fig. 15. Bode plot of the controller $C(s)$

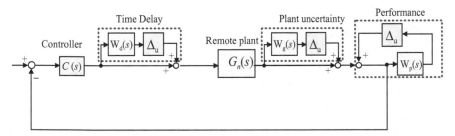

Fig. 16. Block diagram of the system with the conventinal controller

were executed on RT-Linux. RT-Messenger (Sato & Yakoh, 2000) was used to implement the network data-transmission task in Linux kernel mode process. IEEE802.11g compliant wireless LAN device are used, which was connected to PC via USB bus. For the delay measurement, a beacon packet was used as a time stamp. A beacon packet contains a counter value of TSF (timing synchronization function), which is a standard function for IEEE 802.11 compliant devices and resolution of counter is 1 [$\mu$sec]. The function synchronize both timers of local and remote node every 100 [msec] (Uchimura et al., 2007).

To evaluate the performance of the proposed controller, we prepared a controller for comparison purpose, which was also designed by μ-synthesis, however it is designed without the remote plant model $\tilde{G}_m(s)$ and the time delay model, hereinafter referred to as conventional controller. Fig. 16 shows the overall block diagram with the conventional controller. Compareing it with Fig. 9, one may notice that there is no plant model. The conventional controller corresponds to the one which appears in (Leung et al., 1997).

Fig. 17 shows the result of a step response of the velocity control. The blue plot shows the response of the proposed controller and the red plot shows the result by the conventional controller. Comparing these two plots, the proposed controller shows better response in transient response. Fig. 18 shows the result when we intentionally added 200 [msec] delay

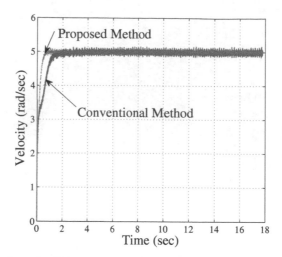

Fig. 17. Experimental results (Step response of velocity control)

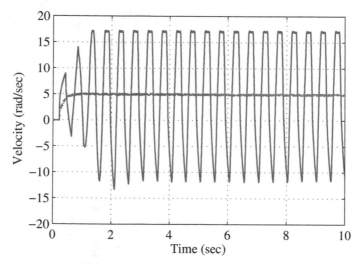

Fig. 18. Experimental results (with intentionally added delay)

in the network transmission path. The delay was virtually emulated by buffering data in memory.

Comparing two plots, the result by the conventional controller shows unstable response, whereas the response by the proposed controller still maintains stability. In fact, we designed both controllers under the assumption of 100 [msec] maximum delay, however the results showed different aspect. These results can be analyzed as following reasons. A $\mu$-synthesis based controller guarantees to maintain robust performance of the system, namely it accomplishes required performance as long as the perturbations of delay and model uncertainty are within the worst case. In terms of robust performance, both proposed and conventional controllers may show similar performance, because they are designed with same $W_p(s)$ for performance weight. In $\mu$-synthesis based design, the obtained controller assures $\mu_{\Delta_r} < 1$ against all possible perturbations. However the system may be stable when one of the perturbations goes beyond the maximum, if it is not the critical one. Namely, the stability margins for different perturbations are not always same. As stated in previous section, model based controller holds more margin in loop gain; hence the deference in the delay margin may appear on the result. As a result, the proposed controller is more robust against time delay than the conventional controller while maintaining same performance.

## 5. Conclusion

In this chapter, a model based controller design by exploiting $\mu$-synthesis is proposed, which is designed for a network based system with time varying delay and the plant model uncertainty. The proposed controller includes the model of the remote plant and time delay. The delay was measured by time-stamped packet. To avoid instability due to model uncertainty and variation of delays, we applied $\mu$-synthesis based robust control method to design a controller. The paper also studied conservativeness on the stability condition based on Lyapnov-Krasovskii functional with LMI and on the robust control including $\mu$-synthesis. Evaluation of the proposed system was carried out by experiments on a motor control system. From the results, we verified the stability and satisfactory performance of the system with the proposed methods.

## 6. References

Anderson,R. J. & Spong, M. W. (1989). Bilateral Control of Teleoperators with Time Delay *IEEE Trans. on Automatic Control*, vol.34, no.5, pp. 494-501.

Borchers, B. (1999). CSDP, A C library for semidefinite programming, *Optimization Methods and Software*, Volume 11, Issue 1 - 4 1999 , pp. 613 - 623.

Chen, J. & Latchman, H. , (1994). Asymptotic stability independent of delays, *American Control Conference*, Vol. 1, pp. 1027 - 1031.

Farsi, M.; Ratcliff, K. & Barbosa, M. (1999). An overview of Controller Area Network, *IEEE Computing and Control Engineering Journal*, Vol.10, pp. 113-120.

Ghodoussi, M.; Butner, S.E. & Wang, Y. (2002). Robotic surgery - the transatlantic case, *Proc. of IEEE Int. Conf on Robotics and Automation*, pp.1882-1888, Vol. 2

Huang, D. & Nguang, S. K. (2007). State feedback control of uncertain networked control systems with random time-delays, *46th IEEE Conf. on Decision and Control*, pp. 3964 - 3969.

Jiang, X. & Han,Q. (2005). On $H_\infty$ control for linear systems with interval time-varying delay, *Automatica*, vol.41, pp 2099 - 2106.

Jun,M. & Safonov, M. G. (2000). Stability Analysis of a System with time delayed States, *IEEE American Control Conference*, pp. 949-952.

Gu, K. ; Kharitonov, V. L. & Che,n J. (2003), Stability of Time-Delay Systems, *1st ed. Boston, MA: Birkhauser.*

Leung, G. ; Franci,s B. ; Apkarian, J. (1997), Bilateral Controller for Teleoperators with Time Delay via $\mu$-Synthesis, *IEEE Trans. on Robotics and Automation*, Vol. 11, No.1, pp. 105-116.

Li, X. & de Souza, C. E. (1996). Robust stabilization and $H_\infty$ control of uncertain linear timedelay systems, *Proc. 13th IFAC World Congress*, pp. 113-118.

Lofberg, J. (2005). YALMIP : a toolbox for modeling and optimization in MATLAB *2004 IEEE International Symposium on Computer Aided Control Systems Design*, , pp. 284 - 289.

Mahmoud, M.S. & Al-bluthairi, N.F. (1994) Quadratic Stabilization of Continuous Time Systems with State delay and Norm-bounded Time-varying Uncertainties, *IEEE Trans. on Automatic Control*, pp. 2135-2139.

Niculescu, S.-I. ; Neto,A. T. ; Dion, J.-M. & Dugard, L. (1995). Delay-dependent stability of linear systems with delayed state: An LMI approach, *Proc. 34th IEEE Conf. Decision Control*, pp. 1495-1497.

Park, P. (1999). A delay-dependent stability criterion for systems with uncertain time-invariant delays, *IEEE Trans. Automat. Contr.*, vol. 44, pp.876-877.

Palmor, Z. (1980), Stability properties of Smith dead-time compensator controllers, *Int. J. of Control*, Vol. 32, No. 6, pp. 937-949.

Richard, J.P. (2003). Time-delay systems: an overview of some recent advances and open problems, *Automatica*, Volume 39, pp. 1667-1694.

Sato, H. & Yakoh, T. (2000). A real-time communication mechanism for RTLinux, *26th Annual Conference of the IEEE Industrial Electronics Society, IECON 2000*, Vol.4, p.p 2437 - 2442.

Skelton, R. E. ; Iwasaki, T. & Grigoriadis, K. (1998) A Unified Algebraic Approach to Linear Control Design, *New York: Taylor & Francis*.

Smith, O. J. M. (1957). Closer Control of Loops with Dead Time , *Chemical Engineering Progress*, 53 , pp. 217 - 219.

Tang, M. Liu, X. (2008). Delay-dependent stability analysis for time delay system, *7th World Congress on Intelligent Control and Automation*, pp. 7260 - 7263.

Tlusty, J. (1985). Machine dynamics, *Handbook of High Speed Machining Technology*, R. I. King, Ed. New York: Chapman & Hall, pp. 48 - 153.

Uchimura, Y. ; Nasu,T. & Takahashi, M. (2007). Time synchronized wireless sensor network and its application to building vibration measurement, *Proc. of 33rd Annual Conference of the IEEE Industrial Electronics Society (IECON2007)*, pp. 2633 - 2638.

Uchimura Y. & Yakoh T. , (2004). Bilateral robot system on the real-time network structure, *IEEE Trans. on Industrial Electronics*, Vol. 51, Issue: 5 , pp.940 - 946.

Verriest, E. I. et.al. (1993). Frequency domain robust stability criteria for linear delay systems, *Proc. 32nd IEEE Conf. Decision Control*, pp. 3473-3478.

Vatanski, N. ; Georges, J.P.; Aubrun, C. ; Rondeau, E. ; Jamsa-Jounela, S. (2009). Networked control with delay measurement and estimation, *Control Engineering Practice*, 17 (2) .

Yue, D. , Han, Q.-L.,Peng, C. (2004). State Feedback controller design for networked control systems, *IEEE Trans. Circ. Sys.*, vol. 51, no. 11, pp. 640-644.

Yeh, S. ; Hsu, C. ; Shih, T. ; Hsiao, J. & Hsu, P. (2008). Remote control realization of distributed rescue robots via the wireless network, *Proc. of SICE Annual Conference*, pp.2928-2932.

Yokokohji, Y. ; Imaida,T. & Yoshikawa, T. (1999). Bilateral teleoperation under time-varying communication delay, *IEEE/RSJ Int. Conf. Intelligent Robots and Systems*, Vol. 3, pp. 1854-1859.

Zhang, J. ; Knopse, C.R. & Tsiotras, P. (2001). Stability of Time-Delay Systems: Equivalence between Lyapunov and Scaled Small-Gain Conditions, *IEEE Transactions on Automatic Control*, Vo. 46 , Issue: 3 , pp. 482 - 486.

# 8

# Identification of Linearized Models and Robust Control of Physical Systems

Rajamani Doraiswami[1] and Lahouari Cheded[2]
*[1]Department of Electrical and Computer Engineering,*
*University of New Brunswick, Fredericton,*
*[2]Department of Systems Engineering,*
*King Fahd University of Petroleum and Minerals, Dhahran,*
*[1]Canada*
*[2]Saudi Arabia*

## 1. Introduction

This chapter presents the design of a controller that ensures both the robust stability and robust performance of a physical plant using a linearized identified model . The structure of the plant and the statistics of the noise and disturbances affecting the plant are assumed to be unknown. As the design of the robust controller relies on the availability of a plant model, the mathematical model of the plant is first identified and the identified model, termed here the nominal model, is then employed in the controller design. As an effective design of the robust controller relies heavily on an accurately identified model of the plant, a reliable identification scheme is developed here to handle unknown model structures and statistics of the noise and disturbances. Using a mixed-sensitivity $H_\infty$ optimization framework, a robust controller is designed with the plant uncertainty modeled by additive perturbations in the numerator and denominator polynomials of the identified plant model. The proposed identification and robust controller design are evaluated extensively on simulated systems as well as on two laboratory-scale physical systems, namely the magnetic levitation and two- tank liquid level systems. In order to appreciate the importance of the identification stage and the interplay between this stage and the robust controller design stage, let us first consider a model of an electro-mechanical system formed of a DC motor relating the input voltage to the armature and the output angular velocity. Based on the physical laws, it is a third-order closed-loop system formed of fast electrical and slow mechanical subsystems. It is very difficult to identify the fast dynamics of this system, and hence the identified model will be of a second-order while the true order remains to be three. Besides this error in the model order, there may also be errors in the estimated model parameters. Consider now the problem of designing a controller for this electro-mechanical system. A constant-gain controller based on the identified second-order model will be stable for all values of the gain as long the negative feedback is used. If, however, the constant gain controller is implemented on the physical system, the true closed-loop third-order system may not be stable for large values of the controller gain. This simple example clearly shows the disparity between the performance of the identified system and the real one and hence provides a strong motivation for designing a robust controller which factors uncertainties in the model.

A physical system, in general, is formed of cascade, parallel and feedback combinations of many subsystems. It may be highly complex, be of high order and its structure may be different from the one derived from physical laws governing its behavior. The identified model of a system is at best an approximation of the real system because of the many difficulties encountered and assumptions made in completely capturing its dynamical behavior. Factors such as the presence of noise and disturbances affecting the input and the output, the lack of persistency of excitation, and a finite number of input-output samples all contribute to the amount of uncertainty in the identified model. As a result of this, high-frequency behavior including fast dynamics may go un-captured in the identified model. The performance of the closed- loop system formed of a physical plant and a controller depends critically upon the quality of the identified model. Relying solely on the robustness of the controller to overcome the uncertainties of the identified plant will result in a poor performance. Generally, popular controllers such as proportional (P), proportional integral (PI) or proportional integral and derivative (PID) controllers are employed in practice as they are simple, intuitive and easy to use and their parameters can be tuned on line. When these controllers are designed using the identified model, and implemented on the physical system, there is no guarantee that the closed-loop system will be stable, let alone meeting the performance requirements. The design of controllers using identified models to ensure robust stability is becoming increasingly important in recent times. In (Cerone, Milanese, and Regruto, 2009), an interesting iterative scheme is proposed which consists of first identifying the plant and employing the identified model to design a robust controller, then implementing the designed controller on the real plant and evaluating its performance on the actual closed-loop system. However, it is difficult to establish whether the identify-control-implement-evaluate scheme will converge, and even if it does, whether it will converge to an optimal robust controller. In this work, each of these issues, namely the identification, the controller design and its implementation on an actual system, are all addressed separately with the clear objective of developing a reliable identification scheme so that the identified model will be close to the true model, hence yielding a reliable controller design scheme which will produce a controller that will be robust enough to ensure both stability and robust performance of the actual closed-loop system. Crucial issues in the identification of physical systems include the unknown order of the model, the partially or totally unknown statistics of the noise and disturbances affecting data, and the fact that the plant is operating in a closed-loop configuration. To tackle these issues, a number of  schemes designed to (a) attenuate the effect of unknown noise and disturbances (Doraiswami, 2005), (b) reliably select the model order of the identified system (Doraiswami, Cheded, and Khalid, 2010) and (c) identify a plant operating in a closed-loop (Shahab and Doraiswami, 2009) have been developed and are presented here for completeness. The model uncertainty associated with the identified model is itself modeled as additive perturbations in both the plant numerator and the denominator polynomials so as to develop robust controllers using the mixed-sensitivity $H_\infty$ controller design procedure (Kwakernaak, 1993). The mixed-sensitivity $H_\infty$ control design procedure conservatively combines and simultaneously solves both problems of robust stability and robust performance using a single $H_\infty$ norm.

This design procedure is sound, mature, focuses on handling the problem of controller design when the plant model is uncertain, and has been successfully employed in practice in recent years (Cerone, Milanese, and Regruto, 2009), (Tan, Marquez, Chen, and Gooden,

2001). The proposed scheme is extensively tested on both simulated systems and physical laboratory-scale systems namely, a magnetic levitation and two-tank liquid level systems. The key contribution herein is to demonstrate the efficacy of (a) the proposed model order selection criterion to reduce the uncertainty in the plant model structure, a criterion which is simple, verifiable and reliable (b) the two-stage closed-loop identification scheme which ensures quality of the identification performance, and (c) the mixed-sensitivity optimization technique in the $H_\infty$-framework to meet the control objectives of robust performance and robust stability without violating the physical constraints imposed by components such as actuators, and in the face of uncertainties that stem from the identified model employed in the design of the robust controller. It should be noted here that the identified model used in the design of the robust controller is the linearized model of the physical system at some operating point, termed the nominal model.

The chapter is structured as follows. Section 2 discusses the stability and performance of a typical closed-loop system. In Section 3, the robust performance and robust stability problems are considered in the mixed-sensitivity $H_\infty$ framework. Section 4 discusses the problem of designing a robust controller using the identified model with illustrated examples. Section 5 gives a detailed description of the complete identification scheme used to select the model order, identify the plant in a closed-loop configuration and in the presence of unknown noise and disturbances. Finally, in Section 6, evaluations of the designed robust controllers on two-laboratory scale systems are presented.

## 2. Stability and performance of a closed-loop system

An important objective of the control system to ensure that the output of the system tracks a given reference input signal in the face of both noise and disturbances affecting the system, and the plant model uncertainty. A further objective of the control system is to ensure that the performance of the system meets the desired time-domain and frequency-domain specifications such as the rise time, settling time, overshoot, bandwidth, and peak of the magnitude frequency response while respecting the constraints on the control input and other variables. An issue of paramount practical importance facing the control engineer is how to design a controller which will both stabilize the plant when its model is uncertain and ensure that its performance specifications are all met. Put succinctly, we seek a controller that will ensure both stability and performance robustness in the face of model uncertainties. To achieve this dual purpose, we need to first introduce some analytical tools as described next.

### 2.1 Key sensitivity functions

Consider the typical closed-loop system shown in Fig. 1 where $G_0$ is the nominal plant, $C_0$ the controller that stabilizes the nominal plant $G_0$; $r$ and $y$ the reference input, and output, respectively; $d_i$ and $d_0$ the disturbances at the plant input and plant output, respectively, and $v$ the measurement or sensor noise. The nominal model, heretofore referred to as the identified model, represents a mathematical model of a physical plant obtained from physical reasoning and experimental data.

Let $w$ and $z$ be, respectively, a (4x1) input vector comprising $r, d_0$, $d_i$ and $v$, and a (3x1) output vector formed of the plant output $y$, control input $u$, and the tracking error $e$, as given below by:

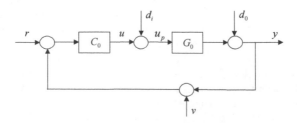

Fig. 1. A typical control system

$$w = \begin{bmatrix} r & d_i & d_0 & v \end{bmatrix}^T \tag{1}$$

$$z = \begin{bmatrix} e & u & y \end{bmatrix}^T \tag{2}$$

The four key closed-loop transfer functions which play a significant role in the stability and performance of a control system are the four sensitivity functions for the nominal plant and nominal controller. They are the system's sensitivity $S_0$, the input-disturbance sensitivity $S_{i0}$, the control sensitivity $S_{u0}$ and the complementary sensitivity $T_0$, given by:

$$S_0 = \frac{1}{1 + G_0 C_0}, \; S_{i0} = \frac{G_0}{1 + G_0 C_0} = S_0 G_0, \; S_{u0} = \frac{C_0}{1 + G_0 C_0} = S_0 C_0, \; T_0 = \frac{G_0 C_0}{1 + G_0 C_0} \tag{3}$$

The performance objective of a control system is to regulate the tracking error $e = r - y$ so that the steady-state tracking error is acceptable and its transient response meets the time- and frequency-domain specifications respecting the physical constraints on the control input so that, for example, the actuator does not get saturated. The output to be regulated, namely $e$ and $u$, are given by:

$$e = S_0(r - d_0) + T_0 v - S_{i0} d_i \tag{4}$$

$$u = S_{u0}(r - v - d_0) - T_0 d_i \tag{5}$$

The transfer matrix relating $w$ to $z$ is then given by:

$$\begin{bmatrix} e \\ u \end{bmatrix} = \begin{bmatrix} S_0 & -S_{i0} & -S_0 & T_0 \\ S_{u0} & -T_0 & -S_{u0} & -S_{u0} \end{bmatrix} \begin{bmatrix} r \\ d_i \\ d_0 \\ v \end{bmatrix} \tag{6}$$

## 2.2 Stability and performance
One cannot reliably assert the stability of the closed-loop by merely analyzing only one of the four sensitivity functions such as the closed-loop transfer function $T_0(s)$ because there may be an implicit pole/zero cancellation process wherein the unstable poles of the plant (or the controller) may be cancelled by the zeros of the controller (or the plant). The cancellation of unstable poles may exhibit unbounded output response in the time domain.

In order to ensure that there is no unstable pole-zero cancellation, a more rigorous definition of stability, termed internal stability, needs to be defined. The closed-loop system is internally stable if and if all the eight transfer function elements of the transfer matrix of Equation (6) are stable. Since there are only four distinct sensitivity functions, $S_0$, $S_{i0}$, $S_{u0}$ and $T_0$, the closed-loop system is therefore internally stable if and only if these four sensitivity functions $S_0$, $S_{i0}$, $S_{u0}$ and $T_0$ are all stable. Since all these sensitivity functions have a common denominator ($1 + G_0 C_0$), the characteristic polynomial $\varphi_0(s)$ of the closed-loop system is:

$$\varphi_0(s) = N_{p0}(s)D_{c0}(s) + D_{p0}(s)N_{c0}(s)$$

(7)

where $N_{p0}(s)$, $D_{p0}(s)$ and $N_{c0}(s)$, $D_{c0}(s)$ are the numerator and the denominator polynomials of $G_0(s)$ and $C_0(s)$, respectively. One may express internal stability in terms of the roots of the characteristic polynomial as follows.

**Lemma 1** (Goodwin, Graeb, and Salgado, 2001): The closed-loop system is internally stable if and only if the roots of $\varphi_0(s)$ all lie in the open left-half of the s-plane.

We will now focus on the performance of the closed-loop system by analyzing the closed-loop transfer matrix given by Equation (6). We will focus on the tracking error $e$ for performance, and the control input $u$ for actuator saturation:

- The tracking error $e$ is small if **(a)** $S_0$ is small in the frequency range where $r$ and $d_0$ are large, **(b)** $S_{u0}$ is small in the frequency range where $d_i$ is large and **(c)** $T_0$ and is small in the frequency range where $v$ is large.
- The control input $u$ is small if **(a)** $S_{u0}$ is small in the frequency range where $r$, $d_0$ and $v$ are large, and **(b)** $T_0$ is small in the frequency range where $d_i$ is large.

Thus the performance requirement must respect the physical constraint that imposes on the control input to be small so that the actuator does not get saturated.

## 3. Robust stability and performance

Model uncertainty stems from the fact that it is very difficult to obtain a mathematical model that can capture completely the behavior of a physical system and which is relevant for the intended application. One may use physical laws to obtain the structure of a mathematical model of a physical system, with the parameters of this model obtained using system identification techniques. However, in practice, the structure as well as the parameters need to be identified from the input-output data as the structure derived from the physical laws may not capture adequately the behavior of the system or, in the extreme case, the physical laws may not be known. The "true" model is a more comprehensive model that contains features not captured by the identified model, and is relevant to the application at hand, such as controller design, fault diagnosis, and condition monitoring. The difference between the nominal and true model is termed as the modeling error which includes the following:

- The structure of the nominal model which differs from that of the true model as a result of our inability to identify features such as high-frequency behavior, fast subsystem dynamics, and approximation of infinite-dimensional system by a finite- dimensional ones.
- Errors in the estimates of the numerator and denominator coefficients, and in the estimate of the time delay

- The deliberate negligence of fast dynamics to simplify sub-systems' models. This will yield a system model that is simple, yet capable enough to capture the relevant features that would facilitate the intended design.

### 3.1 Co-prime factor-based uncertainty model

The numerator-denominator perturbation model considers the perturbation in the numerator and denominator polynomials separately, instead of lumping them together as a single perturbation of the overall transfer function. This perturbation model is useful in applications where an estimate of the model is obtained using system identification methods such as the best least-squares fit between the actual output and its estimate obtained from an assumed mathematical model. Further, an estimate of the perturbation on the numerator and denominator coefficients may be computed from the data matrix and the noise variance. Let $G_0$ and $G$ be respectively the nominal and actual SISO rational transfer functions. The normalized co-prime factorization in this case is given by

$$G_0 = N_0 D_0^{-1}$$
$$G = N D^{-1}$$
(8)

where $N_0$ and $N$ are the numerator polynomials, and both $D_0$ and $D$ the denominator polynomials. In terms of the nominal numerator and denominator polynomials, the transfer function $G$ is given by:

$$G = (N_0 + \Delta_N)(D_0 + \Delta_D)^{-1}$$
(9)

where $\Delta_N$ and $\Delta_D \in RH_\infty$ are respectively the frequency-dependent perturbation in the numerator and denominator polynomials (Kwakernaak, 1993). Fig. 2 shows the closed-loop system driven by a reference input $r$ with a perturbation in the numerator and denominator polynomials. The three relevant signals are expressed in equations (10-12).

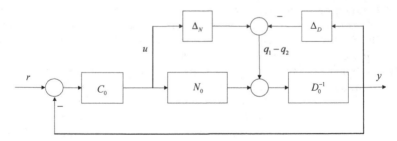

Fig. 2. Co-prime factor-based uncertainty model for a SISO plant

$$u = \frac{C_0}{1 + G_0 C_0} r - \frac{D_0^{-1} C_0}{1 + G_0 C_0} (q_1 - q_2) = S_{u0} r - D_0^{-1} S_{u0} (q_1 - q_2)$$
(10)

$$y = T_0 r + \frac{D_0^{-1}}{1 + G_0 C_0} (q_2 - q_1) = T_0 r + D_0^{-1} S_0 (q_2 - q_1)$$
(11)

$$q_1 - q_2 = \begin{bmatrix} \Delta_N & -\Delta_D \end{bmatrix} \begin{bmatrix} u \\ y \end{bmatrix} \tag{12}$$

## 3.2 Robust stability and performance

Since the reference input does not play any role in the stability robustness, it is set equal to zero and the robust stability model then becomes as given in Fig. 3

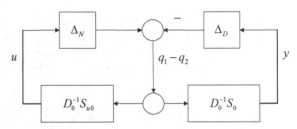

Fig. 3. Stability robustness model with zero reference input

The robust stability of the closed-loop system with plant model uncertainty is established using the small gain theorem.

**Theorem 1:** Assume that $C_0$ internally stabilizes the nominal plant $G_0$. Hence $S_0 \in RH_\infty$ and $S_{u0} \in RH_\infty$. Then the closed-loop system stability problem is well posed and the system is internally stable for all allowable numerator and denominator perturbations, i.e.:

$$\left\| \begin{bmatrix} \Delta_N & \Delta_D \end{bmatrix} \right\| \leq 1 / \gamma_0 \tag{13}$$

If and only if

$$\left\| [S_0 \quad S_{u0}] D_0^{-1} \right\|_\infty < \gamma_0 \tag{14}$$

**Proof:** The SISO robust stability problem considered herein is a special case of the MIMO case proved in (Zhou, Doyle, & Glover, 1996).

Thus to ensure a robustly-stable closed-loop system, the nominal sensitivity $S_0$ should be made small in frequency regions where the denominator uncertainty $\Delta_D$ is large, and the nominal control input sensitivity $S_{u0}$ should be made small in frequency regions where the numerator uncertainty $\Delta_N$ is large.

Our objective here is to design a controller $C_0$ such that robust performance and robust stability of the system are both achieved, that is, both the performance and stability hold for all allowable plant model perturbations $\left\| \begin{bmatrix} \Delta_N & \Delta_D \end{bmatrix} \right\| \leq 1 / \gamma_0$ for some $\gamma_0 > 0$. Besides these requirements, we need also to consider physical constraints on some components such as actuators, for example, that especially place some limitations on the control input. From Theorem 1 and Equation (6), it is clear that the requirements for robust stability, robust performance and control input limitations are inter-related, as explained next:

• Robust performance for tracking with disturbance rejection as well as robust stability in the face of denominator perturbations require a small sensitivity function $S_0$ in the low-frequency region and,

- Control input limitations and robust stability in the face of numerator perturbations require a small control input sensitivity function $S_{u0}$ in the relevant frequency region.

With a view to addressing these requirements, let us select the regulated outputs to be a frequency-weighted tracking error $e_w$, and a weighted control input $u_w$ to meet respectively the requirements of performance, and control input limitations.

$$z_w = \begin{bmatrix} e_w & u_w \end{bmatrix}^T \tag{15}$$

where $z_w$ is a (2x1) vector output to be regulated, $e_w$, and $u_w$ are defined by their respective Fourier transforms: $e_w(j\omega) = e(j\omega)W_S(j\omega)$ and $u_w(j\omega) = u(j\omega)W_u(j\omega)$. The frequency weights involved, $W_S(j\omega)$ and $W_u(j\omega)$, are chosen such that their inverses are the upper bounds of the respective sensitive functions so that weighted sensitive functions become normalized, i.e.:

$$|W_S(j\omega)S_0(j\omega)| \le 1 \,,\, |W_u(j\omega)S_{u0}(j\omega)| \le 1 \tag{16}$$

The map relating the frequency weighted output $z_w$ and the reference input $r$ is shown in Fig. 4:

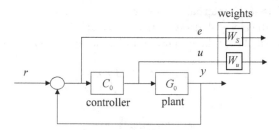

Fig. 4. Nominal closed-loop system relating the reference input and the weighted outputs

The weighting functions $W_s(j\omega)$, and $W_{su}(j\omega)$ provide the tools to specify the trade-off between robust performance and robust stability for a given application. For example, if performance robustness (and stability robustness to the denominator perturbation $\Delta_D$) is more important than the control input limitation, then the weighting function $W_S$ is chosen to be larger in magnitude than $W_{u0}$. On the other hand, to emphasize control input limitation (and stability robustness to the numerator perturbation $\Delta_N$), the weighting function $W_{u0}$ is chosen to be larger in magnitude than $W_S$. For steady-state tracking with disturbance rejection, one may include in the weighting function $W_S$ an approximate but stable 'integrator' by choosing its pole close to zero for continuous-time systems or close to unity for discrete-time systems so as to avoid destabilizing the system (Zhou, Doyle, and Glover, 1996). Let $T_{rz}$ be the nominal transfer matrix (when the plant perturbation $\Delta_0 = 0$) relating the reference input to the frequency-weighted vector output $z_w$, which is a function of $G_0$ and $C_0$, be given by:

$$T_{rz} = D_0^{-1} \begin{bmatrix} \overline{W}_S S_0 & \overline{W}_u S_{u0} \end{bmatrix}^T \tag{17}$$

where $\bar{W}_s = D_0 W_s$ and $\bar{W}_u = D_0 W_u$ so that the $D_0^{-1}$ term appearing in the mixed sensitivity measure $T_{rz}$ is cancelled, thus yielding the following simplified measure $T_{rz} = \begin{bmatrix} W_S S_0 & W_u S_{u0} \end{bmatrix}^T$. The mixed-sensitivity optimization problem for robust performance and stability in the $H_\infty$ – framework is then reduced to finding the controller $C_0$ such that :

$$\left\| T_{rz}\left(C_0, G_0\right) \right\|_\infty \leq \gamma < 1 \tag{18}$$

It is shown in (McFarlane & Glover, 1990) that the minimization of $\left\| T_{rz} \right\|_\infty$ as given by Equation (18), guarantees not only robust stability but also robust performance for all allowable perturbations satisfying $\left\| \begin{bmatrix} \Delta_N & \Delta_D \end{bmatrix} \right\|_\infty \leq 1 / \gamma$.

## 4. $H_\infty$ controller design using the identified model

Consider the problem of designing a controller for an unknown plant G. We will assume however that the system G is linear and admits a rational polynomial model. A number of identification experiments are performed off-line under various operating regimes that includes assumptions on the model and its environment, such as :

- The model order
- The length of the data record
- The type of rich inputs
- Noise statistics
- The plant operates in a closed-loop, thus making the plant input correlated with both the measurement noise and disturbances
- Combinations of any the above

Let $\hat{G}_i$ be the identified model from the $i^{th}$ experiment based on one or more of the above stated assumptions. Let $\hat{C}_i$ be the corresponding controller which stabilizes all the plants in the neighborhood of $\hat{G}_i$ within a ball of radius $1 / \hat{\gamma}_i$. Given an estimate of the plant model $\hat{G}_i$, the controller $\hat{C}_i$ is then designed using the mixed-sensitivity $H_\infty$ optimization scheme , with both the identified model $\hat{G}_i$ and the controller $\hat{C}_i$ based on it, now effectively replacing the nominal plant $G_0$ and nominal controller $C_0$, respectively. Let the controller $\hat{C}_i$ stabilize the identified plant $\hat{G}_i$ for all $\left\| \hat{\Delta}_i \right\|_\infty \leq 1 / \hat{\gamma}_i$ where $\hat{\Delta}_i$ is formed of the perturbations in the numerator and denominator of $\hat{G}_i$. To illustrate the identification-based $H_\infty$-optimization scheme, let us consider the following example. Let the true order of the system G be 2 and assume the noise to be colored. Let $\hat{G}_i : i = 1,2,3$ be the estimates obtained assuming the model order to be 2, 3, and 4, respectively and let the noise be a zero-mean white noise process; $\hat{G}_4$ is obtained assuming the model order to be 2, the noise to be colored but the input not to be rich enough; Let $\hat{G}_5$ be an estimate based on correct assumptions regarding model order, noise statistics, richness of excitation of the input and other factors as pointed out above. Clearly the true plant G may not be in the neighborhood of $\hat{G}_i$, i.e. $G \notin \hat{S}_i$ for all $i \neq 5$ where

$$\hat{S}_i = \left\{ \hat{G}_i : \left\| \hat{\Delta}_i \right\|_\infty \leq 1 / \hat{\gamma}_i \right\} \tag{19}$$

The set $\hat{S}_i$ is a ball of radius $(1 / \hat{\gamma}_i)$ centered at $\hat{G}_i$. Fig. 5 below shows the results of performing a number of experiments under different assumptions on the model order, types of rich inputs, length of the data record, noise statistics and their combinations. The true plant $G$, its estimates $\hat{G}_i$ and the set $\hat{S}_i$ are all indicated by a circle of radius $(1/\hat{\gamma}_i)$ centered at $\hat{G}_i$ in Figure 5. The true plant $G$ is located at the center of the set $\hat{S}_5$.

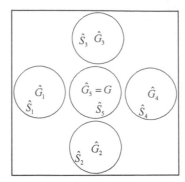

Fig. 5. The set $\hat{S}_i$ is a ball of radius $1/\hat{\gamma}_i$ centered at $\hat{G}_i$

### 4.1 Illustrative example: $H_\infty$ controller design

A plant is first identified and then the identified model is employed in designing an $H_\infty$ controller using the mixed sensitivity performance measure. As discrete-time models and digital controllers are commonly used in system identification and controller implementation, a discrete-time equivalent of the continuous plant is used here to design a discrete-time $H_\infty$ controller. The plant model is given by:

$$G_0(z) = \frac{0.5335\left(1 - z^{-1}\right)}{1 - 0.7859z^{-1} + 0.3679z^{-2}} \qquad (20)$$

The weighting function for the sensitivity and control input sensitivity functions were chosen to be $W_s = \dfrac{0.01}{1 - 0.99z^{-1}}$, $W_u = 0.1$. The weighting function for the sensitivity is chosen to have a pole close to the unit circle to ensure an acceptable small steady-state error. The controller will have a pole at 0.99 approximating a stable integrator. The plant is identified for **(a)** different choices of model orders ranging from 1 to 10 when the true order is 2, and **(b)** different values of the standard deviation of the colored measurement noise $\sigma_v$. Fig. 6 shows the step and the magnitude response of the sensitivity function. The closed-loop system is unstable when the selected order is 1 and for some realizations of the noise, and hence these cases are not included in the figures shown here. When the model order is selected to be less than the true order, in this case 1, and when the measurement noise's standard deviation $\sigma_v$ is large, the set of identified models does not contain the true model. Consequently the closed-loop system will be unstable.

**Comments:** The robust performance and the stability of the closed-loop system depend upon the accuracy of the identified model. One cannot simply rely on the robustness of the $H_\infty$ controller to absorb the model uncertainties. The simulation results clearly show that the model error stems from an improper selection of the model order and the Signal-to-Noise Ratio (SNR) of the input-output data. The simulation results show that there is a need for an appropriate identification scheme to handle colored noise and model order selection to ensure a more robust performance and stability.

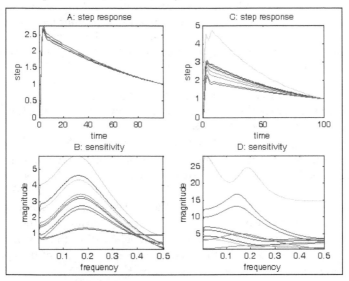

Fig. 6. Figures A and B on the left show the Step responses (top) and Magnitude responses of sensitivity (bottom) when the model order is varied from 2 to 10 when the noise standard deviation is $\sigma_v = 0.001$. Similarly figures C and D on the right-hand show when the noise standard deviation $\sigma_v$ is varied in the range $\sigma_v \in [0.02\ 0.11]$.

## 5. Identification of the plant

The physical system is in general complex, high-order and nonlinear and therefore an assumed linear mathematical model of such a system is at best an approximation of the 'true model'. Nevertheless a mathematical model linearized at a given operating point can be identified and the identified model successfully used in the design of the required controller, as explained below. Some key issues in the identification of a physical system include (a) the unknown statistics of the noise and disturbance affecting the input-output data (b) the proper selection of an appropriate structure of the mathematical model, especially its order and (c) the plants operating in a closed-loop configuration.

For the case (a) a two-stage identification scheme, originally proposed in (Doraiswami, 2005) is employed here. First a high-order model is selected so as to capture both the system dynamics and any artifacts (from noise or other sources). Then, in the second stage, lower-order models are derived from the estimated high-order model using a frequency-weighted estimation scheme. To handle the model order selection, and the identification of the plant, especially an unstable one, approaches proposed in (Doraiswami, Cheded, and Khalid, 2010) and (Shahab and Doraiswami, 2009) are employed respectively.

### 5.1 Model order selection

For mathematical tractability, the well-known criteria based on information-theoretic criteria such as the famous Akaike Information Criterion (Stoica and Selen, 2004), when applied to a physical system, may require simplified assumptions such as long and uncorrelated data records, linearized models and a Gaussian probability distribution function (PDF) of the residuals. Because of these simplifying assumptions, the resulting criteria may not always give the correct model order. Generally, the estimated model order may be large due to the presence of artifacts arising from noise, nonlinearities, and pole-zero cancellation effects. The proposed model order selection scheme consists of selecting only the set of models, which are identified using the scheme proposed in (Doraiswami, 2005), and for which all the poles are in the right-half plane (Doraiswami, Cheded, and Khalid, 2010). The remaining identified models are not selected as they consist of extraneous poles.

**Proposed Criterion:** The model order selection criterion hinges on the following Lemma established in (Doraiswami, Cheded, and Khalid, 2010).

**Lemma:** If the sampling frequency is chosen in the range $2f_c \leq f_s < 4f_c$ , then the complex-conjugate poles of the equivalent discrete-time equivalent of a continuous-time system will all lie on the right-half of the z-plane, whereas the real ones will all lie on the positive real line.

This shows that the discrete-time poles lie on the right-half of the z-plane if the sampling rate ( $f_s$ ) is more than twice the Nyquist rate ( $2f_c$ ). Thus, to ensure that the system poles are located on the right-half and the noise poles on the left-half of the z-plane, the sampling rate $f_s$ must be larger than four times the maximum frequency $f^s_{max}$ of the system, and less than four times the minimum frequency of the noise, $f^v_{min}$ .

$$4f^s_{max} \leq f_s < 4f^v_{min} \tag{21}$$

### 5.2 Identification of a plant operating in closed loop

In practice, and for a variety of reasons (for e.g. analysis, design and control), it is often necessary to identify a system that must operate in a closed-loop fashion under some type of feedback control. These reasons could also include safety issues, the need to stabilize an unstable plant and / or improve its performance while avoiding the cost incurred through downtime if the plant were to be taken offline for test. In these cases, it is therefore necessary to perform closed-loop identification. There are three basic approaches to closed-loop identification, namely a direct, an indirect and a two-stage one. A direct approach to identifying a plant in a closed-loop identification scheme using the plant input and output data is fraught with difficulties due to the presence of unknown and generally inaccessible noise, the complexity of the model or a combination of both. Although computationally simple, this approach can lead to parameter estimates that may be biased due mainly to the correlation between the input and the noise, unless the noise model is accurately represented or the signal-to-noise ratio is high (Raol, Girija, & Singh, 2004). The conventional indirect approach is based on identifying the closed-loop system using the reference input and the system (plant) output. Given an estimate of the system open-loop transfer function, an estimate of the closed-loop transfer function can be obtained from the algebraic relationship between the system's open-loop and closed-loop transfer functions. The desired plant transfer function can then be deduced from the estimated closed-loop transfer function. However, the derivation of the plant transfer function from the closed-loop transfer function may itself be prone to errors due to inaccuracies in the model of the subsystem connected in cascade with the plant. The two-stage approach, itself a form of an indirect method, is based on first identifying the sensitivity and the complementary sensitivity functions using a subspace Multi-Input, Multi-Output (MIMO) identification scheme (Shahab & Doraiswami, 2009). In the second stage, the plant transfer function is obtained from the estimates of the plant input and output generated by the first stage.

## 5.2.1 Two-stage identification

In the first stage, the sensitivity function $S(z)$ and the complementary sensitivity functions $T(z)$ are estimated using all the three available measurements, namely the reference input, $r$, plant input, $u$ and the plant output, $y$ , to ensure that the estimates are reliable. In other words, a Multiple-Input, Multiple-Output (MIMO) identification scheme with one input (the reference input $r$), and two outputs (the plant input $u$ and the plant output $y$) is used here rather than a Single-Input, Single-Output (SISO) scheme using one input $u$ and one output $y$. The MIMO identification scheme is based on minimizing the performance measure, $J$, as:

$$\min_{\hat{z}} J = \|z - \hat{z}\|^2 \tag{22}$$

where $z = \begin{bmatrix} y & u \end{bmatrix}^T$ and $\hat{z} = \begin{bmatrix} \hat{y} & \hat{u} \end{bmatrix}^T$ , $\hat{u}$ is the estimated plant input and $\hat{y}$ is the estimated plant output. The plant input $u$, and the plant output $y$ are related to the reference input $r$ and the disturbance $w$ by:

$$u(z) = S(z)r(z) + S(z)w(z) \tag{23}$$

$$y(z) = T(z)r(z) + T(z)w(z) + v(z) \tag{24}$$

As pointed out earlier, the proposed MIMO identification scheme will ensure that the estimates of the sensitivity and the complementary sensitivity functions are consistent (i.e. they have identical denominators), and hence will also ensure that the estimates of the plant input $u$ and the plant output $y$ , which are both employed in the second stage, are reliable. Note here that the reference signal $r$ is uncorrelated with the measurement noise $w$ and the disturbance $v$, unlike in the case where the plant is identified using the direct approach. This is the main reason for using the MIMO scheme in the first stage. In the second stage, the plant $G(z)$ is identified from the estimated plant input, $\hat{u}$ , and plant output, $\hat{y}$ , obtained from the stage 1 identification scheme, i.e.:

$$\hat{u}(z) = \hat{S}(z)r(z) \tag{25}$$

$$\hat{y}(z) = \hat{T}(z)r(z) \tag{26}$$

Note that here the input $\hat{u}$ and the output $\hat{y}$ are not correlated with the noise $w$ and disturbance term $v$. Treating $\hat{u}$ as the input and $\hat{y}$ as the output of the plant, and $\hat{\hat{y}}$ as the estimate of the plant output estimate, $\hat{y}$ , the identification scheme is based on minimizing the weighted frequency-domain performance measure

$$\min_{\hat{y},} \left\| W(j\omega)\left(\hat{y}(j\omega) - \hat{\hat{y}}(j\omega)\right) \right\|^2 \tag{27}$$

where $W(j\omega)$ is the weighting function. Furthermore, it is shown that:

**Lemma:** If the closed-loop system is stable, then

*   The unstable poles of the plant must be cancelled exactly by the zeros of the sensitivity function if the reference input is bounded.
*   The zeros of the plants form a subset of the zeros of the complementary transfer function

This provides a cross-checking of the estimates of the poles and the zeros of the plant estimated in the second stage with the zeros of the sensitivity and complementary functions in the first stage, respectively.

## 6.1 Evaluation on a physical system: magnetic levitation system (MAGLEV)

The physical system is a feedback magnetic levitation system (MAGLEV) (Galvao, Yoneyama, Marajo, & Machado, 2003). Identification and control of the magnetic levitation system has been a subject of research in recent times in view of its applications to transportation systems, magnetic bearings used to eliminate friction, magnetically-levitated micro robot systems, magnetic levitation-based automotive engine valves. It poses a challenge for both identification and controller design.

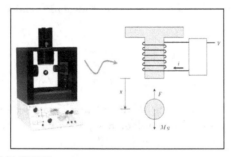

Fig. 7. Laboratory-scale MAGLEV system

The model of the MAGLEV system, shown in Fig. 7, is unstable, nonlinear and is modeled by:

$$\frac{y(s)}{u(s)} = \frac{\beta}{s^2 - \alpha} \tag{28}$$

where $y$ is the position, and $u$ the voltage input. The poles, $p$, of the plant are real and are symmetrically located about the imaginary axis, i.e.: $p = \pm\sqrt{\alpha}$ . The linearized model of the system was identified in a closed-loop configuration using LABVIEW data captured through both A/D and D/A devices. Being unstable, the plant was identified in a closed-loop configuration using a controller which was a lead compensator. The reference input was a rich persistently-exciting signal consisting of a random binary sequence. An appropriate sampling frequency was determined by analyzing the input-output data for different choices of the sampling frequencies. A sampling frequency of 5msec was found to be the best as it proved to be sufficiently small to capture the dynamics of the system but not the noise artifacts. The physical system was identified using the proposed two-stage MIMO identification scheme. First, the sensitivity and complementary sensitivity functions of the closed-loop system were identified. The estimated plant input and output were employed in the second stage to estimate the plant model. The model order for identification was selected to be second order using the proposed scheme. Figure 8 below gives the pole-zero maps of both the plant and the sensitivity function on the left-hand side, and, on the right-hand side, the comparison between the frequency response of the identified model $\hat{G}(j\omega)$, obtained through non-parametric identification, i.e. estimated by injecting various sinusoidal inputs of different frequencies applied to the system, and the estimate of the transfer function obtained using the proposed scheme.

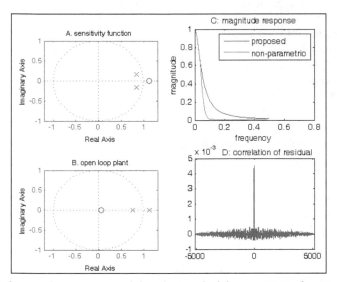

Fig. 8. A and B show pole-zero maps of the plant and of the sensitivity function (left) while C and D (right) show the comparison of the frequency response of the identified model with the non-parametric model estimate, and the correlation of the residual, respectively

The nominal closed-loop input sensitivity function was identified as:

$$S_0(z) = \frac{1.7124\,z^{-1}\left(1 - 1.116z^{-1}\right)}{1 - 1.7076z^{-1} + 0.7533z^{-2}} \tag{29}$$

and the nominal plant model as:

$$G_0(z) = \frac{N_0}{D_0} = \frac{0.0582z^{-1}\left(1 - 0.0687z^{-1}\right)}{\left(1 - 1.116z^{-1}\right)\left(1 - 0.7578z^{-1}\right)} \tag{30}$$

### 6.1.1 Model validation
The identified model was validated using the following criteria:
- The proposed model-order selection was employed. The identifications in stages I and II were performed for orders ranging from 1 to 4. A second-order model was selected in both stages since all the poles of the identified model were located in the right-half of

the z-plane. Note here that the dynamics of the actuator (electrical subsystem) was not captured by the model as it is very fast compared to that of the mechanical subsystem.

- A 4th order model was employed in stage I to estimate the plant input and the output for the subsequent stage II identification.

- The plant has one stable pole located at 0.7580 and one unstable pole at 1.1158. The reciprocity condition is not exactly satisfied as, theoretically, the stable pole should be at 0.8962 and not at 0.7580.

- The zeros of the sensitivity function contain the unstable pole of the plant, i.e. the unstable pole of the plant located at 1.1158 is a zero of the sensitivity function.

- The frequency responses of the plant, computed using two entirely different approaches, should be close to each other. In this case, a non-parametric approach was employed and compared to the frequency response obtained using the proposed model-based scheme, as shown on the right-hand side of Fig. 8. The non-parametric approach gives an inaccurate estimate at high frequencies due to correlation between the plant input and the noise.

- The residual is zero mean white noise with very small variance.

### 6.1.2 $H_\infty$ Mixed sensitivity $H_\infty$ controller design

The weighting functions are selected by giving more emphasis on robust stability and less on robust performance: $W_s(j\omega) = 0.001$ and $W_u(j\omega) = 0.1$. To improve the robustness of the closed-loop system, a feed-forward control of the reference input is used, instead of the inclusion of an integrator in the controller. The $H_\infty$ controller is given by:

$$C_0(z) = \frac{2.5734\left(1+1.113z^{-1}\right)\left(1-0.7578z^{-1}\right)}{\left(1-0.2044z^{-1}\right)\left(1+0.7457z^{-1}\right)} \tag{31}$$

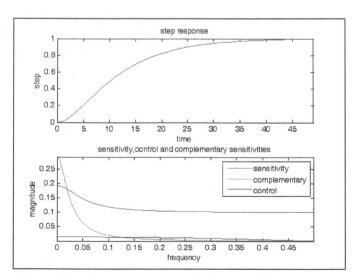

Fig. 9. The step and frequency responses of the closed-loop system with $H_\infty$ controller

It is interesting to note here that there is a pole-zero cancelation between the nominal plant and the controller since a plant pole and a controller zero are both equal to 0.7578. In this case, the $H_\infty$ norm is $\gamma = 0.1513$ and hence the performance and stability measure is $\left\|\begin{bmatrix} W_S S_0 & W_u S_{u0} \end{bmatrix}\right\|_\infty = \gamma = 0.1513$ with $\left\|\begin{bmatrix} \Delta_N & \Delta_D \end{bmatrix}\right\|_\infty \leq 1/\gamma = 6.6087$. The step response and magnitude responses of the weighted sensitivity, complementary sensitivity and the control input sensitivity of the closed-loop control system are all shown above in Fig. 9.

### 6.2 Evaluation on a physical sensor network: a two-tank liquid level system

The physical system under evaluation here is formed of two tanks connected by a pipe. A dc motor-driven pump supplies fluid to the first tank and a PI controller is used to control the fluid level in the second tank by maintaining the liquid height at a specified level, as shown in Fig. 10. This system is a cascade connection of a dc motor and a pump relating the input to the motor, $u$, and the flow $Q_i$. It is expressed by the following first-order time-delay system:

$$\dot{Q}_i = -a_m Q_i + b_m \phi(u) \tag{32}$$

where $a_m$ and $b_m$ are the parameters of the motor-pump subsystem and $\phi(u)$ is a dead-band and saturation-type of nonlinearity. The Proportional and Integral (PI) controller is given by:

$$\begin{aligned} \dot{x}_3 &= e = r - h_2 \\ u &= k_p e + k_I x_3 \end{aligned} \tag{33}$$

where $k_p$ and $k_I$ are the PI controller's gains and $r$ is the reference input.

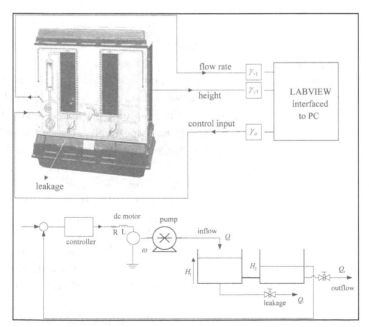

Fig. 10. Two-tank liquid level system

With the inclusion of the leakage, the liquid level system is now modeled by :

$$A_1 \frac{dH_1}{dt} = Q_i - C_{12}\varphi(H_1 - H_2) - C_\ell\varphi(H_1)$$

$$A_2 \frac{dH_2}{dt} = C_{12}\varphi(H_1 - H_2) - C_0\varphi(H_2)$$

(34)

where $\varphi(.) = sign(.)\sqrt{2g(.)}$, $Q_\ell = C_\ell\varphi(H_1)$ is the leakage flow rate, $Q_0 = C_0\varphi(H_2)$ is the output flow rate, $H_1$ is the height of the liquid in tank 1, $H_2$ the height of the liquid in tank 2, $A_1$ and $A_2$ the cross-sectional areas of the 2 tanks, g=980 $cm/sec^2$ the gravitational constant, and $C_{12}$ and $C_o$ the discharge coefficients of the inter-tank and output valves, respectively. The linearized model of the entire system formed by the motor, pump, and the tanks is given by:

$$\dot{x} = Ax + Br$$

$$y = Cx$$

(35)

where x, A, B and C are given by:

$$x = \begin{bmatrix} h_1 \\ h_2 \\ x_3 \\ q_i \end{bmatrix}, A = \begin{bmatrix} -a_1 - \alpha & a_1 & 0 & b_1 \\ a_2 & -a_2 - \beta & 0 & 0 \\ -1 & 0 & 0 & 0 \\ -b_m k_p & 0 & b_m k_I & -a_m \end{bmatrix}, B = \begin{bmatrix} 0 & 0 & 1 & b_m k_p \end{bmatrix}^T, C = \begin{bmatrix} 1 & 0 & 0 & 0 \end{bmatrix}$$

$q_i$, $q_\ell$, $q_0$, $h_1$ and $h_2$ are respectively the increments in $Q_i$, $Q_\ell$, $Q_o$, $H_1^0$ and $H_2^0$, whereas $a_1$, $a_2$, $\alpha$ and $\beta$ are parameters associated with the linearization process, $\alpha$ is the leakage flow rate, $q_\ell = \alpha h_1$, and $\beta$ is the output flow rate, and $q_o = \beta h_2$. The dual-tank fluid system structure can be cast into that of an interconnected system with a sensor network, composed of 3 subsystems $G_{eu}$, $G_{uq}$, and $G_{qh}$ relating the measured signals, namely the error $e$, control input $u$, flow rate $Q$ and the height $h$, respectively. The proposed two-stage identification scheme is employed to identify these subsystems. It consists of the following two stages:

- In Stage 1, the MIMO closed-loop system is identified using data formed of the reference input $r$, and the subsystems' outputs measured by the 3 available sensors.
- In Stage 2, the subsystems $G_{eu}$ $G_{uq}$, and $G_{qh}$ are then identified using the subsystem's estimated input and output measurements obtained from the first stage.

Figure 11 shows the estimation of the 4 key signals $e$, $u$, $Q$ and $h$ in our two-tank experiment, that are involved in the MIMO transfer function in stage I identification. Stage I identification yields the following MIMO closed-loop transfer function given by:

$$\begin{bmatrix} \hat{e}(z) & \hat{u}(z) & \hat{f}(z) & \hat{h}(z) \end{bmatrix}^T = D^{-1}(z)N(z)r(z)$$

(36)

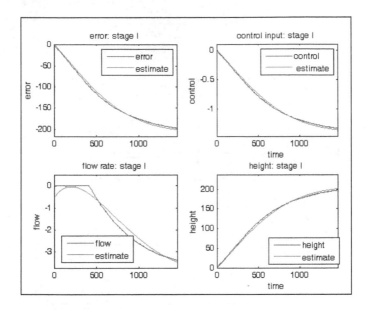

Fig. 11. (Left) The error and flow rate and their estimates and (Right) the control input and height and their estimates.

$$
\text{where } N = \begin{bmatrix}
1.9927 & -191.5216z^{-1} & 380.4066z^{-2} & -190.8783z^{-3} \\
0.0067 & -1.2751z^{-1} & 2.5526z^{-2} & -1.2842z^{-3} \\
-183.5624 & 472.5772z^{-1} & -394.4963z^{-2} & 105.4815z^{-3} \\
-0.9927 & 189.1386z^{-1} & -378.6386z^{-2} & 190.4933z^{-3}
\end{bmatrix}
$$

$$D = 1.0000 \quad - \quad 2.3830z^{-1} \quad + 1.7680z^{-2} \quad - \quad 0.3850z^{-3}$$

The zeros of the sensitivity function, relating the reference input $r$ to the error $e$, are located at 1.02 and 1.0.

Fig. 12 below shows the combined plots of the actual values of the height, flow rate and control input, and their estimates from both stages 1 and 2. From this figure, we can conclude that the results are on the whole excellent, especially for both the height and control input.

Stage II identification yields the following three open-loop transfer functions that are identified using their respective input/output estimates generated by the stage-1 identification process:

$$\hat{G}_{eu}(z) = \frac{u(z)}{e(z)} = 0.0067 + \frac{0.4576z^{-1}}{1 - z^{-1}} \tag{37}$$

$$G_{uq}(z) = \frac{Q(z)}{u(z)} = \frac{0.0104z^{-1}}{1 - 0.9968z^{-1}} \tag{38}$$

$$G_{qh}(z) = \frac{h(z)}{Q(z)} = \frac{0.7856z^{-1}}{1 - 1.0039z^{-1}} \tag{39}$$

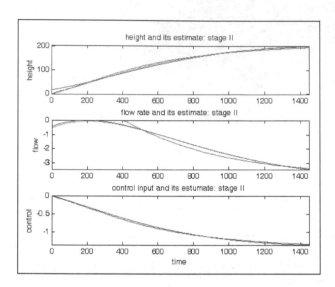

Fig. 12. The actual height (in blue), its estimate from stage 1(in green) and its estimate from stage 2 (in red). Similarly for the flow rate and the control input

**Comments:**

- The two-tank level system is highly nonlinear as can be clearly seen especially from the flow rate profile located at the top right corner of Fig. 11. There is a saturation-type nonlinearity involved in the flow process.

- The subsystems $G_{eu}$ and $G_{qh}$ representing respectively the PI controller and the transfer function relating the flow rate to the tank height are both unstable with a pole at unity representing an integral action. The estimated transfer functions $\hat{G}_{eu}$ and $\hat{G}_{qh}$ have captured these unstable poles. Although the pole of $\hat{G}_{eu}$ is exactly equal to unity, the pole of $\hat{G}_{qh}$, located at 1.0039, is very close to unity. This slight deviation from unity may be due to the nonlinearity effects on the flow rate

- The zeros of the sensitivity function have captured the unstable poles of the open- loop unstable plant with some error. The values of the zeros of the sensitivity function are 1.0178, and 1.0002 while those of the subsystem poles are 1 and 1.0039.

### 6.2.1 Mixed-sensitivity $H_{\infty}$ controller design

The identified plant is the cascade combination of the motor, pump and the two tanks, which is essentially the forward path transfer function formed of the cascade combinations of $G_{uq}$ and $G_{qh}$ , that relates the control input $u$ to the tank height $h$ , and which is given by:

$$G_0(z) = \frac{N_0(z)}{D_0(z)} = \frac{z^{-2}}{1 - 1.997z^{-1} + 0.9968z^{-2}} \tag{40}$$

The weighting functions are selected by giving more emphasis on robust stability and less on robust performance: $W_s(z) = \left[0.01 / \left(1 - 0.99z^{-1}\right)\right]$ and $W_u(z) = 1$ where $z = e^{j\omega}$. The $H_\infty$ controller is then given by:

$$C_0(z) = \frac{0.044029(1 + z^{-1})(1 - 1.98z^{-1} + 0.9804z^{-2})}{(1 - 0.99z^{-1})(1 - 0.6093z^{-1})(1 + 0.6008z^{-2})} \tag{41}$$

The controller has an approximate integral action for steady-state tracking with disturbance rejection and a pole at 0.99 which is very close to unity. In this case, the $H_\infty$ norm is $\gamma = 0.0663$. The step response and the magnitude responses of the sensitivity, complementary sensitivity and the control input sensitivity of the closed-loop control system are all shown in Fig. 13.

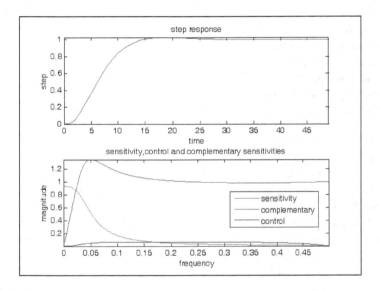

Fig. 13. Step and magnitude freq. res1ponses of the closed-loop system with $H_\infty$ controller

### 6.2.2 Remarks on the mixed-sensitivity $H_\infty$ control design

The sensitivity is low in the low frequency regions where the denominator perturbations are large, the control sensitivity is small in the high frequency regions of the numerator perturbations, and the complementary sensitivity is low in the high frequency region where the overall multiplicative model perturbations are high. As the robustness is related to performance, this will ensure robust performance for steady-state tracking with disturbance rejection, controller input limitations and measurement noise attenuation. When tight performance bounds are specified, the controller will react strongly but may be unstable when implemented on the actual physical plant. For safety reasons, the controller design is started with very loose performance bounds, resulting in a controller with very small gains to ensure stability of the controller on the actual plant. Then, the performance bounds are made tighter to gradually increase the performance of the controller. The design method based on the mixed-sensitivity criterion generalizes some classical control design techniques such as the classical loop-shaping technique, integral control to ensure tracking, performance and specified high frequency roll-off, and direct control over the closed-loop bandwidth and time response by means of pole placement.

## 7. Conclusion

This chapter illustrates, through analysis, simulation and practical evaluation, how the two key objectives of control system design, namely robust stability and robust performance, can be achieved. Specifically, it shows that in order to ensure both robust performance and robust stability of a closed-loop system where the controller is designed based on an identified model of the plant, it is then of paramount importance that both the identification scheme as well as the controller design strategy be selected appropriately, as the tightness of the achieved robustness bound depends on the magnitude of the modeling error produced by the selected identification scheme. In view of this close dependence, a comprehensive closed-loop identification scheme was proposed here that greatly mitigates the effects of measurement noise and disturbances and relies on a novel model order selection scheme. More specifically, the proposed identification consists of (a) a two-stage scheme to overcome the unknown noise and disturbance by first obtaining a high-order model, and then deriving from it a reduced-order model, (b) a novel model-order selection criterion based on verifying the location of the poles and (c) a two-stage scheme to identify first the closed-loop transfer functions of subsystems, and then obtain the plant model using the estimates on the input and output from the first stage. The controller design was based on the well-known mixed-sensitivity $H_\infty$ controller design technique that achieves simultaneously robust stability and robust performance. This technique is able to handle plant uncertainties modeled as additive perturbations in the numerator and denominator of the identified model, and provides tools to achieve a trade-off between robust stability, robust performance and control input limitations. The identification and controller design were both successfully evaluated on a number of simulated as well practical physical systems including the laboratory-scale unstable magnetic levitation and two-tank liquid level systems. This study has provided us with ample encouragement to replicate the use of the powerful techniques used in this chapter, on different systems and to enrich the overall approach with other identification and robust controller design.

## 8. Acknowledgement

The authors acknowledge the support of the department of Electrical and Computer Engineering, University of New Brunswick, the National Science and Engineering Research

Council (NSERC) of Canada , and the King Fahd University of Petroleum and Minerals (KFUPM), Dhahran 31261, Saudi Arabia

## 9. References

Cerone, V., Milanese, M., & Regruto, D. (2009, September). Yaw Stability Control Design Through Mixed Sensitivity Approach. *IEEE Transactions on Control Systems Technology, 17*(5), 1096-1104.

Doraiswami, R. (2005). A two-stage Identification with Application to Control, Feature Extraction, and Spectral Estimation. *IEE Proceedings: Control Theory and Applications, 152*(4), 379-386.

Doraiswami, R., Cheded, L., & Khalid, H. M. (2010). Model Order Selection Criterion with Applications to Physical Systems. Toronto, Canada: Conference on Automation Science and Engineering, CASE 2010.

Doraiswami, R., Cheded, L., Khalid, H. M., Qadeer, A., & Khoki, A. (2010). Robust Control of a Closed Loop Identified System with Parameteric Model Uncertainties and External Disturbances. *International Conference on Systems, Modelling and Simulations.* Liverpool, U.K.

Galvao, R., Yoneyama, T., Marajo, F., & Machado, R. (2003). A Simple Technique for Identifying a Linearized Model for a Didactic Magnetic Levitatiom System. *IEEE Transactions on Education, 46*(1), 22-25.

Goodwin, G. C., Graeb, S. F., & Salgado, M. E. (2001). *Control System Design.* New Jersey, USA: Prentice Hall.

Kwakernaak, H. (1993). Robust Control and H-inf Optimization:tutorial paper. *Automatica, 29*(2), 255-273.

Ljung, L. (1999). *System Identification: Theory for the User.* New Jersey: Prentice-Hall.

McFarlane, D., & Glover, K. (1990). *Robust Controller Design using Normalized Coprime Factor Plant Descriptions.* New York: Springer-Verlag.

Mendel, J. (1995). *Lessons in Estimation Theory in Signal Processing, Communications and Control.* Prentice-Hall.

Pintelon, R., & Schoukens, J. (2001). *System Identification: A Frequency Domain Approach.* New Jersey: IEEE Press.

Raol, J., Girija, G., & Singh, J. (2004). *Modeling and Parameter Estimation.* IEE Control Engineering Series 65, Instituition of Electrical Engineers.

Shahab, M., & Doraiswami, R. (2009). A Novel Two-Stage Identification of Unstable Systems. *Seventh International Conference on Control and Automation (ICCA 2010).* Christ Church, New Zealand.

Skogestad, S., & Poslethwaite, I. (1996). *Multivariable Feedback Control Analysis and Design.* New York, USA: John Wiley and Sons.

Stoica, P., & Selen, Y. S. (2004). Model-Order Selection: A review of Information Criterion Rules. *IEEE Signal Processing Magazine,* 36-47.

Tan, W., Marquez, H. J., Chen, T., & Gooden, R. ( 2001). H infinity Control Design for Industrial Boiler. *Proceedings of The American Control Conference,* (pp. 2537-2542). Viginia, USA.

Zhou, K., Doyle, J., & Glover, K. (1996). *Robust Optimal Control*. New Jersey, USA: Prentice-
Hall.

# 9

# Robust Control of Nonlinear Systems with Hysteresis Based on Play-Like Operators

Jun Fu[1], Wen-Fang Xie[1], Shao-Ping Wang[2] and Ying Jin[3]
*[1]The Department of Mechanical & Industrial Engineering*
*Concordia University*
*[2]The Department of Mechatronic Control, Beihang University*
*[3]State Key Laboratory of Integrated Automation of*
*Process Industry, Northeastern University*
*[1]Canada*
*[2,3]China*

## 1. Introduction

Hysteresis phenomenon occurs in all smart material-based sensors and actuators, such as shape memory alloys, piezoceramics and magnetostrictive actuators (Su, et al, 2000; Fu, et al, 2007; Banks & Smith, 2000; Tan & Baras, 2004). When the hysteresis nonlinearity precedes a system plant, the nonlinearity usually causes the overall closed-loop systems to exhibit inaccuracies or oscillations, even leading to instability (Tao & Kokotovic, 1995). This fact often makes the traditional control methods insufficient for precision requirement and even not be able to guarantee the basic requirement of system stability owing to the non-smooth and multi-value nonlinearities of the hysteresis (Tao & Levis, 2001). Hence the control of nonlinear systems in presence of hysteresis nonlinearities is difficult and challenging (Fu, et al, 2007; Tan & Baras, 2004).

Generally there are two ways to mitigate the effects of hysteresis. One is to construct an inverse operator of the considered hysteresis model to perform inversion compensation (Tan & Baras, 2004; Tao & Kokotovic, 1995; Tao & Levis, 2001). The other is, without necessarily constructing an inverse, to fuse a suitable hysteresis model with available robust control techniques to mitigate the hysteretic effects (Su, et al, 2000; Fu, et al, 2007; Zhou, et al, 2004; Wen & Zhou, 2007). The inversion compensation was pioneered in (Tao & Kokotovic, 1995) and there are some other important results in (Tan & Baras, 2005; Iyer, et al, 2005; Tan & Bennani, 2008). However, most of these results were achieved only at actuator component level without allowing for the overall dynamic systems with actuator hysteresis nonlinearities. Essentially, constructing inverse operator relies on the phenomenological model (such as Preisach models) and influences strongly the practical application of the design concept (Su, et al, 2000). Because of multi-valued and non-smoothness feature of hysteresis, those methods are often complicated, computationally costly and possess strong sensitivity of the model parameters to unknown measurement errors. These issues are directly linked to the difficulties of guaranteeing the stability of systems except for certain special cases (Tao & Kokotovic, 1995). For the methods to mitigate hysteretic effects without constructing the inverse, there are two main challenges involved in this idea. One challenge is that very few hysteresis models are suitable to be fused with available robust adaptive control techniques. And the other is how to fuse the suitable hysteresis model with available control techniques to guarantee the stability of the dynamics systems (Su, et al, 2000). Hence it is usually difficult to construct new suitable hysteresis models to be fused into control plants, and to explore new control techniques to mitigate the effects of hysteresis and to ensure the system stability, without necessarily constructing the hysteresis inverse.

Noticing the above challenges, we first construct a hysteresis model using play-like operators, in a similar way to L. Prandtl's construction of the Prandtl-Ishilinskii model using play operators (Brokate & Sprekels, 1996), and thus name it Prandtl-Ishilinskii-Like model. Because the play-like operator in (Ekanayake & Iyer, 2008) is a generalization of the backlash-like operator in (Su, et al, 2000), the Prandtl-Ishilinskii-Like model is a subclass of SSSL-PKP hysteresis model (Ekanayake & Iyer, 2008). Then, the development of two robust adaptive control schemes to mitigate the hysteresis avoids constructing a hysteresis inverse. The new methods not only can perform global stabilization and tracking tasks of the dynamic nonlinear systems, but also can derive transient performance in terms of $L_2$ norm of tracking error as an explicit function of design parameters, which allows designers to meet the desired performance requirement by tuning the design parameters in an explicit way.

The main contributions in this chapter are highlighted as follows:

i.    A new hysteresis model is constructed, where the play-like operators developed in (Ekanayake & Iyer, 2008) play a role of building blocks. From a standpoint of categories of hysteresis models, this class of hysteresis models is a subclass of SSSL-PKP hysteresis models. It provides a possibility to mitigate the effects of hysteresis without necessarily constructing an inverse, which is the unique feature of this subclass model identified from the SSSL-PKP hysteresis model of general class in the literature;

ii.   A challenge is addressed to fuse a suitable hysteresis model with available robust adaptive techniques to mitigate the effects of hysteresis without constructing a complicated inverse operator of the hysteresis model;

iii.  Two backstepping schemes are proposed to accomplish robust adaptive control tasks for a class of nonlinear systems preceded by the Prandtl-Ishilinskii-Like models. Such control schemes not only ensure the stabilization and tracking of the hysteretic dynamic nonlinear systems, but also derive the transient performance in terms of $L_2$ norm of tracking error as an explicit function of design parameters.

The organization of this chapter is as follows. Section 2 gives the problem statement. In Section 3, we will construct Prandtl-Ishlinshii-Like model and explore its properties. The details about two control schemes for the nonlinear systems preceded by Prandtl-Ishlinshii-Like model proposed in Section 3 are presented in Section 4. Simulation results are given in Section 5. Section 6 concludes this paper with some brief remarks.

## 2. Problem statement

Consider a controlled system consisting of a nonlinear plant preceded by an actuator with hysteresis nonlinearity, that is, the hysteresis is presented as an input to the nonlinear plant. The hysteresis is denoted as an operator

$$w(t) = P[v](t) \tag{1}$$

with $v(t)$ as the input and $w(t)$ as the output. The operator $P[v]$ will be constructed in detail in next section. The nonlinear dynamic system being preceded by the previous hysteresis is described in the canonical form as

$$x^{(n)}(t) + \sum_{i=1}^{k} a_i Y_i(x(t), \dot{x}(t), \cdots, x^{(n-1)}(t)) = bw(t) \tag{2}$$

where $Y_i$ are known continuous, linear or nonlinear function. Parameters $a_i$ and control gain $b$ are unknown constants. It is a common assumption that the sign of $b$ is known. Without losing generality, we assume $b$ is greater than zero. It should be noted that more general classes of nonlinear systems can be transformed into this structure (Isidori, 1989). The control objective is to design controller $v(t)$ in (1), as shown in Figure 1, to render the plant state $x(t)$ to track a specified desired trajectory $x_d(t)$, i.e., $x(t) \to x_d(t)$ as $t \to \infty$. Throughout this paper the following assumption is made.

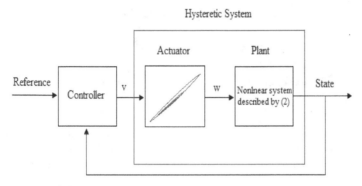

Fig. 1. Configuration of the hysteretic system

**Assumption:** The desired trajectory $X_d = [x_d, \dot{x}_d, \cdots, x_d^{(n-1)}]^T$ is continuous. Furthermore, $[X_d^T, x_d^{(n)}]^T \in \Omega_d \subset R^{n+1}$ with $\Omega_d$ being a compact set.

## 3. Prandtl-Ishlinskii-Like model

In this section, we will first recall the backlash-like operator (Su, et al, 2000) which will serve as elementary hysteresis operator, in other words, the backlash-like operator will play a role of building blocks, then will show how the new hysteresis will be constructed by using the backlash-like operator and explore its some useful properties of this model.

### 3.1 Backlash-like operator
In 2000, Su et al proposed a continuous-time dynamic model to describe a class of backlash-like hysteresis, as given by

$$\frac{dF}{dt} = \alpha \left| \frac{dv}{dt} \right| (cv - F) + B_1 \frac{dv}{dt} \tag{3}$$

where $\alpha, c,$ and $B_1$ are constants, satisfying $c > B_1$.

The solution of (3) can be solved explicitly for piecewise monotone $v$ as follows

$$F(t) = cv(t) + [F_0 - cv_0]e^{-\alpha(v-v_0)\text{sgn}\dot{v}} + e^{-\alpha v\text{sgn}\dot{v}}\int_{v_0}^{v}[B_1 - c]e^{\alpha\zeta(\text{sgn}\dot{v})}d\zeta \qquad (4)$$

for $\dot{v}$ constant and $w(v_0) = w_0$. Equation (4) can also be rewritten as

$$F(t) = \begin{cases} cv(t) + [F_0 - cv_0]e^{-\alpha(v-v_0)} + e^{-\alpha v}\dfrac{B_1 - c}{\alpha}(e^{\alpha v} - e^{\alpha v_0}), & \dot{v} > 0 \\[3mm] cv(t) + [F_0 - cv_0]e^{\alpha(v-v_0)} + e^{\alpha v}\dfrac{B_1 - c}{-\alpha}(e^{-\alpha v} - e^{-\alpha v_0}), & \dot{v} < 0 \end{cases} \qquad (5)$$

It is worth to note that

$$\lim_{v\to+\infty}(F(v) - cv) = -\frac{c - B_1}{\alpha}$$
$$\lim_{v\to-\infty}(F(v) - cv) = \frac{c - B_1}{\alpha} \qquad (6)$$

Hence, solution $F(t)$ exponentially converges the output of a play operator with threshold $r = \dfrac{c - B_1}{\alpha}$ and switches between lines $cv + \dfrac{c - B_1}{\alpha}$ and $cv - \dfrac{c - B_1}{\alpha}$. We will construct a new Prandtl-Ishilinskii-Like model by using the above backlash-like model in next subsection, similar to the construction of the well-known Prandtl-Ishilinskii model from play operators, which is our motivation behind the construction of this new model indeed.

### 3.2 Prandtl-Ishilinskii-Like model

We now ready to construct Prandtl-Ishilinskii-Like model through a weighted superposition of elementary backlash-like operator $F_r[v](t)$, in a similar way as L. Prandtl (Brokate & Sprekels, 1996) constructed Prandtl-Ishilinskii model by using play operators.

Keep $r = \dfrac{c - B_1}{\alpha}$ in mind and, without losing generality, set $F(v(0) = 0) = 0$ and $c = 1$, we rewrite equation (5) as

$$F_r(t) = \begin{cases} v(t) + r - re^{\frac{-(1-B_1)}{r}v}, & \dot{v} > 0 \\[3mm] v(t) - r + re^{\frac{1-B_1}{r}v}, & \dot{v} < 0 \end{cases} \qquad (7)$$

where $r$ is the threshold of the backlash-like operator.

To this end, we construct the Prandtl-Ishilinskii-Like model by

$$w(t) = \int_0^R p(r)F_r[v](t)dr \qquad (8)$$

where $p(r)$ is a given continuous density function, satisfying $p(r) \geq 0$ with $\int_0^\infty p(r)dr < +\infty$, and is expected to be identified from experimental data (Krasnoskl'skill & Pokrovskill, 1983; Brokate & Sprekels, 1996). Since the density function $p(r)$ vanishes for large values of $r$, the choice of $R = +\infty$ as the upper limit of integration in the literature is just a matter of convenience (Brokate & Sprekels, 1996).

Inserting (7) into (8) yields

$$w[v](t) = \begin{cases} \int_0^R p(r)dr\, v(t) + \int_0^R p(r)(r - re^{\frac{-(1-B_1)}{r}v})dr, & \dot{v} > 0 \\ \int_0^R p(r)dr\, v(t) + \int_0^R p(r)(-r + re^{\frac{1-B_1}{r}v})dr, & \dot{v} < 0 \end{cases} \tag{9}$$

the hysteresis (9) can be expressed as

$$w(t) = p_0 v + \begin{cases} \int_0^R p(r)(r - re^{\frac{-(1-B_1)}{r}v})dr, & \dot{v} > 0 \\ \int_0^R p(r)(-r + re^{\frac{1-B_1}{r}v})dr, & \dot{v} < 0 \end{cases} \tag{10}$$

where $p_0 = \int_0^R p(r)dr$ is a constant which depends on the density function $p(r)$.

**Property 1:** Let

$$d[v](t) = \begin{cases} \int_0^R p(r)(r - re^{\frac{-(1-B_1)}{r}v})dr, & \dot{v} > 0 \\ \int_0^R p(r)(-r + re^{\frac{1-B_1}{r}v})dr, & \dot{v} < 0 \end{cases} \tag{11}$$

satisfying $p(r) \geq 0$ with $\int_0^\infty p(r)dr < +\infty$, then for any $v(t) \in C_{pm}(t_0, \infty)$, there exists a constant $M \geq 0$ such that $|d[v](t)| \leq M$.

**Proof:** since (7) can be rewritten as $F_r(t) = v(t) + R(r,v)$ where

$$R(r,v) = \begin{cases} r - re^{\frac{-(1-B_1)}{r}v}, & \dot{v} > 0 \\ -r + re^{\frac{1-B_1}{r}v}, & \dot{v} < 0 \end{cases}$$

Based on the analysis in (Su, et al, 2000), for each fixed $r \in (0, R)$, it is always possible there exists a positive constant $M_1$, such that $|R(r,v)| \leq M_1$. Hence

$$d[v](t) = \int_0^R p(r)R(r,v)dr \leq \int_0^R p(r)|R(r,v)|dr \leq M_1 \int_0^R p(r)dr$$

By the definition of $p(r)$, one can conclude that $M = M_1 \int_0^R p(r)dr$.

**Property 2:** the Prandtl-Ishilinskii-Like model constructed by (9) is rate-independent.
**Proof:** Following (Brokate & Sprekels, 1996), we let $\sigma : [0, t_E] \rightarrow [0, t_E]$ satisfying $\sigma(0) = 0$ and $\sigma(t_E) = t_E$ be a continuous increasing function, i.e. $\sigma(\cdot)$ is an admissible time transformation and define $w_f[v_t]$ satisfying $w_f[v_t] = w[v](t), t \in [0, t_E]$ and $v \in M_{pm}[0, t_E]$ where $v_t$ represents the truncation of $v$ at $t$, defined by $v_t(\tau) = v(\tau)$ for $0 \le \tau \le t$ and $v_t(\tau) = v(t)$ for $t \le \tau \le t_E$, and $w[v](t)$ constructed by (9). For the model (9), we can easily have

$$w[v \circ \sigma](t) = w_f[(v \circ \sigma)_t] = w_f[v_{\sigma(t)} \circ \sigma] = w_f[v_{\sigma(t)}] = w[v](\sigma(t)) = w[v](t) \circ \sigma(t)$$

Hence for all admissible time transformation $\sigma(\cdot)$, according to the definition 2.2.1 in (Brokate & Sprekels, 1996), the model constructed by (9) is rate-independent.
**Property 3:** the Prandtl-Ishilinskii-Like model constructed by (9) has the Volterra property.
**Proof:** it is obvious whenever $v, \overline{v} \in M_{pm}[0, t_E]$ and $t \in [0, t_E]$, then $v_t = \overline{v}_t$ implies that $(w[v])_t = (w[\overline{v}])_t$, so, according to (Brokate & Sprekels, 1996, Page 37), the model (8) has Volterra property.
**Lemma 1:** If a functional $w : C_{pm}[0, t_E] \rightarrow Map([0, t_E])$ has both rate independence property and Volterra property, then $w$ is a hysteresis operator (Brokate & Sprekels, 1996).
**Proposition 1:** the Prandtl-Ishilinskii-Like model constructed by (9) is a hysteresis operator.
**Proof:** From the Properties 1, 2 and Lemma 1, the Prandtl-Ishilinskii-Like model (9) is a hysteresis model.
**Remark 1:** It should be mentioned that Prandtl-Ishilinskii model is a weighted superposition of play operator, i.e. play operator is the hysteron (Krasnoskl'skill & Pokrovskill, 1983), and that backlash-like operator can be viewed as a play-like operator from a 1st order differential equation (Ekanayake & Iyer, 2008). Hence, the model (8) is, with a litter abuse terminology, named Prandtl-Ishilinskii-Like model. As an illustration, Figure 2 shows $w(t)$ generated by (9), with $p(r) = e^{-6.7(0.1r-1)^2}$ $r \in (0, 50]$, $B_1 = 0.505$, and input $v(t) = 7\sin(4t)/(1+t)$, with $F(v(0) = 0) = 0$.

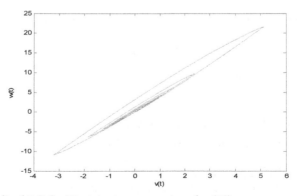

Fig. 2. Prandtl-Ishlinskii-Like Hysteresis curves given by (10)

**Remark 2:** From another point of an alternative one-parametric representation of Preisach operator (Krejci, 1996), the Prandtl-Ishilinskii-Like model falls into PKP-type operator (Ekanayake & Iyer, 2008), as Prandtl-Ishilinskii model into Preisach model. As a preliminary step, in the paper we explore the properties of this model and its potential to facilitate control when a system is preceded by this kind of hysteresis model, which will be demonstrated in the next section. Regarding hysteresis phenomena in which kind of smart actuator this model could characterize, it is still unclear. The future work will focus on, which is beyond of the scope of this paper.

To this end, we can rewrite (9) into

$$w(t) = p_0 v + d[v](t) \tag{12}$$

where $p_0 = \int_0^R p(r)dr$ and $d[v](t)$ is defined by (11).

**Remark 3:** It should be note that (10) decomposes the hysteresis behavior into two terms. The first term describes the linear reversible part, while the second term describes the nonlinear hysteretic behavior. This decomposition is crucial (Su, et al, 2000, Fu, et al, 2007) since it facilitates the utilization of the currently available control techniques for the controller design, which will be clear in next section.

## 4. Adaptive control design

From (10) and Proposition 1 we see that the signal $w(t)$ is expressed as a linear function of input signal $v(t)$ plus a bounded term. Using the hysteresis model of (10), the nonlinear system dynamics described by (2), can be re-expressed as

$$
\begin{aligned}
\dot{x}_1 &= x_2 \\
&\vdots \\
\dot{x}_{n-1} &= x_n \\
\dot{x}_n &= -\sum_{i=1}^{k} a_i Y_i(x_1(t), x_2(t), \cdots, x_n(t)) \\
&\quad + b\{p_0 v(t) - d[v](t)\} \\
&= a^T Y + b_p v(t) - d_b[v]
\end{aligned}
\tag{13}
$$

where $x_1(t) = x(t)$, $x_2(t) = \dot{x}(t), \cdots, x_n(t) = x^{(n-1)}(t)$, $a = [-a_1, -a_2, \cdots, -a_k]^T$, and $b_p = bp_0$

$Y = [Y_1, Y_2, \cdots, Y_k]^T$, and $d_b[v](t) = bd[v](t)$.

Before presenting the adaptive control design using the backstepping technique in (Krisic, et al, 1995) to achieve the desired control objectives, we make the following change of coordinates:

$$
\begin{aligned}
z_1 &= x_1 - x_d \\
z_i &= x_i - x_d^{(i-1)} - \alpha_{i-1}, \quad i = 2, 3, \cdots, n
\end{aligned}
\tag{14}
$$

Where $\alpha_{i-1}$ is the virtual controller in the $i$ th step and will be determined later. In the following, we give two control schemes. In Scheme I, the controller is discontinuous; the other is continuous in Scheme II.

## Scheme I

In what follows, the robust adaptive control law will be developed for Scheme I.
First, we give the following definitions

$$
\begin{aligned}
\tilde{\mathbf{a}}(t) &= \mathbf{a} - \hat{\mathbf{a}}(t) \\
\tilde{\phi}(t) &= \phi - \hat{\phi}(t) \\
M(t) &= M - \hat{M}(t)
\end{aligned}
\tag{15}
$$

where $\hat{\mathbf{a}}$ is an estimate of $\mathbf{a}$, $\hat{\phi}$ is an estimate of $\phi$, which is defined as $\phi := \dfrac{1}{b_p}$, and $\hat{M}$ is an estimate of $M$.

Given the plant and the hysteresis model subject to the assumption above, we propose the following control law

$$
\begin{aligned}
v(t) &= \hat{\phi}(t)v_1(t) \\
v_1(t) &= -c_n z_n - z_{n-1} - \hat{\mathbf{a}}^T Y - \mathrm{sgn}(z_n)\hat{D} + x_d^{(n)} + \dot{\alpha}_{n-1} \\
\dot{\hat{\phi}}(t) &= -\eta v_1(t) z_n \\
\dot{\hat{\mathbf{a}}}(t) &= \Gamma Y z_n \\
\dot{M}(t) &= \gamma |z_n|
\end{aligned}
\tag{16}
$$

where $c_n$, $\eta$, and $\gamma$ are positive design parameters, and $\Gamma$ is a positive-definite matrix. These parameters can provide a certain degree of freedom to determine the rates of the adaptations. And $\alpha_{n-1}$ and the implicit $\alpha_{i-1}$, $i = 2,3,\cdots,n-1$ in (16) will be designed in the proof of the following theorem for stability analysis.

The stability of the closed-loop system described in (13) and (16) is established as:

**Theorem 1:** For the plant given in (2) with the hysteresis (8), subject to Assumption 1, the robust adaptive controller specified by (16) ensures the following statements hold.

i.    The resulting closed-loop system (2) and (8) is globally stable in the sense that all the signals of the closed-loop system ultimately bounded;

ii.   The asymptotic tracking is achieved, i.e., $\lim\limits_{t\to\infty}[x(t) - x_d(t)] = 0$;

iii.  The transient tracking error can be explicitly specified by

$$
\|x(t) - x_d(t)\|_2 \le \sqrt{\dfrac{\left( \dfrac{1}{2}\tilde{\mathbf{a}}(0)^T \Gamma^{-1}\tilde{\mathbf{a}}(0) + \dfrac{b_p}{2\eta}\tilde{\phi}(0)^2 + \dfrac{1}{2\gamma}\tilde{M}(0)^2 \right)}{c_1}}
$$

**Proof:** we will use a standard backstepping technique to prove the statements in a systematically way as follows:

**Step 1:** The time derivative of $z_1$ can be computed as

$$
\dot{z}_1 = z_2 + \alpha_1
\tag{17}
$$

The virtual control $\alpha_1$ can be designed as

$$\alpha_1 = -c_1 z_1$$

where $c_1$ is a positive design parameter.

Hence, we can get the first equation of tracking error

$$\dot{z}_1 = z_2 - c_1 z_1$$

**Step 2:** Differentiating $z_2$ gives

$$\dot{z}_2 = z_3 + \alpha_2 - \dot{\alpha}_1$$

The virtual control $\alpha_2$ can be designed as

$$\alpha_2 = -c_2 z_2 - z_1 + \dot{\alpha}_1$$

Hence the dynamics is

$$\dot{z}_2 = -c_2 z_2 - z_1 + z_3$$

Following this procedure step by step, we can derive the dynamics of the rest of states until the real control appears.

**Step n:** the n-th dynamics are given by

$$\dot{z}_n = b_p v(t) + a^T Y - x_d^{(n)} - \dot{\alpha}_{n-1} + d_b[v](t) \tag{18}$$

We design the real control as follows:

$$\begin{aligned}
v(t) &= \hat{\phi}(t) v_1(t) \\
v_1(t) &= -c_n z_n - z_{n-1} - \hat{a}^T Y - \mathrm{sgn}(z_n) \hat{M} + x_d^{(n)} + \dot{\alpha}_{n-1} \\
\dot{\hat{\phi}}(t) &= -\eta v_1(t) z_n \\
\dot{\hat{a}}(t) &= \Gamma Y z_n \\
\dot{\hat{M}}(t) &= \gamma |z_n|
\end{aligned} \tag{19}$$

Note that $b_p v(t)$ in (19) can be expressed as

$$b_p v(t) = b_p \hat{\phi}(t) v_1(t) = v_1(t) - b_p \tilde{\phi}(t) v_1(t) \tag{20}$$

Hence, we obtain

$$\dot{z}_n = -c_n z_n - z_{n-1} - \tilde{a}^T Y - \mathrm{sgn}(z_n) \hat{M} + d_b[v](t) - b_p \tilde{\phi}(t) v_1(t) \tag{21}$$

To this end, we defend the candidate Lyapunov function as

$$V = \sum_{i=1}^{n} \frac{1}{2} z_i^2 + \frac{1}{2} \tilde{a}^T \Gamma^{-1} \tilde{a} + \frac{b_p}{2\eta} \tilde{\phi}^2 + \frac{1}{2\gamma} \tilde{M}^2 \tag{22}$$

The derivative $\dot{V}$ is given by

$$\dot{V} = \sum_{i=1}^{n} z_i \dot{z}_i + \tilde{\mathbf{a}}^T \Gamma^{-1} \dot{\hat{\mathbf{a}}} + \frac{b_p}{\eta} \tilde{\phi} \dot{\hat{\phi}} + \frac{1}{\gamma} \tilde{M} \dot{\hat{M}}$$

$$\leq \sum_{i=1}^{n} c_i z_i^2 + \tilde{\mathbf{a}}^T \Gamma^{-1} (\Gamma Y z_n - \dot{\hat{\mathbf{a}}}) - \frac{b_p}{\eta} \tilde{\phi}(\eta v_1 z_n + \dot{\hat{\phi}}) - |z_n| \hat{M} + |z_n| \|d_b[v](t)\| + \frac{1}{\gamma} \tilde{M} \dot{\hat{M}}$$

$$\leq -\sum_{i=1}^{n} c_i z_i^2 + \tilde{\mathbf{a}}^T \Gamma^{-1} (\Gamma Y z_n - \dot{\hat{\mathbf{a}}}) - \frac{b_p}{\eta} \tilde{\phi}(\eta v_1 z_n + \dot{\hat{\phi}}) + \frac{1}{\gamma} \tilde{M}(\gamma |z_n| - \dot{\hat{M}}) \tag{23}$$

$$= -\sum_{i=1}^{n} c_i z_i^2$$

Equations (22) and (23) imply that $V$ is nonincreasing. Hence, the boundedness of the variables $z_1, z_2, \cdots, z_n, \hat{\phi}, \hat{\mathbf{a}}$, $\hat{M}$ are ensured. By applying the LaSalle-Yoshizawa Theorem (Krisic, et al, 1995, Theorem 2.1), if further follows that $z_i \to 0$, $i = 1, 2, \cdots, n$ as time goes to infinity, which implies $\lim_{t \to \infty} [x(t) - x_d(t)] = 0$.

We can prove the third statement of Theorem 1 in the following way.
From (23), we know

$$\|z_1\|_2^2 = \int_0^{\infty} |z_1(s)|^2 ds \leq \frac{V(0) - V(\infty)}{c_1} \leq \frac{V(0)}{c_1}$$

Noticing $V(0) = \frac{1}{2} \tilde{\mathbf{a}}(0)^T \Gamma^{-1} \tilde{\mathbf{a}}(0) + \frac{b_p}{2\eta} \tilde{\phi}(0)^2 + \frac{1}{2\gamma} \tilde{M}(0)^2$ after setting $z_i(0) = 0, i = 1, 2, \cdots, n$, hence

$$\|x(t) - x_d(t)\|_2 \leq \sqrt{\frac{\left( \frac{1}{2} \tilde{\mathbf{a}}(0)^T \Gamma^{-1} \tilde{\mathbf{a}}(0) + \frac{b_p}{2\eta} \tilde{\phi}(0)^2 + \frac{1}{2\gamma} \tilde{M}(0)^2 \right)}{c_1}} \tag{24}$$

**Remark 4:** From (24), we know that the transient performance in a computable explicit form depends on the design parameters $\eta, \gamma, c_1$ and on the initial estimate errors $\tilde{\mathbf{a}}(0), \tilde{\phi}(0)$ $\tilde{M}(0)$, which gives designers enough tuning freedom for transient performance.

### Scheme II

In the control scheme above, we notice that in the controller, there is $\text{sgn}(z_n)$ introduced in the design process, which makes the controller discontinuous and this may cause undesirable chattering. An alternative smooth scheme is proposed to avoid possible chattering with resort to the definition of continuous sign function (Zhou et al, 2004). First, the definition of $sg_i(z_i)$ is introduced as follows:

$$sg_i(z_i) = \begin{cases} \dfrac{z_i}{|z_i|}, & |z_i| \geq \delta_i \\[2ex] \dfrac{z_i}{|z_i| + (\delta_i^2 - z_i^2)^{n-i+2}} & |z_i| < \delta_i \end{cases} \tag{25}$$

where design parameter $\delta_i (i=1,\cdots,n)$ is positive. It can be known that $sg_i(z_i)$ has $(n-i+2)$-th order derivatives.

Hence we have

$$sg_i(z_i)f_i(z_i) = \begin{cases} 1, & z_i \geq \delta_i \\ 0, & |z_i| < \delta_i \\ -1, & z_i \leq -\delta_i \end{cases}$$

where

$$f_i(z_i) = \begin{cases} 1, & |z_i| \geq \delta_i \\ 0, & |z_i| < \delta_i \end{cases}$$

Given the plant and the hysteresis model subject to the assumption above, we propose the following continuous controller as follows:

$$\begin{aligned}
v(t) &= \hat{\phi}(t)v_1(t) \\
v_1(t) &= -(c_n+1)(|z_n|-\delta_n)sg_n(z_n) - \hat{a}^T Y - sg_n(z_n)\hat{M} + x_d^{(n)} + \dot{\alpha}_{n-1} \\
\dot{\hat{\phi}}(t) &= -\eta v_1(t)(|z_n|-\delta_n)f_n sg_n(z_n) \\
\dot{\hat{a}}(t) &= \Gamma Y(|z_n|-\delta_n)f_n sg_n(z_n) \\
\dot{\hat{M}}(t) &= \gamma(|z_n|-\delta_n)f_n
\end{aligned} \qquad (26)$$

where, similarly as Control Scheme 1, $c_n$, $\eta$, and $\gamma$ are positive design parameters, and $\Gamma$ is a positive-definite matrix, and $\alpha_{n-1}$ and the implicit $\alpha_{i-1}$, $i=2,3,\cdots,n-1$ in (26) will be designed in the proof of the following theorem for stability analysis.

**Theorem 2:** For the plant given in (2) with the hysteresis (8), subject to Assumption 1, the robust adaptive controller specified by (26) ensures the following statements hold.

i.   The resulting closed-loop system (2) and (8) is globally stable in the sense that all the signals of the closed-loop system ultimately bounded;

ii.  The tracking error can asymptotically reach to $\delta_1$, i.e., $\lim\limits_{t\to\infty}[x(t)-x_d(t)] = \delta_1$;

iii. The transient tracking error can be explicitly specified by

$$\|x(t)-x_d(t)\|_2 \leq \delta_1 + \frac{1}{c_1^{2n}}\left(\frac{1}{2}\tilde{a}(0)^T \Gamma^{-1}\tilde{a}(0) + \frac{b_p}{2\eta}\tilde{\phi}(0)^2 + \frac{1}{2\gamma}\tilde{M}(0)^2\right)^{1/2n} \qquad (27)$$

**Proof:** To guarantee the differentiability of the resultant functions, $z_i^2$ in the Lyaounov functions will be replaced by $(|z_i|-\delta_i)^{n-i+2}f_i$ in Section 3.1 and $z_i$ in the design procedure detailed below will be replaced by $(|z_i|-\delta_i)^{n-i+1}sg_i$ as did in (Zhou et al, 2004).

**Step 1:** We choose a positive-definition function $V_1$ as

$$V_1 = \frac{1}{n+1}(|z_1|-\delta_1)^{n+1}f_1(z_1),$$

and design virtual controller $\alpha_1$ as

$$\alpha_1 = -(c_1+k)(|z_1|-\delta_1)^n sg_1(z_1) - (\delta_2+1)sg_1(z_1) \tag{28}$$

with constant $k$ satisfying $0 < k \le \frac{1}{4}$ and a positive design parameter $c_1$, then compute its time derivative by using (17)(28),

$$
\begin{aligned}
\dot{V}_1 &= (|z_1|-\delta_1)^n f_1(z_1) sg_1(z_1) \dot{z}_1 \\
&\le -(c_1+k)(|z_1|-\delta_1)^{2n} f_1(z_1) + (|z_1|-\delta_1)^n (|z_2|-\delta_2-1) f_1(z_1)
\end{aligned}
\tag{29}
$$

**Step 2:** We choose a positive-definition function $V_1$ as

$$V_2 = V_1 + \frac{1}{n}(|z_2|-\delta_2)^n f_2(z_2),$$

and design virtual controller $\alpha_2$ as

$$\alpha_2 = -(c_2+k+1)(|z_2|-\delta_2)^{n-1} sg_2(z_2) + \dot{\alpha}_1 - (\delta_3+1)sg_2(z_2) \tag{30}$$

with a positive design parameter $c_2$, then compute its time derivative,

$$
\begin{aligned}
\dot{V}_2 &\le -\sum_{i=1}^{2} c_i(|z_i|-\delta_i)^{2(n-i+1)} f_i(z_i) - k(|z_1|-\delta_1)^{2n} f_1(z_1) + (|z_1|-\delta_1)^n (|z_2|-\delta_2-1) f_1(z_1) \\
&\quad - (|z_2|-\delta_2)^{2(n-1)} f_2(z_2) + (|z_2|-\delta_2)^{n-1}(|z_3|-\delta_3-1) f_2(z_2)
\end{aligned}
$$

By using inequality $2ab \le a^2 + b^2$, we have

$$
\begin{aligned}
\dot{V}_2 &\le -\sum_{i=1}^{2} c_i(|z_i|-\delta_i)^{2(n-i+1)} f_i(z_i) + \frac{1}{4k}(|z_2|-\delta_2-1)^2 \\
&\quad - (|z_2|-\delta_2)^{2(n-1)} f_2(z_2) + (|z_2|-\delta_2)^{n-1}(|z_3|-\delta_3-1) f_2(z_2)
\end{aligned}
$$

for both cases $|z_2| \ge \delta_2+1$ and $|z_2| < \delta_2+1$, we can conclude that

$$\dot{V}_2 \le -\sum_{i=1}^{2} c_i(|z_i|-\delta_i)^{2(n-i+1)} f_i(z_i) + (|z_2|-\delta_2)^{n-1}(|z_3|-\delta_3-1) f_2(z_2) \tag{31}$$

**Step n:** Following this procedure step by step, we can derive the real control

$$
\begin{aligned}
v(t) &= \hat{\phi}(t) v_1(t) \\
v_1(t) &= -(c_n+1)(|z_n|-\delta_n) sg_n(z_n) - \hat{\mathbf{a}}^T Y - sg_n(z_n)\hat{M} + x_d^{(n)} + \dot{\alpha}_{n-1} \\
\dot{\hat{\phi}}(t) &= -\eta v_1(t)(|z_n|-\delta_n) f_n sg_n(z_n) \\
\dot{\hat{\mathbf{a}}}(t) &= \Gamma Y(|z_n|-\delta_n) f_n sg_n(z_n) \\
\dot{\hat{M}}(t) &= \gamma(|z_n|-\delta_n) f_n
\end{aligned}
\tag{32}
$$

where $\alpha_{n-1}$ can be obtained from the common form of virtual controllers $\alpha_i = -(c_i + k + 1)(|z_i| - \delta_i)^{n-i+1} sg_i(z_i) + \dot{\alpha}_{i-1} - (\delta_{i+1} + 1) sg_i(z_i)$, $(i = 3, \cdots, n-1)$ with positive design parameters $c_i$.

We define a positive-definition function as

$$V = \sum_{i=1}^{n} \frac{1}{n-i+2} (|z_i| - \delta_i)^{(n-i+2)} f_i(z_i) + \frac{1}{2} \tilde{a}^T \Gamma^{-1} \tilde{a} + \frac{b_p}{2\eta} \tilde{\phi}^2 + \frac{1}{2\gamma} \tilde{M}^2$$

and compute its time derivative by using (13), (28), (30) and (32),

$$\dot{V} = \dot{V}_{n-1} + (|z_n| - \delta_n)^2 f_n(z_n) sg_n(z_n) \dot{z}_n + \tilde{a}^T \Gamma^{-1} \dot{\tilde{a}} + \frac{b_p}{\eta} \tilde{\phi} \dot{\tilde{\phi}} + \frac{1}{\gamma} \tilde{M} \dot{\tilde{M}}$$

$$\leq -\sum_{i=1}^{n} c_i (|z_i| - \delta_i)^{2(n-i+1)} f_i(z_i) + \tilde{a}^T \Gamma^{-1} (\Gamma Y z_n - \dot{\hat{a}})$$

$$- \frac{b_p}{\eta} \tilde{\phi} (\eta v_1 z_n + \dot{\hat{\phi}}) - |z_n| \hat{M} + |z_n| |d_b[v](t)| + \frac{1}{\gamma} \tilde{M} \dot{\tilde{M}}$$

$$\leq -\sum_{i=1}^{n} c_i (|z_i| - \delta_i)^{2(n-i+1)} f_i(z_i) + \tilde{a}^T \Gamma^{-1} (\Gamma Y z_n - \dot{\hat{a}}) - \frac{b_p}{\eta} \tilde{\phi} (\eta v_1 z_n + \dot{\hat{\phi}}) + \frac{1}{\gamma} \tilde{M} (\gamma |z_n| - \dot{\hat{M}})$$

$$= -\sum_{i=1}^{n} c_i (|z_i| - \delta_i)^{2(n-i+1)} f_i(z_i)$$

Thus we proved the first statement of the theorem. The rest of the statements can be easily proved following those of the proof of theorem 1, hence omitted here for saving space.

**Remark 5:** It is now clear the two proposed control schemes to mitigate the hysteresis nonlinearities can be applied to many systems and may not necessarily be limited to the system (2). However, we should emphasize that our goal is to show the fusion of the hysteresis model with available control techniques in a simpler setting that reveals its essential features.

## 5. Simulation results

In this section, we illustrate the methodologies presented in the previous sections using a simple nonlinear systems (Su, et al, 2000; Zhou et al, 2004) described by

$$\dot{x} = a \frac{1 - e^{-x(t)}}{1 + e^{-x(t)}} + bw(t) \tag{33}$$

where $w$ represents the output of the hysteresis nonlinearity. The actual parameter values are $a = 1$, and $b = 1$. Without control, i.e., $w(t) = 0$, (33) is unstable, because $\dot{x} = (1 - e^{-x(t)}) / (1 + e^{-x(t)}) > 0$ for $x > 0$, and $\dot{x} = (1 - e^{-x(t)}) / (1 + e^{-x(t)}) < 0$ for $x < 0$. The objective is to control the system state $x$ to follow the desired trajectory $x_d = 12.5 \sin(2.3t)$.

In the simulations, the robust adaptive control law (19) of Scheme I was used, taking $c_1 = 0.9$, $\gamma = 0.2$, $\eta = 0.1$, $\Gamma = 0.1$, $\hat{\phi}(0) = 0.8/3$, $\hat{M}(0) = 2$, $\hat{x}(0) = 3.05$, $v(0) = 0$, $B_1 = 0.505$,

$p(r) = e^{-6.7(0.1r-1)^2}$ for $r \in (0,50]$. The simulation results presented in the Figure 3 is the comparison of system tracking errors for the proposed control Scheme I and the scenario without considering the effects of the hysteresis. For Scheme II, we choose the same initial values as before and $\delta = 0.35$. The simulation results presented in the Figure 4 is the comparison of system tracking errors for the proposed control Scheme II and the scenario without considering the effects of the hysteresis. Clearly, the all simulation results verify our proposed schemes and show their effectiveness.

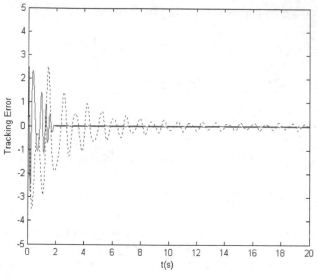

Fig. 3. Tracking errors -- control Scheme I (solid line) and the scenario without considering hysteresis effects (dotted line)

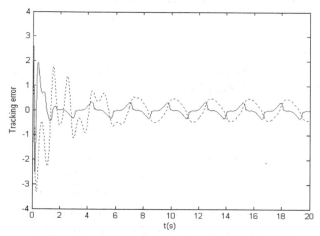

Fig. 4. Tracking errors -- control Scheme II (solid line) and the scenario without considering hysteresis effects (dotted line)

## 6. Conclusion

We have for the first time constructed a class of new hysteresis model based on play-like operators and named it Prandtl-Ishlinshii-Like model where the play-like operators play a role of building blocks. We have proposed two control schemes to accomplish robust adaptive control tasks for a class of nonlinear systems preceded by Prandtl-Ishlinshii-Like models to not only ensure stabilization and tracking of the hysteretic dynamic nonlinear systems, but also derive the transient performance in terms of $L_2$ norm of tracking error as an explicit function of design parameters. By proposing Prandtl-Ishlinshii-Like model and using the backstepping technique, this paper has address a challenge that how to fuse a suitable hysteresis model with available robust adaptive techniques to mitigate the effects of hysteresis avoid constructing a complicated inverse operator of the hysteresis model. After this preliminary result, the idea in this paper is being further explored to deal with a class of perturbed strict-feedback nonlinear systems with unknown control directions preceded by this new hysteresis model.

## 7. Acknowledgement

This work was supported by the NSERC Grant, the National Natural Science Foundation of China (61004009, 61020106003), Doctoral Fund of Ministry of Education of China (20100042120033), and the Fundamental Research Funds for the Central Universities (N100408004, N100708001).

## 8. References

Su, C. Y.; Stepanenko, Y.; Svoboda, J. & Leung, T. P. (2000). Robust Adaptive Control of a Class of Nonlinear Systems with Unknown Backlash-Like Hysteresis, *IEEE Transactions on Automatic Control*, Vol. 45, No. 12, pp. 2427-2432.

Fu, J.; Xie, W. F. & Su, C. Y. (2007). Practically Adaptive Output Tracking Control of Inherently Nonlinear Systems Proceeded by Unknown Hysteresis, *Proc. of the 46th IEEE Conference on Decision and Control*, 1326-1331, New Orleans, LA, USA.

Banks, H. T. & Smith, R. C. (2000). Hysteresis modeling in smart material systems, *J. Appl. Mech. Eng*, Vol. 5, pp. 31-45.

Tan, X. & Baras, J. S. (2004). Modelling and control of hysteresis in magnetostrictive actuators, *Automatica*, Vol. 40, No. 9, pp. 1469-1480.

Tao G. & Kokotovic P. V. (1995). Adaptive control of Plants with Unknown Hysteresis, *IEEE Transactions on Automatic Control*, Vol. 40, No. 2, pp. 200-212.

Tao G. & Lewis, F., (2001). Eds, *Adaptive control of nonsmooth dynamic systems*, New York: Springer-Verlag, 2001.

Zhou J.; Wen C. & Zhang Y. (2004). Adaptive backstepping control of a class of uncertain nonlinear systems with unknown backlash-like hysteresis, *IEEE Transactions on Automatic Control*, Vol. 49, No. 10, pp. 1751-1757.

Wen C. & Zhou J.(2007). Decentralized adaptive stabilization in the presence of unknown backlash-like hysteresis, *Automatica*, Vol. 43, No. 3, pp. 426-440.

Tan X. & Baras J. (2005). Adaptive Identification and Control of Hysteresis in Smart Materials, *IEEE Transactions on Automatic Control*, Vol. 50, No. 6, pp. 827-839.

Iyer R.; Tan X., & Krishnaprasad P.(2005), Approximate Inversion of the Preisach Hysteresis Operator with Application to Control of Smart Actuators, *IEEE Transactions on Automatic Control*, Vol. 50, No. 6, pp. 798-810.

Tan X. & Bennani O. (2008). Fast Inverse Compensation of Preisach-Type Hysteresis Operators Using Field-Programmable Gate Arrays, *in Proceedings of the American Control Conference*, Seattle, USA, pp. 2365-2370.

Isidori A. (1989). *Nonlienar Control Systems: an Introduction*, 2nd ed. Berlin, Germany: Springer-Verlag.

Krasnoskl'skii M. A. & Pokrovskii A. V. (1983). *Systems with Hysteresis*. Moscow, Russia: Nauka.

Brokate, M. & Sprekels, J. (1996). *Hysteresis and Phase Transitions*, New York: Springer-Verlag.

Krejci P. (1996) *Hysteresis, convexity and dissipation in hyperbolic equations*, Gakuto Int. Series Math. Sci. & Appl. Vol. 8, Gakkotosho, Tokyo.

Ekanayake D. & Iyer V. (2008), Study of a Play-like Operator, *Physica B: Condensed Matter*, Vol. 403, No.2-3, pp. 456-459.

Krisic M.; Kanellakopoulos I. & Kokotovic P. (1995). *Nonlinear and Adaptive Control Design*. New York: Wiley.

# Permissions

The contributors of this book come from diverse backgrounds, making this book a truly international effort. This book will bring forth new frontiers with its revolutionizing research information and detailed analysis of the nascent developments around the world.

We would like to thank Andreas Mueller, for lending his expertise to make the book truly unique. He has played a crucial role in the development of this book. Without his invaluable contribution this book wouldn't have been possible. He has made vital efforts to compile up to date information on the varied aspects of this subject to make this book a valuable addition to the collection of many professionals and students.

This book was conceptualized with the vision of imparting up-to-date information and advanced data in this field. To ensure the same, a matchless editorial board was set up. Every individual on the board went through rigorous rounds of assessment to prove their worth. After which they invested a large part of their time researching and compiling the most relevant data for our readers. Conferences and sessions were held from time to time between the editorial board and the contributing authors to present the data in the most comprehensible form. The editorial team has worked tirelessly to provide valuable and valid information to help people across the globe.

Every chapter published in this book has been scrutinized by our experts. Their significance has been extensively debated. The topics covered herein carry significant findings which will fuel the growth of the discipline. They may even be implemented as practical applications or may be referred to as a beginning point for another development. Chapters in this book were first published by InTech; hereby published with permission under the Creative Commons Attribution License or equivalent.

The editorial board has been involved in producing this book since its inception. They have spent rigorous hours researching and exploring the diverse topics which have resulted in the successful publishing of this book. They have passed on their knowledge of decades through this book. To expedite this challenging task, the publisher supported the team at every step. A small team of assistant editors was also appointed to further simplify the editing procedure and attain best results for the readers.

Our editorial team has been hand-picked from every corner of the world. Their multi-ethnicity adds dynamic inputs to the discussions which result in innovative outcomes. These outcomes are then further discussed with the researchers and contributors who give their valuable feedback and opinion regarding the same. The feedback is then collaborated with the researches and they are edited in a comprehensive manner to aid the understanding of the subject.

Apart from the editorial board, the designing team has also invested a significant amount of their time in understanding the subject and creating the most relevant covers. They scrutinized every image to scout for the most suitable representation of the subject and create an appropriate cover for the book.

The publishing team has been involved in this book since its early stages. They were actively engaged in every process, be it collecting the data, connecting with the contributors or procuring relevant information. The team has been an ardent support to the editorial, designing and production team. Their endless efforts to recruit the best for this project, has resulted in the accomplishment of this book. They are a veteran in the field of academics and their pool of knowledge is as vast as their experience in printing. Their expertise and guidance has proved useful at every step. Their uncompromising quality standards have made this book an exceptional effort. Their encouragement from time to time has been an inspiration for everyone.

The publisher and the editorial board hope that this book will prove to be a valuable piece of knowledge for researchers, students, practitioners and scholars across the globe.

# List of Contributors

**Kai Zenger and Juha Orivuori**
Aalto University School of Electrical Engineering, Finland

**Cristina Ioana Pop and Eva Henrietta Dulf**
Technical University of Cluj, Department of Automation, Cluj-Napoca, Romania

**Ciprian Lupu**
Department of Automatics and Computer Science, University "Politehnica" Bucharest, Romania

**Anna Filasová and Dušan Krokavec**
Technical University of Košice, Slovakia

**Hidetoshi Oya**
The University of Tokushima, Japan

**Kojiro Hagino**
The University of Electro-Communications, Japan

**Kazuhiro Yubai, Akitaka Mizutani and Junji Hirai**
Mie University, Japan

**Yutaka Uchimura**
Shibaura Institute of Technology, Japan

**Rajamani Doraiswami**
Department of Electrical and Computer Engineering, University of New Brunswick, Fredericton, Canada

**Lahouari Cheded**
Department of Systems Engineering, King Fahd University of Petroleum and Minerals, Dhahran, Saudi Arabia

**Jun Fu and Wen-Fang Xie**
The Department of Mechanical & Industrial Engineering, Concordia University, Canada

**Ying Jin**
State Key Laboratory of Integrated Automation of Process Industry, Northeastern University, China

**Shao-Ping Wang**
The Department of Mechatronic Control, Beihang University, China

Printed in the USA
CPSIA information can be obtained
at www.ICGtesting.com
JSHW011359221024
72173JS00003B/353

9 781632 402028